COMMUNICATING IN BUSINESS

Joseph Buschini

Richard R. Reynolds
University of Connecticut

Houghton Mifflin Company • Boston

Atlanta   Dallas   Geneva, Illinois   Lawrenceville, New Jersey
Palo Alto   Toronto

S0-AKE-712

Consultants

June St. Clair Atkinson
Associate Director
Program Development
  Division of Vocational
  Education
State Department of
  Public Instruction
Raleigh, North Carolina

Thomas E. Beck
Visiting Professor
Anglo-American Department
Tokyo University of
  Foreign Studies
Tokyo, Japan

Anne Benaquist
Writer/Editor
Formerly Instructor
English Department
Keene State College
Keene, New Hampshire

Eleanor Bergholz
Curriculum Specialist
  for English and Speech
Big Bend Community College
  European Division
New York, New York

Alan J. Berman
Professor
English Department
LaGuardia Community College
Long Island City, New York

Judith Shultz Byfield
Assistant to the Vice President
  of Academic Affairs
Southern Ohio College
Cincinnati, Ohio

Nancy Clair
Writer/Editor
Formerly Language
  Coordinator
The Experiment in
  International Living
Brattleboro, Vermont

Gerald Fiske
Formerly Vice President
Information Systems
Boston Five Cents Savings,
  Federal Savings Bank
Boston, Massachusetts

Mildred I. Johnson
Lecturer
Department of Management
College of Business
Colorado State University
Fort Collins, Colorado

Kenji Kitao
President of the Japan
  Association of Language
  Teachers
Associate Professor
Department of English
Doshisha University
Kyoto, Japan

Frank Malgesini
Executive Director
Maria Ines Gomez Madrid
Master Teacher
Aida A. Olivas
Master Teacher
Mexican North American
  Institute of Cultural
  Relations
Chihuahua, Mexico

L. Ann Masters
President of the National
  Association of
  Business Education
  State Supervisors
Director of Business
  Education
Nebraska Department of
  Education, Vocational
  Division
Lincoln, Nebraska

Ardith Meier
Instructor
Anglo-American Institute
University of Vienna
Vienna, Austria

Gregory L. Metcalf
Credit Officer
John Hancock Financial
  Services, Inc.
Boston, Massachusetts

Mary Perkins
Teaching Master
Business Division
Durham College
Oshawa, Ontario, Canada

Anne M. Rosen
Lecturer
Secretarial Studies
College of the Bahamas
Nassau, Bahamas

Nancy C. Schlemminger
Business Teacher
Shrewsbury High School
Shrewsbury, Massachusetts

Katherine Slusher
Program Director
English for Professionals
Institute of North
  American Studies
Barcelona, Spain

Cheryl A. Walsh
Instructor
International Language
  Center
University of South Florida
Tampa, Florida

Sue Wanwig
Writing Program Supervisor
Pegasus Language Services
c/o Mobil Sekiyu
Tokyo, Japan

Editorial Advisor

Mikito F. Nakamura, Professor of Business at Kwansei Gakuin University, Nishinomiya, Japan, is the author of a number of books and articles on the theory of business communications. Dr. Nakamura is President of the Japan Business English Association and Honorary Fellow of the American Business Communication Association.

Design and Art PC&F, Inc.
Cover Original photograph by R. Krubner/H. Armstrong Roberts; computer generated images by Creative Technologies, Inc.

Copyright © 1986 by Houghton Mifflin Company

All rights reserved. No part of this work may be reproduced or transmitted in any form or by any means, electronic or mechanical, including photocopying and recording or by any information storage or retrieval system, except as may be expressly permitted by the 1976 Copyright Act or in writing by the Publisher. Requests for permission should be addressed to: Permissions, Houghton Mifflin Company, One Beacon Street, Boston, Massachusetts, 02108.

Printed in U.S.A.

ISBN: 0-395-36005-6

ABCDEFGHIJ-DP-898765

AUTHORS

Joseph Buschini

Joseph Buschini is an author of several textbooks and has contributed to articles, journals, and reports in a variety of fields. Mr. Buschini has been a consultant to Houghton Mifflin company for a number of years and lives and Newburyport, Massachusetts.

Richard R. Reynolds

Richard R. Reynolds, Associate Professor of English at the University of Connecticut, Storrs, Connecticut, practiced law for twelve years. Dr. Reynolds leads business writing seminars sponsored by Boston University and by Fordham University.

CONTENTS

PREFACE

Communicating in Business is a first course in Business English. It should help students improve their writing skills as they work within a business-oriented context and develop competence in other forms of business communication. An Instructor's Manual and a set of transparencies accompany the text.

Communicating in Business emphasizes concepts and practices that students can use throughout their careers. These concepts and practices are developed gradually within contextualized situations that reflect current trends in business communications. Throughout the text, students are encouraged to apply their language skills in a way that will produce specific results within a given business situation.

Although the text covers all major forms of business communication, it emphasizes the process of writing. Function, not format, is the primary concern. In a clear, concise, and easy-to-understand manner, *Communicating in Business* shows students how to compose successful business correspondence. The text systematically involves students in the communication process by asking them to improve, write, revise, or respond to problems, questions, and practice exercises.

Organization   The text is organized into ten chapters, each dealing with a general area of business communication. There are two or more lessons in each chapter. Each lesson opens with a model of a specific type of correspondence. As students proceed through the text, they'll soon notice that these models of correspondence interrelate. By following a single employee who encounters increasingly difficult communication problems, students gain insight into the circumstances and relationships that generate business communications.

After the model correspondence, the text discusses the purpose, strategy, and method of composing the correspondence. Then students are asked to revise poorly written examples of the target correspondence. A checklist follows, summarizing the main points of the lesson. Next, students are confronted with a business situation and asked to write an appropriate response. Students proceed by defining the desired goal of their message, identifying their audience, and writing a first draft. They complete the assignment by preparing a final draft on the appropriate stationery.

The lesson continues with a "Style and Structure" section, which presents strategies and methods of good writing, and developmental exercises. Many of the topics covered in the "Style and Structure" section are incorporated into the "Revising" section. Consequently, in many cases it is helpful for students to complete the "Style and Structure" section before they attempt the revisions.

Each lesson concludes with a vocabulary-building exercise and a "Guidelines" section that reviews basic grammar and punctuation. Practice exercises for the "Guidelines" can be found at the end of the book.

At the end of each chapter, a "Communication Workshop" allows students to express and expand their awareness of business practices and procedures, and it provides the instructor with interesting, structured material for class discussion and activities.

TEXTBOOK FEATURES

Communicating in Business combines ease of presentation with maximum flexibility in classroom procedure and homework assignments. Clear learning objectives, listed at the beginning of each lesson, describe what students should have accomplished after completing the lesson. Checklists provide a quick review of the lesson's main points, and each "Writing Assignment" can be adapted into a typing simulation to broaden the scope of the text.

The text contains several appendices which cover the practice exercises for the "Guidelines," letter formats, international monetary units, common abbreviations, and metric conversion tables. A glossary defines business terms and includes relevant computer terminology.

Instructor's Manual
with Tests

The manual recommends methods of classroom presentation, provides alternative activities and expansion assignments, and includes suggested answers to all exercises and assignments. It also contains a complete test bank of chapter tests.

Transparencies

Transparencies of model correspondence and lesson checklists are available to help the instructor present important concepts.

Acknowledgements

The authors would like to thank the Editorial Advisor, the Consultants, and the many students and colleagues for constructive comments and criticisms. Their contributions have greatly improved the text. For constant support and encouragement from family and friends, the authors are profoundly grateful.

COMMUNICATING IN BUSINESS

INTRODUCTION

All business depends upon the exchange of information, and our success in business often depends upon how successfully information is exchanged. We trade most of our information through language, language that is based on numbers or on words. Today, much of the word-based information upon which the world's business depends is exchanged in English. Perhaps, then, we can conclude that improving our use of English will improve our business.

Think of English as a tool, one that you use to complete specific jobs. These jobs can include making introductions, placing orders for service or merchandise, selling, negotiating with associates, and collecting money. Whatever the job, the skill with which you use the tool will determine how quickly and effectively the job is done. So let's get to work.

Define Your Goal

The first step in beginning a job is to decide what kind of job it is. You should always begin by asking yourself the following question: "What results do I want my message to bring?" Sometimes the answer to this question comes easily: "I want Welch Enterprises to pay me for the machine parts I sent them two years ago!" Other times, the problem is more complex: "I want our overseas distributors to increase this year's orders to offset a higher tariff and diminished profitability." Before you pick up your pencil or feed a sheet of paper into your typewriter or punch the "On" button of your word processor, make sure that you've got a clear idea of the job you want to do. The next step, of course, is to determine the best way to get the job done.

Know Your Audience

Who you are writing to determines what you will write, so always remember your reader. Never begin a business letter without a clear idea of the person who will have to read it. What is your relationship with this reader? What do you want the reader to do with the information you are sending? How will the reader react to your message? Try to understand your reader. If you can anticipate your reader's reaction, you can work to influence it.

The way in which you organize and present your message determines the way in which it will be received. But don't plan the best way to present your message – think about the best way for your reader to receive it. Concentrate on the reader, and be sensitive to your relationship with him or her. This relationship, as well as the context of the message, will determine the appropriate *tone* of your writing.

The tone of your writing reveals your attitude toward your reader and your subject. Too many writers try to conform to an "official" formal and impersonal tone in all their business communications. Successful writers, however, select a tone that will help achieve their goals and influence their readers. The ability to

| Return Address | **OMNICOMP INTERNATIONAL** |
| | 17 BUNKER HILL ROAD, SHREWSBURY MA 01545 |

| Date Line | November 21, 19.. |

| Mailing Notation | SPECIAL DELIVERY |

Inside Address	Mr. Marvin Webster
	Ainsley Data Processing Associates
	1442 Miller Street
	North Sydney, NSW 2060 AUSTRALIA

| Salutation | Dear Mr. Webster: |

| Subject Line | Subject: Improved Service for Our Distributors |

| The Body | As part of our plan to improve our operations, we are expanding the staff here at the home office. In this way we hope to speed our order-processing functions and to make any necessary corrections or adjustments to your account immediately. |

I'd also like to announce the appointment of Elvira Benway as operations manager. Ms. Benway has been with Omnicomp International for four years as a sales correspondent.

Also, we are enclosing a price list, which has been updated for the coming year. If you wish to place an order based on this year's prices, please send it no later than December 15.

| Complimentary Close | Sincerely yours, |

Signature and Typed Name	*Larry Fine*
	Larry Fine
	Sales Manager

| Reference Initials | LF/mh |

| Carbon Copy Notation | cc: Ms. Elvira Benway |

| Enclosure Notation | Enclosure |

manipulate the tone of your writing will grow with your ability to control the language, and there are plenty of exercises in this book to help you. But your writing skills will be wasted if you don't use them with your reader in mind.

First Draft

Not many writers can produce effective, finished prose in their first draft. Always begin with a first draft and plan to rewrite it. Once you have a clear idea of your goal, your reader, and your organizational strategy (we'll talk about this later), write your message as clearly and directly as possible. Don't worry if your wording isn't entirely satisfactory or if your sentences aren't phrased correctly – just get your basic message down on paper! State your message in the simplest, most straightforward way; there will be plenty of time to correct it in your finished copy.

When you finish your first draft, examine it critically. Is the message clear? Is it organized correctly? Does it sound right? (In this book, we hope you'll find the information to help you answer questions like these and that you'll learn the importance of asking them.) Make the necessary changes in your final copy and check it again. Each sentence should contribute to your goal and to your reader's understanding. If it doesn't, or if you are in doubt, don't hesitate to throw it out.

Format

The appearance of your letter is important. A crumpled, dirty page with erasures, smudges, and misspellings will prevent you from achieving your goal, unless your goal is to convince the reader of your incompetence. Always make sure that your communications are neatly typed and error-free.

The basic format of business letters may vary slightly, but the parts of the business letter and their functions are usually the same.

The printed letterhead or return address: A printed letterhead usually contains the company's name and address, and it oftens includes its telephone number as well. If you are writing a business letter on blank paper, begin with your address. Depending on the style of your letter, the return address is placed at the left or right margin.

The date: The date on which the letter is written appears three to six spaces below the return address or letterhead. It provides an easy reference to your letter.

Mailing notation (optional): If you are using a special postal service to send your letter, you may want to add a mailing notation two spaces below the date line at the left margin.

Inside address: This includes the complete name, official title (if any), and address of the person to whom you are writing. It appears two spaces below the previous entry.

Attention line (optional): The attention line is used to direct the letter to a specific department or individual whose name does not appear in the inside address. It generally appears two spaces below the inside address.

The salutation: The salutation is a polite greeting that opens your letter. It always appears at the left margin, two spaces below the line above it. The form of the salutation depends upon the relationship between the writer and the reader.

To an individual:

Dear Dr. Jones:	Dear Mr. Jones:
My dear Dr. Jones:	Dear Ms. Jones:
Dear John:	Dear Customer:
Dear Professor Jones:	Dear Salesperson:

Avoid using *Dear Sir* or *Dear Madam*.

To a mixed-gender group:

Dear Ladies and Gentlemen:	Dear Management:
Dear Omnicomp International:	Dear Sales Department:

The subject line (optional): A subject line can be used to call attention to the topic of the letter. It appears two spaces below the salutation and is used primarily in sales letters or promotional announcements.

The body: The body contains the actual message of the letter. Typewritten letters are usually single-spaced, with double spacing between paragraphs.

The complimentary close: The complimentary close is a polite way of concluding your message, and it appears two spaces below the last line in the body. The first word of the close is capitalized. The most commonly used closes are the following:

Most informal (for a close personal relationship):

Cheers,	As ever,
Regards,	Kindest wishes,
Best regards,	Kindest regards,

Informal and friendly (for a first-name relationship):

Yours,	Cordially,
Most cordially,	Cordially yours,

Friendly but rather neutral (for all but the most formal letters):

Sincerely,	Sincerely yours,
Very sincerely,	Most sincerely,
Yours sincerely,	Most sincerely yours,

Polite, neutral, and somewhat formal (for general business correspondence):

Very truly yours,	Yours truly,
Respectfully yours,	Respectfully,

Signature and typed name: A handwritten signature is placed between the complimentary close and the typed name of the writer. If desired, one's job title can be placed below the typed name.

Reference initials: The typist's lower-case initials are typed two lines below the typed name, flush with the left margin, and may be preceded by the writer's capitalized initials and a slash or colon.

Carbon copy notation: If copies of the letter are sent to others, a carbon copy notation (cc) is typed two lines below the previous entry, usually in lower-case letters, with or without a colon between *cc* and the recipient's name.

    cc Legal Department   cc: Mr. John Gray

Enclosure notation: If something is included with the letter, one of the following notations, placed two lines below the carbon copy notation, will remind the reader to check the envelope's contents:

Enclosure   Enclosures (2)

British and American Format

Years ago, the differences between British and American letter formats were considerably greater than they are now. Although letter styles have been evolving into a common, international format, you can still find some differences. The British style, for example, does not punctuate the date and salutation of the reader. Titles, such as *Mr* and *Ms,* appear without periods. Both sets of reference initials are capitalized and placed opposite the date, and the order of the date line is day, month, and year.

Block Letter

The letter on page 2 is an example of a block letter – a format in which all parts of the letter are aligned with the left margin. In the appendix, you can find examples of other commonly used business letters, such as the simplified letter, the modified block letter, the modified semi-block letter, the executive letter, the hanging-indent letter, and the half-sheet letter.

1

THE APPLICATION SERIES

Letters of Application

Résumés

Follow-up Letters

1.1 LETTERS OF APPLICATION

Objectives

1. Write letters of application.
2. Understand parts of the sentence.
3. Revise sentences.
4. End sentences appropriately.

Accounts Correspondent

Growing computer company seeks qualified individual to oversee all aspects of our order-fulfillment process, including preparation of customer purchase orders, monitoring inventory control, providing appropriate documentation to shipping department, customer communications and support, credit memos, and promotional mailings. Good communication skills and experience with computer workstations necessary. Degree preferred. Send résumé to Elena O'Malley, our Personnel Director. Omnicomp International, 17 Bunker Hill Road, Shrewsbury, MA 01545.

Ms. Elena O'Malley
Personnel Director
Omnicomp International
17 Bunker Hill Road
Shrewsbury, MA   01545

Dear Ms. O'Malley:

Define the job and express an interest in it.

Your advertisement for an accounts correspondent in this week's issue of Computer Times interests me very much. I hope that you will consider me for the position.

Describe your present situation, experience, and qualifications.

As the current assistant manager of the Personal Computer Center in Warwick, Rhode Island, I supervise the shipping and receiving process, provide customer support, and sell to the public. Since one of our most popular items is the Omnicomp ML420, I have become quite familiar with its operation and its compatible software.

Refer to the qualifications requested in the advertisement.

As you can see from my enclosed résumé, I received a bachelor's degree in English from Nebraska College, with minor concentrations in marketing and in computer science. I am confident that I have the qualifications necessary to become a successful accounts correspondent at Omnicomp.

Suggest an interview and tell how the reader can contact you.

Please let me know when we can talk further about the job. You can reach me at the above address or by telephone at (401) 555-2022. Thank you for your time and consideration.

Sincerely yours,

Edgar P. Fowler

Edgar P. Fowler

Enclosure

Purpose　　　The most common way to begin finding a job is to write an application letter to a prospective employer. The primary purpose of the letter is to obtain an interview, but the letter also provides the employer with an example of your communication skills and creates a first impression.

Most applications are solicited, which means that they are written in response to an advertisement for a specific job. In such cases, you should study the advertisement carefully and find out as much as you can about the company to which you are applying. Try to imagine the person who will read your letter and focus on him or her. It is not an impersonal company that will read your letter but a person who needs to find someone to fill a job.

Of course your reader will probably receive many letters applying for the same job. Make your letter one that will be remembered. Be confident, enthusiastic, and show that you have all the qualifications necessary for the job. Obviously, your letter should be neat and free of mistakes.

Organization　　　A typical application letter has three parts, and you can arrange these parts into three or four paragraphs. The opening paragraph defines the job that you are applying for and expresses your interest in it. The middle paragraphs briefly describe your present position, your experiences, and your qualifications. Your last paragraph should suggest an interview and tell your reader how to contact you.

When your reader examines your application, he or she will try to determine how closely your qualifications fit those required for the job. Your middle paragraph, therefore, should emphasize the strongest reasons for hiring you. There is no need to mention any weaknesses.

Let's say, for example, that you are applying for a job that requires five years' experience and you only have three. Don't make a negative statement, such as "Although I have been working in the field for only three years, I feel that I can do the job." State the negative factor in a positive manner: "Because of my experience in the field, I am confident that I can do the job well." Remember that you are only trying to get an interview. There will be plenty of time later to make qualifying statements.

If you have had experience in the field in which you are applying, it is usually helpful to refer to some detailed, technical aspect of the job. If you are applying for your first job, then make a statement that shows you understand what will be required of you. It's also helpful to mention a specific achievement.

Close the letter by telling the reader you would like to talk more about the job at an interview. Provide enough information for your reader to contact you easily. End your letter by thanking your reader for considering your application.

A common procedure is to attach a résumé (also called curriculum vitae or data sheet) to your letter of application (see Lesson 2.1). If you do so, you may want to call attention to a particular detail on your résumé by referring to it in the letter. When a résumé or other material is sent with a letter, the word *Enclosure* is placed below the writer's name at the lower left side of the page. If you do not include a résumé with your application letter, tell your reader that you will be happy to provide one upon request.

Some applications are unsolicited, which means that they don't respond to an advertised job opening. In such cases, simply state your career objective, describe your qualifications, and ask for an interview.

REVISING

Revise the following letters of application that were written in response to the advertisements. Improve the style and make the content conform to the standards discussed in this lesson. You may invent fictional details to improve the letter.

Case A

> **Retail Petroleum Coordinator**
>
> A subsidiary of a major oil company is actively recruiting retail supervisors for the Sydney area. The applicant should possess a successful background in the following industry-related skills: multi-unit operations, personnel management, revenue control, sales and promotion, and merchandising. Salary of 26000, monthly bonus, company auto, and expenses. Rush letter and résumé to Personnel Dept., Portway Products Ltd., 407 Warrenton Park, Sydney, NSW 2100.

President
Portway Products Ltd.
407 Warrenton Park
Sydney, NSW 2100

Dear Sir:

I am writing to let you know that I will accept the position you advertised several weeks ago. It was a difficult decision because the pay was not quite as much as I wanted, but I felt that working for your company would be a significant step in the advancement of my career.

I will be moving to Sydney soon, so please write quickly. If I don't hear from you, I'll just stop by your office when I arrive.

After you look at my enclosed data sheet, I'm sure you will see why I am unquestionably the most qualified and talented person available. By hiring me, you will be greatly improving your company.

Humbly yours,

Quentin Quigley

REVISION A

_____

_____

_____

_____

_____

_____

_____

_____

_____

Case B

January 10, 19..

Sales Engineer
Opportunity with the Bevis Machine Corp. for aggressive sales engineer trainee. Mechanical knowledge and college degree preferred, and some prior sales experience helpful. Territory located in Southern Florida. Competitive salary, excellent benefits. Write Ms. Mary Jane Benzing, P.O. Box 104, Ft. Lauderdale, FL 80124

Ms. M. J. Benzing
Ft. Lauderdale
Florida

Dear Ms. Benzing:

I am answering your company's advertisement in the Fort Lauderdale Sentinel. At present I am in my final year at Connolly Community College and would like to have such a job. I have worked a lot of different places while in high school and here, as you will see on my enclosed résumé. I didn't much like being a waiter, but I feel sure I could do as well as a salesman because your products are outstanding. Hoping you will give me a call at the number below so we can talk about it. I'm good at fixing cars.

Sincerely yours,

Marvin Noodles
235-8754

REVISION B

_____

_____

_____

_____

_____

_____

_____

_____

_____

_____

_____

_____

_____

CHECKLIST

Letters of Application

1. Remember your goal: to obtain a personal interview. ☐

2. Study the job description or advertisement carefully. Find out as much as you can about the employer. ☐

3. Focus on your reader. Write to a person, not to a company. ☐

4. Use the first paragraph to identify the job and to express your interest in it. Use a positive, confident tone. ☐

5. Use the middle paragraph(s) to describe your experience, qualifications, and present situation. Never provide negative information. ☐

6. Conclude by requesting an interview. Provide the details necessary for the employer to contact you easily. ☐

7. Remember – your letter forms an employer's first impression of you. Check it carefully. ☐

WRITING ASSIGNMENT

Background

The following advertisement appeared in yesterday's *Daily Journal*.

Video Consulting

Unique opportunity for an entry-level position in the Video Game industry. The position involves the processing of systems development reports and the handling of confidential information. Assist in putting together reports, provide customer support, and aid in all aspects of operations. Good communications skills and strong typing are essential. Write Roberta Pierce, Arim-Haddad Associates, 814 Federation Ave., Winnepeg, Manitoba, I4I 2A4.

G. Wolff, of 12 High Street, St. John, New Brunswick, E4Q, 4L1, is interested in applying for the job. Prepare a letter of application. Write the goal of your letter and identify your audience. Then write your first draft on a separate piece of paper. Use the page on your right for your final copy.

You (G. Wolff) have recently graduated from Chandler Junior College, where you received an associate degree in management. You are now working in Willard's Appliance Shop as a salesperson. It is a part-time job, and you have been there for two years.

In your letter, include some interests and abilities that you feel would help you in the job you are applying for. Present yourself as someone who can help the company.

Goal: _____

Audience: _____

12 High Street
St. John, New Brunswick E4Q 4L1

October 27, 19..

Ms. Roberta Pierce
Arim-Haddad Associates
814 Federation Avenue
Winnipeg, Manitoba I4I 2A4

STYLE AND STRUCTURE
The Sentence

Every sentence contains a subject and a verb or verb phrase, and it expresses a complete thought. A sentence can be **declarative, interrogative, imperative,** or **exclamatory**.

Declarative sentences make statements:

> Mr. Wolff came into the office.

Interrogative sentences ask questions:

> Did Mr. Wolff come into the office?

Imperative sentences issue orders or directions:

> Come into the office, please.

Exclamatory sentences express strong feelings:

> How nice to see you, Mr. Wolff!

The **subject** of a sentence names the person or thing that is the topic of the sentence. The **verb** or **verb phrase** describes the action or condition of the subject. The **complement** is a word or group of words that completes the meaning of the sentence. These three – subject, verb, and complement – are the main parts of the sentence, and they usually appear in that order.

> The company (*subject*) earned (*verb*) large profits (*complement*).
> Ms. Watson (*subject*) should have reported (*verb phrase*) these profits (*complements*).

Use only complete sentences in your writing and avoid the incorrect use of sentence fragments. A sentence fragment is an incomplete idea or part of a sentence that is written as if it were a complete sentence. Two parts of a sentence that often appear as fragments are the phrase and the clause. A **phrase** is a group of related words without both a subject and a verb. Here are some fragments that are phrases:

> INCORRECT: Operating the computer.
> By August 8.
> After the meeting.
> Preparing the tax return.

Certainly you would not mistake a phrase for a sentence.

A **clause**, however, can be a complete sentence if it expresses a complete thought because a clause contains a subject and a verb. Clauses are classified as either **independent** or **dependent**. A dependent clause may stand alone as a complete sentence. However, a dependent clause that is used alone is a **fragment** and must be joined to a main clause.

> INDEPENDENT CLAUSE: Sales have climbed.
>
> DEPENDENT CLAUSE: Although sales have climbed
>
> DEPENDENT CLAUSE
> AND MAIN CLAUSE: Although sales have climbed, profits have fallen.

PRACTICE A Identify the following sentences as either declarative, interrogative, imperative, or exclamatory. Then change each sentence to a different type.

Example
1. We must see the head of their purchasing department soon. *(Declarative)*

    Should we see the head of their purchasing department soon?

    (Interrogative)

2. It is essential that the engineering team meet this deadline!_____

    _____

    _____

3. After you tested the new computers, were you fully satisfied?_____

    _____

    _____

4. Be at the plant at 8:00 a.m. tomorrow, so we can review the quarterly reports.

    _____

    _____

5. I will call you Monday morning to set up an interview._____

    _____

    _____

6. Let me know your decision._____

    _____

    _____

PRACTICE B In each of the following sentences, underline the subject and write *S* above it, underline the verb or verb phrase and write *V* above it, and underline the complement and write *C* above it.

Example

         S   *V*   *C*

1. The auditors questioned our accounting methods.

2. The computers were down most of the day.

3. They sent their invoice March 15.

4. Did you receive the complete list at the end of the month?

5. Omnicomp is expanding its staff.

6. We must receive your order.

PRACTICE C

Distinguish complete sentences from fragments by labeling each of the following *C* (complete) or *F* (fragment).

Example

1. Although we carefully inspected every one of the new machines after they arrived. ___F___

2. Basic to a sentence are subject, verb, and complement. _____

3. Our profits for the period are up, despite the rise in interest rates. _____

4. Whether we can increase efficiency by adding another mainframe computer or by hiring extra personnel, at least temporarily. _____

5. When you've checked your letter for punctuation, spelling, and style. _____

6. It's a short assignment. _____

Sentence Variety

If you repeat the same sentence pattern over and over again, you'll probably bore or confuse your reader. Varying sentences within a paragraph makes your ideas easier to follow and lets you emphasize important points. The following techniques can help you achieve sentence variety:

1. Vary the length of your sentences. The average sentence contains about sixteen words. Within a paragraph, for example, you might mix sentences of twenty-eight words, five words, and fifteen words. In a five-sentence paragraph expressing some fairly difficult ideas, you might drop in as the middle sentence something extremely simple, such as "Let me explain" or "That approach won't work."

2. Open sentences different ways. Not every sentence needs to begin with its subject. You might start with a phrase or an adverb:

   Despite our sales increase, profits fell.

   Eventually the cost of rubber will level off.

   To reach overseas markets, we must find better means of distribution.

3. Alternate simple sentences with compound and complex sentences. A simple sentence has a subject and a verb or verb phrase:

   We have reached overseas markets.

   Profits fell throughout the fiscal year.

   Ms. Johnson's résumé impressed the committee members.

4. A compound sentence has two main clauses.

   We have reached overseas markets; now we must find better means of distribution.

5. A complex sentence contains a main clause and a subordinate clause.

Although we have reached overseas markets, we must find better means of distribution.

Although sales increased, profits fell.

Since Ms. Johnson's résumé impressed the committee members, they decided to hire her.

PRACTICE D

Revise the sentences below to provide variety in length, style, and structure.

Example

1. Our engineers inspected the wiring. They reported some wires were crossed. We wrote the company about that. They have not answered our letter.

When our engineers inspected the wiring, they noticed some wires were

crossed. We wrote the company about the wiring problem, but they

haven't answered our letter.

2. To write a good letter of application, picture your reader. To impress your reader, describe your credentials. To get an interview, enclose your telephone number. To get hired, show interest in the company.

3. Getting a job is difficult for most people. Writing the application letter is painful for many job seekers. Going for the interview is nerve-wracking for timid applicants. Adjusting to a new company is often difficult.

4. Having had extensive experience in sales, I would like a job in that field. After two years describing pension plans to prospective customers, I feel I know that side of the work. Although my degree is in French literature, I believe I have the ability to explain difficult concepts to people.

5. The new 408 computer can do several calculations the old 214 could not do, and the 408 can do the old calculations faster. We should write the manufacturer and find out the price of the 408. It may be hard to have a 408 in place by the end of June, but we should try.

_____

_____

_____

_____

_____

WORDS IN ACTION

A Choose the best answer.

1. I feel that I have the necessary _____ for the job.
   a. employment
   b. application
   c. qualifications
   d. emphasis

2. In order to improve the _____ of our department, we have decided to hire an administrative assistant.
   a. experience
   b. efficiency
   c. employment
   d. software

3. The position _____ a person with proven managerial abilities.
   a. assumes
   b. associates
   c. applies
   d. requires

4. I would _____ an opportunity to talk further with you about the job.
   a. demand
   b. appreciate
   c. expect
   d. require

5. I am writing in _____ to your advertisement in *The Daily News*.
   a. expectation
   b. response
   c. enthusiasm
   d. application

6. You can reach me at the above _____ or by telephone at 555-1242.
   a. telephone
   b. office
   c. address
   d. interview

7. As you can see from my _____ résumé, I graduated with honors from Louisiana State University.
   a. applied
   b. wonderful
   c. enclosed
   d. letter

8. Our company's _____ director will be interviewing several job applicants next week.
   a. efficiency
   b. operation
   c. correspondent
   d. personnel

9. Although we received a number of applications, none of the _____ possessed the necessary qualifications.
   a. jobs
   b. applicants
   c. applications
   d. applied

10. I have had five years' _____ in field sales and consulting, and during that time I have developed a number of important contacts.
    a. experience
    b. working
    c. supervisory
    d. accounting

B Write the word that best matches each definition: advertisement, appropriate, compatible, consideration, promote.

1. a notice designed to attract public attention to a product   _____

2. careful thought; deliberation   _____

3. suitable   _____

4. capable of living or performing well with another or others   _____

5. attempting to sell or gain recognition for a product   _____

GUIDELINES

Final Punctuation

Period	Use a period after a complete declarative sentence. Most abbreviations are followed by periods:

Period — Use a period after a complete declarative sentence. Most abbreviations are followed by periods:

> The interview is scheduled for tomorrow morning.

> Mr., Ms., Dr.

Question Mark — Use a question mark after a direct question.

> Did you see the invoices?

Be careful to distinguish between a direct question and a request that is worded like a question. Do not use a question mark after a request.

> REQUEST: Would you please bring your résumé.

> QUESTION: Should I bring in letters of recommendation as well as my résumé?

Exclamation Point — Use an exclamation point to express strong feeling or excitement. The exclamation point is also used for emphasis or to express irony. Use exclamation points sparingly.

> Your performance of last month was outstanding!

1.2 RÉSUMÉS

1. Prepare a résumé.
2. Use infinitives correctly.
3. Use complete forms of verbs.
4. Use progressive tenses correctly.

State your
career interest.

Summarize your previous
work experience.

Summarize your
education and list
degrees you received.

EDGAR P. FOWLER
23 Skedrowe Street
Cornhill, RI 01685
Telephone (401) 555-2022

Career Objective
A sales operations position in the computer industry, with opportunities for creative input and advancement.

Experience
September 1984–present

PERSONAL COMPUTER CENTER
Warwick, Rhode Island
Assistant Manager.

Responsibilities include supervising the shipping and receiving department, providing customer service and support, retail selling, and handling related correspondence.

October 1983–May 1984

CAMPUS STEREO & CAMERA
Lincoln, Nebraska
Salesperson (part-time).

Responsibilities included making retail sales presentations of stereo and video equipment, processing orders, and handling complaints. Received award for best sales record April 1984.

Education
1982–1984

Bachelor of Arts in English, with minor course concentrations in Computer Science and Marketing.
Nebraska Wesleyan College
Lincoln, Nebraska

1980–1982

Associate degree in Liberal Arts.
Cornhill Community College
Cornhill, Rhode Island

References furnished upon request.

20

Purpose	A résumé presents a summary of your experience and qualifications in outline form. It allows the employer to quickly see the extent of your education, training, and background. Like the letter of application, the résumé should stimulate an employer's interest and lead to an interview.

Organization	The first step in writing an effective résumé is to define the position you want. If you don't know the exact title of the job, at least determine the general area in which you would like to work. Then analyze your skills and background and identify the things that qualify you for the job. Put yourself in the place of your prospective employer. What qualities would you look for in a new employee?

Organize your résumé so that your strongest points are emphasized. If your job experience qualifies you for the position, begin your résumé with your employment history. If your educational background is more suited to the job than your work experience, begin with your educational qualifications.

Your résumé should be attractive in format, neat and uncluttered, and typed on white or conservative pastel paper. Try to limit yourself to one page, but never allow the résumé to run longer than two pages. Your résumé should be well organized, easy to read, and, of course, free of errors. Do not use abbreviations in the résumé or application letter.

Using sentence fragments in a résumé is not only acceptable but preferred. Use verbs of action and limit the use of personal pronouns and articles. For example, you would write "Promoted to public affairs division, August 19..," not "I was promoted to the public affairs division in August 19.."

List your education and experience in reverse chronological order, that is, beginning with the most recent. When you list your work experience, give the name and location of the company and give your duties, emphasizing the aspects of your job that relate to the position you are applying for. Under the heading "Education," list the institutions you have attended and the diplomas or degrees that you have received. In addition, you may want to mention any honors you have earned or any memberships in professional organizations.

"References" refers to persons who will provide a recommendation of your character and ability. Always obtain an individual's permission before you use him or her as a reference. If you have obtained a reference from a person who is respected in the field in which you are applying or who is acquainted with your prospective employer, give the name and address of that person in your résumé. If not, it is a common practice to wait for a response from the employer before providing references.

Functional Résumé	An alternative to the chronological résumé is the functional résumé, effective for people who have held many different kinds of jobs, because it emphasizes skills rather than job history. If Edgar Fowler wanted to change his chronological résumé to a functional résumé, he would keep the name, address, telephone number, career objective, education, and references the same, but list his occupational experience in separate categories under the headings "Administration," "Communications," and "Technical Skills."

REVISING

Reorganize and edit the following résumés. You can create details that might improve them.

Case A

Rosanna Cornatto
Telephone (410) 555-4120
821 Montego Boulevard, Houston TX   77002
Age 20

School Diploma 19..	John Copeland High School, Houston
19.. – present	I am now enrolled at Conway College. I have finished courses in history, sociology, introductory commerce, rock and roll music, marketing, management strategy, photography, data processing, and sculpture.
Jobs	When I was in high school, I worked at Burger Heaven on Tomane Street in Houston. I waited on customers and cleaned up after closing.
	Now I work at Vincent's Video Village. I am interested in computers and I know something about them.
	Desire job selling computers. Reference: Vincent's, 875 Las Olas Boulevard, Houston.

REVISION A

Case B

The Official Résumé of Quentin Q. Quigley

Education

Beaver Elementary School Grades 1–6	Excellent grades in all courses
Robert Johnson Jr. High School, Grades 7—8	Excelled in mathematics
Hosmer High School	Received diploma, captain of basketball team, president of chess club
Wolfe University	Bachelor's degree

Jobs

President Quigley Enterprises	Basically involved in the promotion of capital, as well as public relations
Custodial engineer Wiltflake Apartments	Accomplished the successful maintenance of a multi-unit dwelling and effected the biweekly disposal of waste materials
Distributor of The Daily Journal	Responsible for the dispersal of news and information throughout a four-block territory, as well as for the collection of subscription fees on a weekly basis

Occupational Aspirations

A top-level executive position with maximum prestige and opportunities for rapid advancement.

REVISION B

_____

_____

_____

_____

_____

_____

_____

_____

_____

_____

_____

_____

_____

WRITING ASSIGNMENT

Choose one of the following job descriptions and prepare a résumé for "yourself." Remember to emphasize the experiences that qualify you for the job you are applying for. You can create fictional experiences.

Background

1. CUSTOMER SERVICE MANAGER — Major airline offers both in-flight and on-the-ground positions for responsible, articulate, success-oriented individuals with some college education. In-flight, you'll direct on-board ticketing and provide a variety of professional services for our passengers. On-the-ground positions involve reservations, station operations, and key support functions.

2. ADMINISTRATIVE ASSISTANT — Well-known fashion design company is looking for a "self-starter" with excellent typing and steno skills to assist a key executive department. You must be extremely detail-oriented and organized to succeed in this challenging position. Responsibilities include correspondence, phones and a number of special projects.

3. PERSONNEL INTERVIEWER — Major teaching hospital has entry-level personnel position for a personable individual with strong communication skills. The duties involve interviewing/ screening applicants, administering pre-employment tests, checking references, and assisting in various employee-relations projects.

4. DIAMOND SALES TRAINEE — Unique opportunity to learn the diamond business. Applicant must have available references. Prior sales experience or training preferred.

5. PUBLICIST — Excellent opportunity in growing film distribution company. We need a bright individual to act as our in-house publicist and handle all press relations, stockholder relations, press releases, celebrity appearances, and promotions. Experience in theatrical publicity a plus.

6. MANAGEMENT TRAINEE — Opportunities for college graduates to manage personnel and equipment in a marine environment. Fully paid training program leads to responsible position. Positions require a BS/BA degree in any major, with 3.0 average or above preferred. Applicants must be available for international travel. Aptitude test is required.

7. BILINGUAL CORRESPONDENTS — Major multinational corporation needs a number of individuals with strong language skills. Openings exist in virtually all languages, but strong communication skills in English are necessary. Duties involve correspondence, translating, and proofreading contract and other legal documents.

Résumé

Infinitives

Present Infinitives

Use the present infinitive to express an action occurring at the same time as that of the main verb:

> I **am disappointed** because I had hoped **to be** (not **to have been**) finished by now.

Perfect Infinitive

Use the perfect infinitive to express an action occurring before the action of the main verb:

> I am happy **to have been** (not **to be**) of service last week.

Complete Verb Forms

Be certain to use all forms of a verb necessary in any one sentence.

> WRONG: They always **have** and always will be **impressed** by increased production.
>
> RIGHT: They always **have been** and always will be **impressed** by increased production.

Consistency of Tense

Importance

A verb's tense indicates the time of its action. When you use two verbs, their tenses should be consistent with each other so your reader can understand your message easily. This means that you should not change the tense without good reason.

> UNCLEAR: We **sold** more products last year, but we **earn** less profit.
>
> CLEAR: We **sold** more products last year, but we **earned** less profit.

Whenever possible, use the same verb tense within a sentence or paragraph. Use different tenses only when they are necessary for your meaning.

> CLEAR: Last year we **manufactured** only machine parts, but now we **manufacture** complete engines as well.

Progressive Tenses

The progressive tense of a verb indicates an action in progress, either in the past, present, or future. To form this tense, use a form of the verb *be* with the present participle (*-ing* form) of the main verb. Remember that the progressive tense describes an ongoing or continuing action.

Writers often use a progressive tense where it is inappropriate. For example:

> CHANGE: We will be calling you next week.
>
> TO: We will call you next week.

A telephone call will take so little time that it should not be regarded as an ongoing action. On the other hand, a construction job might well demand the progressive tense, as in:

> They have been working there since last year, and will probably still be working there next year.

Progressive tenses can indicate continuing action in the past, present, or future.

1. The present progressive is used for an action that is happening now:

   > I am waiting for your check to arrive.

2. The past progressive is used to describe an action that was in progress at a certain time:

   > I was working yesterday afternoon.

3. The future progressive refers to the progress of activities or conditions in the future:

   > Our company will be moving to the new office next month.

4. The present perfect progressive emphasizes the duration of an action that began in the past and has continued into the present:

   > We have been waiting for your check for two weeks.

5. The past perfect progressive describes the continuation of a past event or condition over a period of time prior to another:

   > We had been waiting for your check, but it arrived yesterday.

6. The future perfect progressive expresses the continued duration of an action or condition from the present into the future:

   > As of next week, we will have been waiting for your check for six months.

1.3 FOLLOW-UP LETTERS

1. Write follow-up letters.
2. Organize paragraphs.

Thank the reader
and refer to the
interview.

Briefly mention
your strongest
qualifications.

End on an
optimistic note.

23 Skedrowe Street
Cornhill, RI 01685

12 January, 19..

Mrs. Elvira Benway
Operations Manager
Omnicomp International
17 Bunker Hill Road
Shrewsbury, MA 01545

Dear Mrs. Benway:

Thank you for giving me the opportunity to speak with you
and learn more about Omnicomp International. I was quite
impressed by the organization, and the position of accounts
correspondent provides exactly the type of opportunity that I
am looking for.

I realize that my experience in wholesale marketing is
somewhat limited, but I am confident that my experience and
training, as well as my familiarity with Omnicomp's excellent
products, will enable me to learn quickly.

Thank you again, and please express my appreciation to Ms.
O'Malley. I look forward to hearing from you soon.

Sincerely,

Edgar P. Fowler

Edgar P. Fowler

Purpose	A follow-up letter should express your appreciation for an interview, and it serves the purpose of placing your name before the interviewer one more time. The letter lets the employer know that you find the job attractive and that you are confident of your ability to perform it. The follow-up letter is usually written a day or two after the interview.

Your follow-up letter should be short, sincere, and optimistic. Make a specific reference to the interview and provide any relevant information that you may have forgotten to mention earlier. You can restate your strongest qualifications, but do it subtly. Any overstatement can produce a negative effect.

Organization	If you receive a job offer at your interview, your follow-up letter will be a letter of acceptance, or if you decide against the job, one of refusal. In the former case, begin by accepting the job and thanking the employer. Identify the job by title and state the salary agreed upon. A second paragraph might discuss when you will assume your new duties. Your conclusion should indicate that you are pleased with your new position. You might write as follows:

> I'm writing to accept the position of . . . at the agreed-upon salary of . . . . I look forward to working at . . . .
>
> As we discussed, I will start work on . . . .

If you refuse the offer, your letter should be tactful and appreciative. Thank the employer for his or her offer and give a logical and polite reason for your refusal. This letter should be courteous and brief. It might begin this way.

> Thank you for offering me the position of retail supervisor at . . . . However, after thinking it over, I've decided I can't relocate from . . . to . . . at this time.

If you do not get the job but you are still interested in working for the company, you can send another follow-up letter two or three months after you submitted your initial application. This letter can serve as a reminder that you are still interested in working for the company, and it provides an update on any recent activities or experiences that might add to your desirability as an employee. Such a letter might begin as follows:

> Although several months have passed since I first submitted my application, I'd like you to know that I am still very much interested in working for . . . . I hope that you will keep my application in your "active" file and consider me if an appropriate position becomes available.
>
> Since our last meeting, I've completed several courses in marketing techniques and an introductory course in computer programming.

There is no need, however, to restate any information from your original application.

REVISING

Revise the follow-up letters below. Make the style smoother and the content more tactful and confident. Use appropriate salutations and closings.

Case A

> Sir:
>
> What's the story? It has been three weeks since my interview and I've heard nothing from you people. Don't you know talent when you see it?
>
> I enjoyed our interview very much, and I was looking forward to working for Gutierrez Consulting Corporation. I know that I would have found the work interesting and rewarding. Apparently you thought otherwise.
>
> Thank you for taking the time to meet with me, and please be expressing my appreciation to Mr. Gutierrez and Ms. Ortega. I hope you are still considering my application.
>
> You'd better call me soon, or it will be too late.
>
> Impatiently yours,
>
>
> Edwina Arcarro

REVISION A

This letter is also much too short. Rewrite it to make it more memorable.

Case B

March 12, 19..

Ms. M. J. Benzing
Computrol Company
Ft. Lauderdale, FL

Dear Miss Benzing:

I thought our interview went successfully and am writing to tell you how glad I would be if you will soon be making me an offer for the job.

Thanking you again.

Gratefully yours,

"Marv" Noodles

REVISION B

_____

_____

_____

_____

_____

_____

_____

_____

_____

_____

_____

_____

_____

_____

_____

_____

_____

CHECKLIST

Follow-up Letter

1. Be brief. Remember that your letter serves only as a reminder. ☐

2. Thank the interviewer for taking the time to meet with you. ☐

3. Express your increased interest in the job and in the company. ☐

4. Briefly mention your suitability for the position. ☐

5. End with a positive, confident tone. ☐

WRITING ASSIGNMENT

Prepare a follow-up letter for J. Daniels, 7 Motlow Drive, Lynchburg, Tennessee 37202. Continue your first draft on separate paper.

Background

On November 4 you (J. Daniels) had a job interview with Music City Magazine, 402 Williams Avenue, Nashville, TN 37214, for the position of production assistant in the Graphics and Photography Department. You met with Wilbur Nelson, the production manager. He explained that the job would require you to handle all incoming requests for graphic design and photography, telephone traffic, and paperwork.

You are a recent graduate with no related job experience, but you have taken a number of art and photography courses in school and are an amateur photographer. This job would be a perfect opportunity for you to get experience in the field. The company would prefer a person with experience, but no experience is necessary.

You feel that the interview was successful and that you made a good impression, but Mr. Nelson told you that he would be interviewing several other applicants before making his decision.

Goal: _____

Audience: _____

FIRST DRAFT

_____

_____

_____

_____

_____

_____

107 Motlow Drive
Lynchburg, TN 37202

November 17, 19..

Mr. W. Nelson
Production Manager
Music City Magazine
402 Williams Avenue
Nashville, TN 37214

Dear Mr. Nelson:

STYLE AND STRUCTURE
The Paragraph

Definition A paragraph is a group of sentences that develops a single idea. The first sentence usually announces the topic of the paragraph, the middle sentence(s) develops the topic or idea, and the final sentence states a conclusion and prepares the way for the next paragraph. Consider, for example, the following paragraph:

> Our delivery schedule is causing problems. We have not yet delivered the full line of products, so we appear to be late. The delivery is not really overdue, because the buyer has changed certain specifications.

The first sentence introduces the topic, "delivery schedule." In the second sentence, the writer develops the idea further by mentioning that the delivery "appears to be late." The final sentence further develops the idea and then concludes that the supplier is not actually late. It also suggests that the next paragraphs will clarify the uncertainty.

Length Most paragraphs contain three to five sentences. Three is the minimum necessary to announce, develop, and conclude. Five allows room for several topic-developing sentences in the middle. The length of your paragraphs can vary according to the subject matter and to the number and length of clauses in the sentences. Try to vary the lengths of your paragraphs. This will make your writing more interesting.

If you write too many short paragraphs, your reader will be frustrated by your failure to connect facts and thoughts that are logically related. On the other hand, very long paragraphs tend to blur their points and confuse their readers.

PRACTICE A

Number these sentences to make a properly organized paragraph.

_____ You will note from my enclosed résumé that I have assisted in an office and worked in the college library. _____ Your advertisement indicates that your office needs an assistant to type correspondence and do research at the courthouse. _____ Through my job at the library and in various courses, I've developed research skills. _____ Typing letters daily has brought my speed to sixty words a minute.

PRACTICE B

Write a topic sentence that could introduce a paragraph on each of the following topics. Then, using one of those sentences, write a paragraph. You can create suitable facts to develop the idea.

1. an interview you had for employment

_____

2. excessive downtime of your company's leased computers

_____

3. the delivery of a certain order to your company

_____

4. the introduction of a new product

_____

Paragraph:

_____

_____

_____

_____

_____

PRACTICE C   The following paragraph is too long. Find the best place to divide it into two paragraphs.

As you requested, I investigated the relative merits of two computer systems to see which would be our best buy in terms of maintenance and repair. The Pineapple system, according to representatives of ten companies that have used it, has frequent breakdowns. Customer service engineers from Pineapple usually arrive quickly and have nearly always managed to get the system working again. As a result, little time has been lost. The Minute system, on the other hand, has not often failed to function properly for the three companies where I inquired. However, all three stated that occasional breakdowns had been followed by long delays of operation. In some cases, it seemed that the repairmen were unable to locate the trouble, either because they were badly trained or because the system was difficult to work on. In other cases, the parts needed to correct the trouble were neither on hand nor easily obtainable. I conclude, therefore, that the Pineapple system would cause us considerably less downtime than the Minute system.

The second paragraph should begin with

_____

WORDS IN ACTION _____

A   Choose the best answer.

1. Oscar is considering a _____ in marine engineering.
   a. salary   c. career
   b. subsidiary   d. capital

2. Mr. Yasuda has asked that we call the customer to _____ the unusual number of replacement filters that were ordered.
   a. clarify   c. schedule
   b. enroll   d. submit

3. Robert's interview is _____ for three o'clock.
   a. enrolled
   b. chronological
   c. wholesale
   d. scheduled

4. The Webb Corporation is trying to raise additional _____ to finance its new venture.
   a. salary
   b. capital
   c. desirability
   d. acceptance

5. Rosebud Provisions Company is a _____ of Corporal Foods Corporation.
   a. concentration
   b. subsidiary
   c. wholesale
   d. recommendation

6. Mrs. Wagner would like all department directors to _____ their proposals by November 15.
   a. enroll
   b. submit
   c. mention
   d. schedule

7. I agree with the committee's _____ to create a separate department to deal with international sales.
   a. subsidiary
   b. concentration
   c. acceptance
   d. recommendation

8. Anita chose not to accept the job at Cheapway Company because she wasn't satisfied with the _____.
   a. subsidiary
   b. salary
   c. capital
   d. concentration

9. Although many of us agreed with him, we felt that it was _____ to make such hostile remarks at the committee meeting.
   a. inappropriate
   b. cumulative
   c. tactful
   d. subtle

10. Many distributors are waiting _____ for the back-ordered items to be delivered.
    a. apparently
    b. impatiently
    c. subtly
    d. wholesale

B   Write the word that best matches each definition: necessary, occasional, relevant, submit, tactful.

1. essential; needed   _____

2. pertinent; related   _____

3. happening from time to time   _____

4. to commit something to another's
   consideration or judgment   _____

5. diplomatic; considerate   _____

COMMUNICATION WORKSHOP
The Interview

After personnel departments have initially examined applicants through their application letters and résumés, they schedule the remaining candidates for interviews. The interview allows the applicants to present their qualifications and to obtain specific information about the company and the job. It gives the interviewer an opportunity to personally evaluate the applicants and decide whether they are appropriate candidates for the job.

In many companies, the applicant is interviewed twice; first by the personnel department, and then by someone in the department that has the job opening. Let's take a look at Fowler's interview at Omnicomp.

Discussion Activities

1. You are a personnel interviewer at Omnicomp. You have been asked to screen Edgar Fowler (another student) for the accounts representative position. Review the position description and Fowler's résumé. Your primary responsibility is to find out if Fowler meets the specific skill and educational requirements.

   Ask Fowler five questions when he comes in. Ask some questions that relate to the position description and to Fowler's résumé. Ask some broader questions to determine the applicant's attitude, expectations, and work habits. Ask another person to be Fowler and to respond to your questions.
   a. Why are you interested in working at our company?
   b. What are your short-term and long-term goals?
   c. What are your strengths and weaknesses?

2. A successful interview usually involves questions from both sides of the desk. You (Fowler) are to make up five other questions. Ask another person to be the personnel interviewer and to respond to your questions.
   a. Is this a newly created position or a vacancy?
   b. What are the opportunities for growth in this position?
   c. What do you see as the major challenges this position presents?

3. Your appearance and behavior are also important in making a good impression at an interview. Below are some guidelines. Discuss others that you feel are important.
   a. Dress appropriately–not too casually or too formally.
   b. Go to the interview alone.
   c. Plan to arrive a few minutes before the scheduled time. Don't arrive too early, and never arrive late.
   d. Bring a copy of your résumé.
   e. Give your name and the name of the person you are meeting to the receptionist, then wait for instructions.
   f. Introduce yourself to the interviewer. Shake hands, and remember to smile.
   g. Do not chew gum or smoke, even if you are invited to do so.
   h. Answer all questions clearly and completely. Don't hesitate to talk about your abilities and accomplishments, but don't elaborate too much.
   i. Don't be afraid to ask questions about the job, its salary, and its opportunities for advancement.

j. Leave as soon as the interview is over, and thank the interviewer for discussing the job with you.

4. Take roles in pairs as the interviewer at Omnicomp and as Fowler. Do the entire interview from beginning to end. Be prepared to ask and answer questions developed in Exercises 1 and 2.

5. You are the interviewer at Omnicomp and have just completed Fowler's interview. Complete and discuss Section I of the Interview Analysis Form.

6. You have just interviewed Fowler for a position as account correspondent. Complete and discuss Section II of the Interview Analysis Form.

OMNICOMP INTERNATIONAL / Interview Analysis Form

Name of Applicant _____   Date _____

Source _____

Section I — Interview in Personnel Department

Position Title:

Does applicant meet specific skill requirements?
Does applicant meet specific educational requirements?
Is applicant interested?
Is starting salary range acceptable to applicant?

☐ Applicant referred to _____
                              Supervisor/Department   Interview Date

☐ Applicant not referred to hiring department. Explain fully.

   Explanation:

                                              _____   _____
                                                    Interviewer   Date

Section II — Interview in Hiring Department

Any questions regarding this applicant should be directed to the personnel department interviewer named above. After you have interviewed this applicant, please complete this section and return it with all application data to the personnel department.

Applicant selected   ☐ Yes   ☐ No

Reason not selected (Check appropriate box. Explain fully below.):

☐ Skills   ☐ Evaluation of candidate's adaptability
☐ Education   ☐ Applicant not interested
☐ Related experience   ☐ Other

   Explanation:

Would you consider this applicant for future openings in your department?
        ☐ Yes   ☐ No

                              _____   _____
                                       Supervisor   Date

2
ROUTINE CORRESPONDENCE

Letters of Inquiry

Letters of Response

2.1 LETTERS OF INQUIRY

1. Write letters of inquiry.
2. Incorporate participial phrases in sentences.
3. Avoid dangling participles and misplaced modifiers.

M.K.Chatterjee, Ltd.

201 Netaji Subhash Marg   Daryaganj, New Delhi

4 January 19..

OMNICOMP INTERNATIONAL
17 Bunker Hill Road
Shrewsbury, MA 01545

Dear Sales Department:

State the topic and give the reason for the inquiry.

I am very much interested in the OMNI 409 data base management system advertised in the November issue of Data World. Our brokerage firm is planning to implement a new system to be used with our QBL mainframe, and the OMNI 409 appears to be the one best suited to our needs. Before making our final decision, however, we need to obtain more information.

Specifically, please answer the following questions:

State clearly the information you request.

1. Does the 409's financial system have the capacity for an unlimited number of different currencies?
2. Can you link our executives' microcomputers directly to the mainframe and still provide security?
3. What networking options for capital expenditure forecasting and tracking are available to us in New Delhi?

Thank the reader.

In addition, please send the details of your customer training program to help us set up the system.

If it is at all possible, may I please have your response by 1 February. Thank you very much.

Respectfully yours,

Ravi Kumar

Ravi Kumar
Business Manager

Purpose   People write letters of inquiry to obtain information or to make a request. A direct inquiry asks a company about its products or services. Any business should be happy to respond to a direct inquiry. The writer is a potential customer, and his or her questions should be answered quickly, completely, and courteously.

Organization   In order to obtain the information you want, you should inquire specifically. Therefore, your first step is to define exactly what it is that you want to know. Then you must provide the necessary details that your reader will need in order to answer your questions completely. Always try to make your reader's job as easy as possible.

Let's say that your company is planning to hold its annual sales conference, and you have been asked to find out which hotel would be the best location for the event. You would not write "Please send me information on your conference facilities and group rates." Such a request would make it very difficult for the hotel manager to offer you a competitively priced package suited to your needs.

Therefore, you'll want to provide more details. Your reader needs to know the date and duration of the conference, the number of people that will attend, the number and size of the conference rooms you will need, and the number of meals served, if any. The hotel surely wants your business, and by providing these details, you will enable the manager to make the most attractive offer possible.

Another type of inquiry asks a favor of a reader who is not selling a product or service. Instead, the writer asks for information needed for his or her own purposes. You might, for example, want to write for information about a job applicant. Or perhaps you are planning to open a factory and you want to know how many unemployed machinists live in a certain area. You would then write to a regional planning center for the appropriate demographic statistics.

Whatever the favor, be especially specific and clear so that granting your request will take as little of the reader's time as possible. Most requests for information are responded to as a common courtesy, particularly those asking for credit or employment references. Businesses would expect similar responses in return.

If you are requesting detailed information as a favor, you should be courteous and considerate of your reader. You might offer to send a copy of any report that is based, even in part, on the information you requested. If you enclose a self-addressed envelope, you may speed the response.

Order of Paragraphs   Begin your letter of inquiry by identifying yourself and stating why you want the information you are asking for. Then, in the second paragraph, ask your questions, keeping them to a minimum and writing as concisely as possible. Conclude by thanking the reader for taking the time to answer your inquiry.

REVISING

Revise the following letters of inquiry.

Case A

Dear Mr. Webber:

In making my decision, would you please provide the following information. What is the price of your E-Z Model 19 hydraulic tailgate, including its installation on Morton 340 refrigerated trailers. I am also interested in its gross weight, hoping to maintain fuel efficiency.

We are a major distributor of frozen seafood, operating a fleet of twenty-four trucks. Primarily, our trucks are late-model Peterworth 410's, pulling 30-foot Morton refrigerated trailers. I am conducting a feasibility study on the benefits of equipping our trailers with hydraulic tailgates. Estimating our needs, the average delivery lowered by the tailgate would weigh 600 lbs.

Send me your response quickly.

Yours truly,

Marlon DiMare
Shipping Director

REVISION A

Case B

Manager
Mister Burger Restaurant
1650 West Parson Street
Vancouver, BC V6E

Dear Manager:

I have been thinking about getting a Mister Burger franchise and opening a restaurant in Yellowknife, N.W.T. Before making my final decision, I wanted to contact other franchisors asking about their experiences with Mister Burger.

How has business been for you? How many hours do you work each week? What percentage of your total sales constitutes your annual pretax profit? Have you received adequate support from the Mister Burger Corporation?

I'm in a hurry, so you'd better answer my letter immediately.

Respectfully yours,

R. MacDonald

REVISION B

CHECKLIST

Letters of Inquiry

1. Define the information that you want to obtain ☐

2. Begin by identifying yourself and stating the reason you are requesting information. ☐

3. Be specific and clear. ☐

4. Organize your request in a way that makes it easy for your reader to respond. If you have several specific questions, present them in a numbered list. ☐

5. Be courteous. Thank your reader. ☐

6. If you are requesting information for personal reasons, enclose a self-addressed envelope. ☐

WRITING ASSIGNMENT

Prepare a letter of inquiry for R. Swizzler of Wallabee Consulting Associates, Bowman Road, Bentley, 6102 Western Australia. Continue your first draft on a separate piece of paper.

Background

You (R. Swizzler) are a research analyst, currently working on a marketing survey for a publishing company planning an optometry textbook. You have developed a list of questions that you would like to send to as many optometrists and professors of optometry as possible.

Dr. Kenji Yamada, of 16-6 Ichijoji-Nakanotacho, Sakyoku, Kyoto 606, Japan, is the current president of the International Association of Optometrists. The association publishes a monthly newsletter. Write to Dr. Yamada and ask if he will provide you with the names and addresses of the members of his organization. Ideally, you would like the mailing list of the IAO Newsletter. There is probably an expense involved in preparing the list and sending it to you, so offer to pay.

Goal: _____

Audience: _____

FIRST DRAFT

_____

_____

_____

_____

_____

Wallabee Consulting Associates, Ltd.

Bowman Road
Bentley, 6102 Western Australia

STYLE AND STRUCTURE
Participial Phrases

A participle is a verb form; present participles end in *-ing,* and past participles (of regular verbs) end in *-ed.* A participial phrase consists of a participle and its related words, such as its object and any modifiers. The participial phrase acts as an adjective, modifying a noun or pronoun.

> The computers **experiencing the least downtime** became popular.
>
> The sales representative, **watching the clock nervously**, reported on the conference.
>
> **Recorded last week**, the minutes of Friday's meeting were distributed today.

A perfect participle uses the present participle of *have* and the past participle of the main verb:

> **Having completed the necessary groundwork,** they drew up the contract.
>
> **Having returned all her phone calls**, she wrote the requested letter, ordering the new disks.

Participial phrases provide a way to write one good, flowing sentence in place of several choppy ones.

> CHOPPY: The company found its sales had declined. It discovered deliveries were slow. As a result, the shipping department was reorganized.
>
> EFFECTIVE: **Finding** its sales had declined and **discovering** deliveries were slow, the company reorganized the shipping department.

PRACTICE A   Combine each of the following pairs of sentences, using participial phrases.

Example   1. Make the adjustments necessary to match the analysis entries. We can then begin the program.
After making the adjustments necessary to match the analysis entries, we _____
can begin the program. _____

2. I have worked for the company for the past year. During that time I have conducted a number of presentations on electrode technology.

_____

_____

_____

_____

_____

3. I have researched various computer systems this past year. During that time I reviewed several systems for *Computer Magazine.*

_____

_____

_____

4. Mr. Sullivan was infuriated by the decison. He quit his job.

_____

_____

_____

5. Analyze the profits from the first quarter. We can make budget projections.

_____

_____

_____

6. Mrs. Jones was concerned by the deadline. She decided to work late.

_____

_____

_____

Dangling Participles

Beware of the dangling participle, a common mistake that can get your reader hopelessly lost. Every participial phrase modifies a noun or pronoun. If the noun or pronoun is missing or if it is placed so that its relation to the phrase is not clear to the reader, the participle "dangles." It either modifies nothing or it appears to modify the wrong noun or pronoun. Avoid confusion by inserting the appropriate noun or pronoun as close as possible to the modifying participle.

DANGLING: **Using the computer,** information can be put in and easily retrieved. (Who is using the computer?)

CORRECT: Using the computer, **you can put in information** and easily retrieve it.

DANGLING: **Realizing your concern about the performance tests,** you will soon receive a full report. (Who is realizing your concern?)

CORRECT: Realizing your concern about the performance tests, **we will soon send you** a full report.

DANGLING: **Having reviewed the flow chart,** the problem is in the analysis entries. (Who has reviewed the flow chart?)

CORRECT: Having reviewed the flow chart, **I think** the problem is in the analysis entries.

Misplaced Participles   If the noun or pronoun that you intend to modify is present in the sentence but is farther from the participle than another noun or pronoun, the participle will seem to modify the closer noun or pronoun. The participle will, therefore, be considered misplaced. To correct dangling participles and misplaced modifiers, move the participial phrase next to the noun or pronoun that it should modify.

MISPLACED: That man just delivered a package **holding a clipboard.** (Is the package holding a clipboard?)

CORRECT: That man **holding a clipboard** just delivered a package.

Sometimes you need to know the writer's meaning to identify which noun or pronoun is supposed to be modified.

MISPLACED: The committee hired a new vice president **knowing new research was necessary.** (Who knew new research was necessary—the committee or the vice president?)

CORRECT: **Knowing new research was necessary,** the committee hired a new vice president.

Other Misplaced Modifiers   In addition to participial phrases, other grammatical constructions can modify words. Notice how the position of the modifier can change the meaning of the sentence:

ADVERB: The machine **almost** broke down every time we used it. (It never quite did.)

The machine broke down **almost** every time we used it. (It did often.)

PREPOSITION: The agent opened the door **with the briefcase.** (How did the agent open the door?)

The agent **with the briefcase** opened the door. (Tells which agent opened the door.)

The following suggestions will help you avoid dangling participles and misplaced modifiers.

1. Test whether an adjective phrase is being used properly by reading it with the nearest noun or pronoun.

WRONG: **Walking around the department,** a crumpled memo caught her eye. (Did the memo walk around the department?)

RIGHT: **Walking around the department,** she noticed a crumpled memo.

2. Test whether an adverb phrase is being used properly by reading it with the nearest verb.

WRONG: He looked at the letter he had typed **with his hands in his pockets.** (Did he type with his hands in his pockets?)

RIGHT: **With his hands in his pockets,** he looked at the letter he had typed.

PRACTICE B

Revise the following sentences to eliminate dangling participles and misplaced modifiers.

Example
1. Having read about your special price on drill presses, will you please send me Catalog Item 463A, shown on page 324.
   Having read about your special price on drill presses, I'd like you to send me Catalog Item 463A, shown on page 324, please.

2. We would like to know your opinion of Mr. Manson's work for you before employing him.

3. Can you send us details about the disks, not having seen your brochure?

4. We want to order a tractor, considering the discount you have made available.

5. Having received your new Omni 320 data system, will you please send me information on your customer training seminars.

6. Having taken the first Computer Seminar, please enroll me in the next course.

7. Returning to my office, several clients were waiting.

8. I would like to cancel my order, considering the substantial delay in shipment.

WORDS IN ACTION

A Choose the best answer.

1. Ms. Ogden must obtain additional _____ before making her final decision.
   - a. currency
   - b. forecasting
   - c. data
   - d. profit

2. As a professional _____, our company answers all credit and personnel inquiries.
   - a. courtesy
   - b. analyst
   - c. expenditure
   - d. franchise

3. The Alpha Company is offering a 10-percent _____ on all prepaid orders.
   - a. profit
   - b. currency
   - c. potential
   - d. discount

4. The International Data Processors' Association will be holding its next annual _____ in Tokyo.
   - a. facility
   - b. network
   - c. expenditure
   - d. conference

5. Group registrations are not allowed. Each member must register for the conference _____.
   - a. individually
   - b. competitively
   - c. facility
   - d. respectfully

6. Because of an unusually slow third quarter, this year's _____ were lower than we expected.
   - a. analysts
   - b. profits
   - c. currencies
   - d. presentations

7. Western Europe _____ one third of its overseas market.
   - a. discounts
   - b. constitutes
   - c. franchises
   - d. facilitates

8. Our regional director feels that the product has great _____ for success in his territory.
   - a. potential
   - b. facility
   - c. expenditure
   - d. implementation

9. The original motors were not powerful enough and had to be replaced, creating an additional manufacturing _____.
   - a. profit
   - b. expenditure
   - c. discount
   - d. machinist

10. The Palmer Company has an excellent _____ for recycling aluminum.
    - a. brokerage
    - b. analyst
    - c. facility
    - d. presentation

B Write the word that matches each definition: adequate, facilitate, financial, mainframe, microcomputer.

1. able to fulfill a requirement; suitable _____

2. the central processing unit of a computer exclusive of remote devices _____

3. involving finance; monetary _____

4. a very small computer _____

5. to aid; to ease _____

2.2 LETTERS OF RESPONSE

Objectives

1. Write letters of response.
2. Enliven sentences with active verbs.
3. Make subjects and verbs agree.
4. Use modal auxiliaries correctly.

Refer to the reader's inquiry and the subject of your response.

Provide the information requested. Be specific and complete.

Close with an offer of further assistance.

OMNICOMP INTERNATIONAL
17 BUNKER HILL ROAD, SHREWSBURY MA O1545

January 20, 19..

Mr. Ravi Kumar
Business Manager
M.K. Chatterjee, Ltd.
201 Netaji Subhash Marg
Daryaganj, New Delhi

Dear Mr. Kumar:

Thank you for your letter of January 4 in which you expressed an interest in the OMNI 409 DBMS. We are very proud of the system, and we believe you will find it to be the most effective and efficient available.

Let me respond to your questions one by one:

1. Our World Trade and Exchange program has the capacity to accept any number of foreign currencies. When on-line, the system can perform up-to-the-minute conversions and equations involving as many as thirty currencies, and changes in exchange rates are immediately adjusted.

2. The OMNI 3683 modem, combined with an individualized software interface, can provide a direct and complete interface with your QBL mainframe from any location with telephone facilities. Information is released through five levels of limited access, and at each level is protected by a state-of-the-art security system made up of interlocking, alternating entry codes.

3. Your questions concerning networking options and our customer training program can best be answered by Mr. Gaston Portier, our local representative. I have forwarded your inquiry to him, and you can expect to hear from him before February 1.

I have also enclosed several related brochures and a copy of the OMNI 409 User's Guide.

Again, let me thank you for your interest in the system, and if I can be of any further help to you, please contact me.

Sincerely yours,

Edgar P. Fowler

Edgar P. Fowler
Account Correspondent

Enclosure
cc: Gaston Portier

Purpose   Good business sense and common courtesy require that you answer all letters of inquiry, even if the response simply tells the reader that you are unable to provide the information requested. Response letters should answer all questions as completely as possible and should be sent without delay.

Remember that an inquiry concerning your product or service represents a person already interested in doing business with you. Therefore, it is important that you prepare your response carefully. The strategy of such a response is similar to that of a sales letter (see Chapter 5). If you are asked questions that you can answer positively, then there is no problem—just answer the questions directly, point by point, and as completely as possible.

Strategies   In some cases, however, you may be asked to provide information that shows a weakness of your product. Rather than responding in a straightforward, negative manner, you may want to present the negative information in a positive way. Begin your letter by answering any questions that you can respond to positively. Then answer the negative question. If possible, present the negative information in a basically positive or neutral sentence.

NEGATIVE: Our model E17 electric motors are not energy-efficient and are expensive to operate.

POSITIVE: Although the E17 motors are not as energy-efficient as others, they are the most durable, problem-free electric motors available.

Without actually misleading your readers, this strategy will help to maintain their interest in the other, more positive features of your product.

Inquiries that do not involve potential sales should still be answered completely and promptly. Accurate, pleasant responses create good public relations and establish business contacts and associations. No matter how trivial, unnecessary, or ridiculous an inquiry might seem, good business sense requires a polite response.

Before you answer an inquiry, therefore, make sure that you are the person who can give the best response. Perhaps another person in your company has greater expertise or access to more complete information than you do. The future of an important sale may hinge on your ability to determine this point. If you do forward the inquiry to an associate and are not sure the associate will respond immediately, write and let the inquirer know that you have forwarded his or her letter.

Organization   Begin your letter by directly referring to the inquiry and to the subject of your response. You may want to thank your reader for the interest he or she has shown in your product. Then answer any questions specifically, providing any other details that might be helpful. If you are unable to answer any questions, explain why and, if possible, suggest where the information might be found. At the end of the letter, offer to answer any additional questions that your reader may have.

REVISING

Revise the following response letters. If necessary, replace any weak verbs with strong ones. Present all negative information in a positive way.

Case A

> Wolfe J. Flywheel
> Western Investigation and Surveillance
> 2100 L Street, Northwest
> Washington, DC 20037
>
> Mr dear Mr. Flywheel:
>
> Thank you for making an inquiry about the Lexam 240 four-hour recording cassettes, and if I can be the provider of further help, please feel free to place a call to me.
>
> You were certainly correct in questioning the quality of the Lexam 240's plastic casing. The casings are made from a lightweight, inexpensive plastic that can easily crack when dropped. The tape, on the other hand, is of the finest quality, designed for distortion-free reproduction and durability. The cassette's rotating mechanism is designed to prevent tangling and damage to the tape.
>
> Yours truly,

REVISION A

Case B

Mr. Wallace Sprout
62 Avenue Du Closseau
1180 Bruxelles
Belgium

Sir:

I have received your inquiry of March 15 concerning the combined use of underwater strobe lights and depth sounders. We are a marine construction firm involved in dredging, pile-driving, and making underwater foundations. We do not collect any of the information in your request, and we are much too busy to waste time gathering data for you.

Why don't you contact Marine Research Associates at 1412 Strand Street, Neptune Beach, Florida. Those people have nothing better to do than answer a lot of foolish questions, so I'm sure they will be glad to assist you.

Should you have any questions, I hope you will keep them to yourself.

Affectionately yours,

REVISION B

CHECKLIST

Letters of Response

1. Make sure that you are the person most qualified to respond. ☐

2. Respond as quickly as possible. ☐

3. Begin by directly referring to the inquiry and to the subject of your response. ☐

4. Answer all questions specifically and as completely as possible. If you are unable to answer, explain why and suggest where an answer may be found. ☐

5. Offer to answer any further questions your reader may have. ☐

WRITING ASSIGNMENT

You have just received the following letter of inquiry:

Background

Sales Manager
Cheng Lee Lock Company
40-48 Yee Wo Street
Causeway Bay, Hong Kong

Dear Sales Manager:

For several years now, we have been using your 525A interchangeable core locks with great success. We are currently constructing a new facility at Palmerston, New Zealand, and we would like to use 525A locks there as well.

We will require 423 standard locksets and 8 cross-bolt locks for 12-foot overhead steel doors. Could you please quote me a price for this order and include the amount of time needed for delivery?

Thank you for your prompt reply.

Sincerely,

Reginald Duff
Plant Development Manager

Unfortunately, the Cheng Lee Lock Company has discontinued production of the 525A locks and is now making locks only for automobiles. Answer Mr. Duff's inquiry politely. You may want to let him know that Lian Lock Ltd., Tung Ho Building, 28–34 Chen St., Mongkok, Kowloon, manufactures a lockset that is very similiar to the 525A. Write your first draft on a separate sheet of paper.

Goal: _____

Audience: _____

STYLE AND STRUCTURE
Emphasizing Verbs

Action Verbs

One of the best ways to write clear and concise sentences is to make the verb carry your meaning. Some verbs express more than others do. Usually, forms of the verb *be* require nouns and prepositions to accompany them; the verb *be* describes a condition, not an action. Action verbs, on the other hand, describe something happening. They make sentences more vivid, more direct, and more concise than do the *be* forms.

WORDY AND DULL: **The cost** of this computer **is** more than it was last month.

BETTER: This computer **costs** more than it did last month.

As the example shows, the action verb may already be hiding in the sentence, disguised as another part of speech (usually a noun). In the first example above, the writer used the word *cost* as a noun when it would have worked better as a verb.

Wordiness

Although forms of *be* most frequently cause wordiness, there are a number of other weak verbs that do the same thing (*make, have, seem, occur, take, place, become*). It is not possible to list all the weak verbs, because a verb's strength often depends on the writer's meaning. If you look closely at the main verb or verbs in a sentence, you'll probably be able to tell quickly whether the verb is strong enough to express the meaning concisely. You will often find a better verb nearby, disguised as a noun.

WEAK: Please **subject** the report to careful analysis.
STRONG: Please **analyze** the report carefully.

WEAK: Our goal **is** the reorganization of the shipping department.
STRONG: We will **reorganize** the shipping department.

WEAK: The manager **made** an attempt to increase production.
STRONG: The manager **attempted** to increase production.

In the examples above, the sentences are short and simple, and you can revise them easily. A strong verb can become a noun by the addition of such endings as *-tion, -sis, -ment, -ence, -ance, -ism.*

NOUN: agreement, presentation
VERB: agree, present

Missing Subject

When the subject of the verb does not appear in the sentence, the writer must supply it.

WEAK: The accounting department **must be enlarged** if it is to deal with the new tax regulations.

STRONG: **We** must **enlarge** the accounting department to deal with the new tax regulations.

PRACTICE A   Change the following nouns to verbs.

    Example   1. analysis   *analyze* _____

                2. plagiarism   _____

                3. conference   _____

                4. acceptance   _____

                5. criticism   _____

                6. assurance   _____

                7. concentration   _____

                8. opposition   _____

                9. improvement   _____

              10. transaction   _____

PRACTICE B   Revise the following sentences by replacing weak verbs with action verbs. Supply the subject of the action verb where necessary.

    Example   1. This division is involved in the manufacturing of ultrasound hardware.
                    This division manufactures ultrasound hardware.

                2. The review of the applications was conducted by the vice president.

                3. More information will be sent from our main office next week.

                4. We are most desirous of meeting with you and your associates.

                5. A need exists for us to address the solution to the problem.

                6. Ms. Jones got expert advice from an efficiency consultant.

                7. Thank you for making inquiry about our word processors.

8. Although I cannot provide you with an answer to your question, I have forwarded your letter to our chief engineer, Mr. Wilson.

_____

_____

9. The recommendation we usually suggest is to insulate the wires.

_____

_____

10. We believe the new disk will effect improvements in the system's performance.

_____

_____

WORDS IN ACTION

A   Choose the best answer.

1. Our seat covers are made of the most _____ fabrics available.
   a. durable   c. trivial
   b. alternate   d. neutral

2. I have a meeting this afternoon with a _____ of the Snerd Corporation.
   a. brochure   c. manufacturer
   b. representative   d. subordinate

3. Their accounting department is very _____.
   a. durable   c. efficient
   b. foreign   d. trivial

4. The Berman Company is closing two branch offices in a(n) _____ to save money.
   a. quote   c. alternate
   b. disguise   d. attempt

5. Since I am not qualified to answer your question, I will _____ your inquiry to Miss Wisess.
   a. accept   c. discontinue
   b. forward   d. interface

6. Although Rita is a competent architect, her real area of _____ is marine engineering.
   a. disguise   c. expertise
   b. distortion   d. surveillance

7. We will not _____ delivery of an incomplete order.
   a. disguise   c. construct
   b. forward   d. accept

8. A complete description of the system and its many features is contained in the new _____.
   a. brochure   c. equation
   b. disguise   d. representative

B Write the word that matches each definition: brochure, efficient, foreign, mechanism, trivial.

1. pamphlet   _____

2. acting or producing with a minimum
   of waste or expense   _____

3. a machine; interacting parts   _____

4. of little importance or concern   _____

5. away from one's native country; not
   domestic   _____

GUIDELINES

Verbs: Modal Auxiliaries

Use *might, could, would,* and *should* after an independent clause containing a past-tense verb. Do not use *may, can, will* or *shall* with the past tense:

Examples

> Eve **told** me that she **might** not be home this weekend.
>
> BUT: Herb **thinks** he **may** be home, however.
>
> I **thought** I **could** find a simple solution to your problem.
>
> BUT: I **think** I **can** help if I have more time.
>
> Megan **said** she **would** check with the Nassau office next week.
>
> BUT: Bob **thinks** he **will** buy a boat next week.
>
> I **thought** I **should** try to get tiokoto for tho oxhibit.
>
> BUT: We **feel** we **will** be better ott alone.

Subject-Verb Agreement

A verb form must always agree in number with its subject.

1. Singular subjects require singular verbs:

> **The item** I received **was** damaged.

2. Plural subjects require plural verbs:

> **The items** I received **were** damaged.

3. For most subjects, the plural is formed by adding *-is* or *-es* to the end of the word. An *-s* or *-es* is added to the end of many present-tense verbs with singular subjects:

> **The machines work** properly.
>
> **The machine works** properly.

4. Collective nouns usually require a singular verb form:

> **The board** of directors **supervises** the expansion.
>
> **The company manufactures** ball bearings.
>
> **The group** of experts **presents** its findings tomorrow.

5. Subjects joined by the conjunction *and* are usually plural:

> **Mr. Tanaka and Mr. Yoshida arrive** today.

6. Do not be distracted by intervening words:

> **The mud,** as well as the heavy rains, **makes** our progress slow.
>
> **The incidence** of errors, tardiness, and expressions of discontent **is** increasing.

7. Single subjects joined by *either/or, neither/nor,* and *or* are usually singular:

Either Mr. Ogden **or** Miss Watson **responds** to complaints.

Neither extreme heat **nor** extreme cold **affects** the engine's performance.

The management committee **or** the personnel department **handles** employee relations.

8. When there is a mixture of singular and plural nouns with *or* or *nor,* the verb agrees with the nearest noun:

Neither the buildings **nor the garden has** been preserved.

Either she **or her associates are** usually here.

9. *Each, every, either, neither, anyone, anybody, everyone, everybody, someone, somebody, no one, nobody,* and *one* all take singular verbs:

Each of the contractors **has** only one chance to bid.

10. *None* takes either a singular or a plural verb, depending in its meaning in the sentence. When *none* means "no individuals" (people or things), it takes a plural verb. When *none* means "no amount," it takes a singular verb. When *none* means "not a single one," it is better to say *not one* than *none*:

None of the employees **know** the answer.

Not one of our guests **was** late.

None of the water **has** spilled.

11. *Number* is singular when preceded by *the,* plural when preceded by *a:*

The number of responses **has** surpassed our expectations.

A number of the customers **have** expressed their dissatisfaction.

COMMUNICATION WORKSHOP
Dictation and Transcription

Dictation is the process of giving a communication orally to another person, who then prepares a written document. You should follow certain guidelines when you give or take dictation. For example, if you are dictating a letter, you must plan it in advance, either by writing a rough draft or by making notes. If you are taking dictation, you must be organized and have the appropriate equipment ready for the job.

Remember to consider the ability of the person taking dictation. Don't hesitate to ask if your rate of speaking is too fast, or if you need to clarify anything. If you are dictating into a machine or word-processing center, make sure you state your name, department, and telephone extension.

The transcriber should consider the ability of the person dictating. If necessary, ask for additional clarification. Check for style, spelling, and structure, and proofread for punctuation and grammar. Feel free to make suggestions concerning tone, missing information, or any other matter you notice.

Transcription is the process of typing communications after they have been dictated. Whether you are transcribing from a machine or from your notes, you'll have to use your language skills to make sure that the message appears in the proper written form. Pay attention to details and look for any errors or inconsistencies in the document. By proofreading and examining a letter's content, an alert transcriber helps make each communication a successful one.

Discussion Activities

1. When giving dictation, you should first write a rough draft or make notes. Discuss four more guidelines you should follow.

2. When taking a dictation, you (the transcriber) should always be organized. Discuss four more guidelines.

3. Discuss some possible errors, other than spelling and grammar, that might appear on a dictated letter.

4. Ask someone to dictate a sentence to you. Suggest ways to improve the dictation. Reverse roles.

5. Ask someone to dictate a letter in this chapter to you. Comment on the effectiveness of the dictation. Pay particular attention to the guidelines.

6. What seems to be the most difficult part in giving a dictation? What can you do to avoid these difficulties?

7. What seems to be the most difficult part in taking a dictation? What can you do to avoid these difficulties?

8. How is modern technology (for example, word processors) affecting dictation?

3
INTEROFFICE COMMUNICATIONS

Memorandums

Transmittals

3.1 MEMORANDUMS

1. Write memorandums.
2. Use the active and the passive voice correctly.
3. Use colons correctly.

State the subject accurately.

Give the main message in the first sentence.

Provide necessary details and background information.

Limit the memo to one page.

OMNICOMP INTERNATIONAL
17 BUNKER HILL ROAD, SHREWSBURY MA 01545

Memorandum

TO: Ed Fowler   DATE: February 14, 19..
FROM: Elvira Benway *EB*
SUBJECT: Problems with the S. W. Briggs, Ltd. Account

Please send me copies of all documents relating to the S. W. Briggs account, and let me know if you notice anything unusual in the file.

We've been having continual difficulties in servicing this account. During the past year we've billed them incorrectly, and we've sent the wrong merchandise on several occasions.

Also, please process their current order for an SP106 EPP as quickly as possible.

Purpose   The memorandum (or memo) is the most common form of written communication between persons within a company. While letters represent a company to the public, memorandums (or *memoranda*) represent the writer to his or her co-workers. The memo allows you to transmit information accurately, and it provides you with a record of the message for future reference. You should, therefore, keep copies of all the memorandums you write.

Form   The standard form of the memo is designed to save time – no return address, salutation, or complimentary close is used. This form contains the following headings: *To, From, Date,* and *Subject.* Since the memo is designed to save time, it is important that you state the subject accurately and that you give the memo's most important information immediately. There is no need to make introductory statements such as "The purpose of this memo is to . . . ."

Organization   For your first sentence, always determine the main point of your message and write it as simply and directly as possible. If your memo is in response to a question, give the basic answer in the first sentence. If you are making a request or asking for information, begin with a question. The remaining body of the memo should be used to provide necessary details and background information. Your message should be complete, but it should also be brief. Each sentence should relate to the topic stated in the subject line.

Always try to limit your memo to one page. This rule will encourage you to focus clearly on your subject and to eliminate anything that does not help you express your main point. In most cases, you will find that a subject you cannot limit to one page is probably too complex for the memo form. In that case, the report form is probably best (see Chapter 8).

As in a letter, the tone of your memo depends upon your relationship with the reader. There is really no standard formula for writing in one style to your superiors in the company and in another style to your subordinates. Effective communication is based on personal relationships, not job titles. When you are in doubt, use a friendly, informal style. Although you should compose your memo carefully, your message should appear as though it had been written quickly and efficiently. You can achieve this effect by eliminating unnecessary words and by occasionally using verb contractions. Remember that the memo is designed to save time.

REVISING

Revise the content and style of these memos as needed.

Case A

Interoffice Memorandum

TO: William M. Tweed, President
FROM: Rocco Porcelli
DATE: April 1, 19..
SUBJECT: A suggestion

I have prepared this memorandum in order to make a suggestion. The suggestion concerns a way of improving the efficiency of our office. Have you noticed the number of workers loitering around the copy machine. Supposedly, they are waiting to use the machine, but this is merely an excuse to socialize with each other. If there were two copy machines, they wouldn't have this excuse and they would have to work harder. The amount of time saved would surely justify the cost of the machine. I know because my desk is near the copy machine, and I watch everyone who uses it and listen to their conversations. Therefore, a new copy machine should be bought by the company.

REVISION A

Case B

**BOWSER BEEFY
DOG FOOD COMPANY**
Memorandum

TO: Lionel Basenji, Assistant Vice President   Date: 10/31/19..
FROM: Phil Doberman, General Manager

Something really must be done about the problem discussed
by us last week at our division meeting. I remember that some
good suggestions were made by you. The trouble is
implementing them.

Production was off by nearly 20 percent last month. Too
much mechanical failure must be the reason for that. Even our
deliveries are now behind schedule, and we are beginning to get
complaints from customers and even cancellations.

If you get an idea about the mechanical failure problem,
please let me know. Maybe it relates to difficulties with the
maintenance budget or the hiring freeze.

We should think about making our monthly newsletter a
biweekly. Fred Bassett in the sales department is especially
eager to do that.

REVISION B

CHECKLIST

Interoffice Memorandums

1. Define your subject and state it accurately. ☐

2. Consider your reader when you determine the tone of the memo. In most cases, use a friendly, informal style. ☐

3. Put the main point of your memo in the first sentence. ☐

4. Use the body of the memo to provide necessary details and background information. All sentences should be directly related to the topic stated in the subject line. ☐

5. Limit your memo to one page. If you can't, then re-examine your subject. It is probably too complex for the memo format. ☐

6. Keep copies of the memos you write. They are often useful for future reference. ☐

WRITING ASSIGNMENT

Background

The Takai Company plans to buy seven new copy machines for its office. Two different types of copier have been recommended: the Repro ND400 and the Zero 112. Alphonse DeFilippo, the company's business manager, has asked O. Fallon, his administrative assistant, to compare the two models and make a recommendation. Prepare a memo for O. Fallon answering Mr. DeFilippo's request. Use the following information to make your decision.

The machines are comparable in price and in the length of their service contracts. You (O. Fallon) have sent a number of inquiries to companies that are using these machines. Their responses indicate that the users of both machines were basically satisfied. You learned, however, that the Zero 112 tends to need repairs more frequently than the Repro ND400 does. These repairs are usually completed quickly by the Zero service representatives.

The Repro ND400 is more reliable, but it is slower than the Zero 112. The Repro is capable of making thirty-six copies per minute, while the Zero is capable of forty-four. The Zero has a copy enlarger, a feature that the Repro does not have. You have checked with the company's department managers, however, and have found that the advertising department is the only department that would ever need enlarged copies.

Write your first draft on a separate sheet of paper.

Goal: _____

Audience: _____

TAKAI CO.   Interoffice Memorandum

From: Date:
To:
Subject:

STYLE AND STRUCTURE
The Active and the Passive Voice

Definition

Many verbs require an object to complete their meaning. They are referred to as transitive verbs. Transitive verbs can have one of two voices: active or passive. When a verb has a direct object, it is in the active voice:

ACTIVE: Ms. Wilson *wrote* a letter.

But when the writer uses the direct object as the subject, the verb is said to be in the passive voice:

PASSIVE: A letter *was written* by Ms. Wilson.

The passive voice always requires a verb phrase. This consists of a form of the verb *be* (or occasionally *get*) followed by the past participle form of the main verb.

You will probably notice that the two examples above say the same thing but that the second sentence requires two extra words, *was* and *by*. That is one disadvantage of using the passive voice: it is wordy. Often a writer drops the *by* phrase when using the passive voice, feeling the meaning is clear without it:

A letter *was written.*

Usage

Thus the overall effect of the passive voice is to emphasize the object or action, and to minimize the subject, or actor. By leaving out the *by* phrase and completely hiding the actor, the writer loses a certain amount of clarity.

In some instances, however, you may want to obscure the actor. Most writers would feel more comfortable using the passive voice in the following sentence:

ACTIVE: I *made* a careless mistake that cost the company thousands of dollars.

PASSIVE: A careless mistake that cost the company thousands of dollars *was made.*

As you can see, the passive voice is a great way to avoid responsibility in your writing. When you use the passive habitually, your writing becomes wordy and unclear, and soon loses all contact with your individual personality.

As a general rule, then, use the active voice whenever possible. Use the passive only when there is a good reason for it, such as when the actor is unimportant (*The new copy machine has been installed*) or when you want to avoid naming the actor (*An error was made in the accounting department*).

PRACTICE A

In each of the following sentences, change the underlined verb from the passive to the active voice. Add the missing subject if necessary.

Example

1. Last year's losses have been accounted for by Mr. Crawley.
   Mr. Crawley accounted for last year's losses.

2. Half of the merchandise was damaged by the fire.

   _____

   _____

3. The responsibility for promotions was delegated to him.

   _____

   _____

4. We expect that sales will be continued in St. Louis.

   _____

   _____

5. There is a service fee, which is charged to your account.

   _____

   _____

6. The program will be started by our technology section.

   _____

   _____

7. The terminal won't be delivered by our company until next week.

   _____

   _____

8. It is required by law that the contents be listed accurately by you.

   _____

   _____

9. Significant progress has been made by the administration.

   _____

   _____

PRACTICE B   In each of the following sentences, substitute a new verb in the active voice for the underlined passive verb, and revise to make the meaning clear.

Example   1. It was discovered by an audit that equipment had disappeared.
   An audit showed that equipment had disappeared.

2. Your letter was not received in our office.

   _____

   _____

3. Operation is greatly enhanced by the new features.

_____

_____

4. Public concern has been initiated by the findings of the commission.

_____

_____

5. The need to resolve this problem should be addressed.

_____

_____

6. Tasks must have a date by which they are to be accomplished.

_____

_____

7. The profits were lost through inflation.

_____

_____

8. Mr. Ogata's inquiry was responded to.

_____

_____

9. Five new typewriters were purchased by the management.

_____

_____

10. A replacement part was shipped to Houston.

_____

_____

WORDS IN ACTION

A   Choose the best answer.

1. We welcome any _____ from our employees concerning the problem.
   a. excuse   c. suggestion
   b. maintenance   d. purchase

2. Our problems with production have resulted in the _____ of several orders.
   a. cancellation
   b. maintenance
   c. reference
   d. progress

3. The assembly _____ is actually quite simple.
   a. complex
   b. representative
   c. progress
   d. process

4. Ms. Antrope makes _____ visits to the company's regional sales offices.
   a. accurate
   b. frequent
   c. overall
   d. current

5. Mr. Fowler will have to _____ his large entertainment expenses.
   a. initiate
   b. delegate
   c. socialize
   d. justify

6. Mrs. Regardie's _____ include processing payments and collecting overdue accounts.
   a. references
   b. responsibilities
   c. services
   d. administration

7. The initial cost is quite reasonable, but the _____ cost can be very expensive.
   a. maintenance
   b. purchase
   c. current
   d. informal

8. After the presentation, the speakers held an _____ meeting to answer individual questions.
   a. accurate
   b. informal
   c. overall
   d. occasional

9. The report showed an _____ increase in net profits for the third quarter.
   a. overall
   b. informal
   c. initial
   d. accurate

10. After the conference, the attendants were able to _____ at the reception.
    a. eliminate
    b. minimize
    c. terminate
    d. socialize

B   Write the word that matches each definition: eliminate, minimize, purchase, terminate, transmit.

1. get rid of; leave out; remove   _____

2. send   _____

3. decrease to the smallest possible size, amount, value   _____

4. discontinue; halt; bring to an end   _____

5. buy   _____

1. The colon formally introduces a list or a statement. It clarifies and calls attention to the information that follows it. The colon usually requires a word of introduction or a summarizing statement:

> Our system includes the following: a terminal, a processing unit, and a printer.
>
> The company's activities can be divided into three categories: production, marketing, and distribution.

2. The colon follows the salutation and subject line in a business letter:

> Dear Mr. Fowler:
>
> *Subject:* Our upcoming meeting in . . . .

3. Use a colon to separate two independent clauses in a sentence when the first clause introduces or leads to or promises the second:

> The decision was made: they would leave in the morning.
>
> The rule is this: Never say "never."

4. Use a colon after *as follows* or *the following* when the expression immediately precedes the statement of a rule or definition:

> The principle of inflation can be stated as follows: It is a sustained and significant increase in the general price level.

5. Use a colon to introduce a direct quotation:

> The author described the effects of inflation: "It can cause bracket creep as taxpayers are forced into higher-rate brackets in progressive tax systems."

6. Do not use colons after the expressions *that is, for example, such as, namely,* and *for instance.*

INCORRECT: A substance may undergo a change of phase, that is: a change from solid to liquid or from liquid to gas.

CORRECT: A substance may undergo a change of phase, that is, a change from solid to liquid or from liquid to gas.

7. Never use a colon after a verb or preposition:

INCORRECT: We need to buy: a truck, a van, and a forklift.

CORRECT: We need to buy the following: a truck, a van, and a forklift.

INCORRECT: On my next trip, I have appointments in: London, Toronto, and New York.

CORRECT: On my next trip, I have appointments in three cities: London, Toronto, and New York.

3.2 TRANSMITTALS

Objectives

1. Write transmittals.
2. Use the correct personal pronoun throughout a sentence or paragraph.
3. Use subordinate conjunctions effectively.
4. Identify restrictive nonrestrictive clauses.

Identify what you are sending and give your reason for sending it.

Specify the action that you want the reader to take. Give any necessary background information.

OMNICOMP INTERNATIONAL
17 BUNKER HILL ROAD, SHREWSBURY MA O1545

Memorandum

TO: Elvira Benway   DATE: February 15, 19..
FROM: Edgar Fowler EF
SUBJECT: S. W. Briggs Account File

Here is the material you requested in your memo of 2/14. I've attached copies of the following documents:

1. Orders of October 22, 19.., March 15, 19.., August 16, 19.., and November 1, 19..
2. Invoices 1295, 1647, 1722, and 2001
3. Annual account statement for 19..
4. Customer claim letters of 8/30/19.. and 11/22/19..
5. Adjustment letters of 9/5/19.. and 11/30/19..

Please check these documents carefully. I have processed the latest order, but I haven't been able to find the cause of our problems with this account. Let me know if you notice any irregularities in these documents.

Purpose   When you send information or material, you should always attach a covering transmittal. If the material is being sent to another person in the same company, the transmittal write in the memo form. Use the standard business letter format is used when you are sending something outside the company. The transmittal simply identifies what you are sending and gives your reason for sending it.

The transmittal achieves two goals. First, it lets the reader know that he or she has received everything that you have sent, along with specific instructions concerning what to do with it. Second, the transmittal provides a record of where and when the material was sent and determines the responsibility for its care. Always keep a copy of the transmittal for your files.

Organization   The first paragraph of the transmittal should simply identify the material that you are sending and your reason for sending it. There is no need to use formal language in your transmittal:

AVOID: Attached please find . . .
           Enclosed is . . .
           Herewith the following . . .

USE: Here is . . .
     I have enclosed . . .
     This is the information . . .

If you are sending one or two items, identify them in a sentence. For three or more items, use a numbered list. Identify the enclosed material accurately and completely, using document numbers or dates if necessary.

Although many writers conclude their transmittals at this point, most readers appreciate a second paragraph. The second paragraph can be used to give instructions, to make recommendations, or to highlight any important or unusual elements of the enclosed material. A second paragraph should always define any action required of the reader.

REVISING

This writer is sending five photographic negatives to the company's graphic service department. She wants to have three prints made of each negative. Rewrite the transmittal.

Case A

Memorandum

TO: Matt Brady
FROM: Cecilia B. DeMille
DATE: June 6, 19..
SUBJECT: what we talked about on the phone yesterday morning

Herewith, please find the attached stuff that I asked you about.
I hope you can complete the job as soon as possible.

REVISION A

_____
_____
_____
_____
_____
_____
_____
_____
_____
_____
_____
_____
_____
_____
_____
_____
_____
_____
_____
_____
_____

Correct the organization, content, and style of the following letter of transmittal.

Case B

DRYDOCK ENTERPRISES
Box 112 G.P.O. Sydney, NSW 2001 AUSTRALIA

Professor Waldo Moronne
Center for East-West Studies
2-7-5 Yamamotodai
Nerima-ku, Tokyo 177 Japan

Dear Professor Moronne:

I have enclosed: the original and a copy of the agreement to publish your article, "East Is East, but Is West West?," in November issue of Southern Business Review. Please follow the following instructions:

1. Sign both the original agreement and the copy.
2. Return the original to me.
3. Keep the copy for your files.

When the article is published, I will send you copy of them. Also, here is a check for $500 which was for payment.

Sincerely

Rupert Drydock
September 5, 19..

REVISION B

_____
_____
_____
_____
_____
_____
_____
_____
_____
_____
_____

CHECKLIST

The Transmittal

1. Accurately identify what you are sending. ☐

2. State your reason for sending the material. ☐

3. Specify any action that you want the reader to take. Give any necessary instructions for the disposition of the material. ☐

4. Point out any important or unusual elements of the enclosed material. ☐

5. Keep a copy to remember the transaction and to determine responsibility for the materials that were sent. ☐

WRITING ASSIGNMENT

Background

R. Jimenez is the account manager for Madison Pressley Associates, an advertising firm. Several weeks ago, you (R. Jimenez) contracted an artist, Anna Patterson, of 118 Franklin St., New York, NY 10013, to produce a series of drawings to be used in your advertising campaign. Today the six drawings arrived.

Prepare a transmittal memo to Ted Cleaver in your company's graphic service department. Instruct him to prepare a photostat of each of the drawings, enlarging them by 30 percent. Then send a letter of transmittal to Anna Patterson to accompany a check for $900 as payment for her work. Be sure to let her know how happy you are with the drawings.

Goal: _____

Audience: _____

FIRST DRAFT

_____

_____

_____

_____

_____

_____

_____

_____

_____

MADISON PRESSLEY ASSOCIATES
228 East Harris Street
San Francisco, CA   94080

From: Date:
To:
Subject:

STYLE AND STRUCTURE

Consistency

Consistency of Person

Consistency of person requires you to use the correct personal pronoun throughout a sentence or paragraph. The pronoun must be related to the subject it refers to, and it should not be changed unless you want to change the meaning. Avoid confusing shifts between the first person (I, we), the second person (you), and the third person (he, she, it, they).

> UNCLEAR: A *customer* can learn to operate the tool in five minutes if *they* have the owner's manual.
>
> UNCLEAR: A *customer* can learn to operate the tool in five minutes if *you* have the owner's manual.
>
> CLEAR: A *customer* can learn to operate the tool in five minutes if *he* or *she* has the owner's manual.
>
> BETTER: *Customers* can learn to operate the tool in five minutes if *they* have the owner's manual.

Consistency of Number

There should not be any shifts between singular and plural within a sentence or paragraph. The same number should be used throughout.

> UNCLEAR: The *company* sent a memorandum to *their* employees.
>
> CLEAR: The *company* sent a memorandum to *its* employees.

PRACTICE

Correct the inconsistencies in the following sentences by eliminating any confusing shifts in person and number.

Example

1. Consumers have difficulty assembling the machine because you can't follow these directions easily.
   Consumers have difficulty assembling the machine because they can't follow these directions easily.

2. If you notice what happened to second-quarter sales, it shows a sharp decline.

3. Everyone should report the number of defects they see in any product.

4. Neither the foreman nor the plant superintendent are willing to take responsibility for this.

5. None of the experiments with reprocessed tapes have proved successful.

_____

_____

6. The chief chemist, the division manager, and the vice president, despite the opposition of the president, insists the formula will work.

_____

_____

7. This report is one of those that issues from the home office every month.

_____

_____

8. Each worker knows that they are responsible for the success of the product.

_____

_____

9. Our production costs are higher than it was three years ago.

_____

_____

10. As I was leaving the secured area, I saw that the alarm system wasn't working. You could see the warning light flash.

_____

_____

WORDS IN ACTION

A   Choose the best answer.

1. The committee has _____ that we submit our proposals before Friday.
   a. assembled   c. declined
   b. appreciated   d. requested

2. In order to comply with the customer's specifications, we had to make several _____ in the design.
   a. adjustments   c. formulas
   b. statistics   d. defects

3. We have recently hired two technical writers to help prepare the operator's _____ for the HAL200 computer.
   a. annual   c. material
   b. agreement   d. manual

4. I have _____ a check for $954.76 in payment of your invoice number 1044.
   a. achieved   c. declined
   b. enclosed   d. assembled

5. The slow sales can be blamed on a _____ in the world's economy.
   a. decline   c. formula
   b. document   d. statistic

6. Although we wanted to rent a larger office, we discovered that the cost was

   _____.
   a. appreciated   c. prohibitive
   b. great   d. consistent

7. We sell the bicycles in parts, and the customer must _____ them.
   a. appreciate   c. attach
   b. decline   d. assemble

8. The engine was returned because of a(n) _____ in the starting mechanism.
   a. chemist   c. agreement
   b. defect   d. formula

9. The company has decided to hold two sales conferences, one in September
   and one in April, instead of one _____ conference, which has always been
   held in November.
   a. prohibitive   c. biweekly
   b. consistent   d. annual

10. I _____ your help and cooperation in this matter.
    a. conclude   c. appreciate
    b. decline   d. achieve

B   Write the word that matches each definition: conclude, enclose, inconsistency, necessary, opposition.

1. the state of being not regular or
   predictable   _____

2. the act of being in conflict   _____

3. indispensable; essential or vital to
   achieve a result or effect   _____

4. to reach a decision; to determine; to
   close   _____

5. to place within a package or
   container; to close in   _____

GUIDELINES

Subordination

You can often avoid using too many short, simple sentences by subordinating one idea to another. Consider the following examples:

The items were damaged. They weren't handled carefully.

The shipper is responsible. I cannot accept the delivery.

The shipper sends replacement items. We can do business again.

These sentences can be connected by linking the ideas with subordinating conjunctions:

The items were damaged *because* they weren't handled carefully.

Although the shipper is responsible, I cannot accept the delivery.

When the shipper sends the items, we can do business again.

The Comma The subordinating conjunctions make one idea subordinate to, or dependent upon, another. A comma is used only when the subordinate part of the sentence comes first.

Until we get the replacements, our stocks will be low.

Our stocks will be low until we get the replacements.

Here is a list of some subordinating conjunctions:

after	before	unless	where
although	if	until	wherever
as	once	when	while
because	since	whenever	

Restrictive and Nonrestrictive Clauses

Restrictive Clauses

A restrictive clause limits the meaning of the noun it modifies. Restrictive clauses are necessary in the meaning of the sentence. As you can see, restrictive clauses are not set off by commas.

> The person *who stole my account* is in for a big surprise.
>
> The reports *that come from the marketing department* always seem well written.

Nonrestrictive Clauses

A nonrestrictive clause supplies additional information about the noun it modifies, but it is not really necessary to the basic meaning of the sentence. Nonrestrictive clauses are set off by commas.

> Arnold Grant, *who used to work down the hall from me,* was awarded this year's top bonus.
>
> The controversy, *which was becoming more and more heated,* finally forced the employee to resign.

That* and *Which

The choice between *that* and *which* to introduce restrictive and nonrestrictive clauses can sometimes be a difficult one. For clauses not referring to people, use *that* to introduce all restrictive clauses and *which* to introduce all nonrestrictive clauses.

> The machine *that we really wanted* was far too expensive.
>
> Today that computer, *which cost ten thousand dollars originally,* is worth two thousand dollars.

COMMUNICATION WORKSHOP
Minutes of Meetings

Within most companies, several committees or groups address certain problems or perform specific functions. Such committees generally appoint a secretary to record the minutes (prepare a summary) of their meetings. These minutes provide a record of the meeting's events, serve as reminders to committee members, inform members who may have missed meeting of what has been accomplished, and establish responsibility for decisions and actions. Copies of the minutes are usually sent to all persons who attended the meeting, to committee members who were not present, and to any individual or officer in the company who may be interested in the meeting's proceedings.

The format of the minutes can vary, but the document should always include the name of the meeting; the time, date, and place of the meeting; who attended; and what discussions took place. It can also remind members of the date of the committee's next meeting.

The person who is assigned to record the minutes must take accurate notes during the meeting and be able to identify the main points of each speaker's remarks. The reporter can then use the notes to write a brief summary of these points in the body of the minutes.

Summary of Software Development Committee Meeting

TIME AND PLACE The meeting was held on Friday, July 13, 19.., in the executive conference room. The committee's chairperson, Bert Traven, called the meeting to order at 10:00 A.M.

ATTENDANCE Those attending were E. Benway, R. Drake, L. Fine, S. Jones, M. Melle, A. Mason, S. Robinson, B. Traven, and S. Van Zandt.

DISCUSSIONS Marty Melle explained the recent divisional reorganization, under which the Educational Software and Industrial Graphics Departments are grouped under Development Director Steve Christenson.

Anne Mason explained the key issues covered in a June 12 meeting on software marketing. Her group is helping its sales representatives understand our new software offerings.

Sylvia Robinson mentioned that the Marmot Company's software list is up for bids, since Marmot has announced it is discontinuing software distribution.

Sylvia also described the Bilateral Video Disc program (BVD) submitted by Dr. Milton Boyle of Oxford University. The program, currently being evaluated by Mr. Christenson's group, is an interactive video program designed for elementary education.

Sam Jones described GRAPH, a graphing package now under development. The program can produce up to 150 presentation-quality charts and graphs on a single diskette.

NEXT MEETING   The committee will meet Thursday, August 16, at 10:00 A.M., in the executive conference room.

ADJOURNMENT   The meeting was adjourned at 11:55 A.M.

J. Boswell
Recorder

DISCUSSION ACTIVITIES

1. Form three committees of five persons and discuss one of the following topics. Choose a chairperson and appoint someone to record the minutes.
   Topics:
   a. the effect of modern technology in today's business office
   b. the greatest concern facing business today
   c. the relationship between business and our community

2. You (the recorder) have been asked to take notes on one of the topics in question 1. Prepare the minutes and distribute them to the members of the committee for their approval. You (a committee member) are expected to suggest corrections or to approve the minutes as stated.

3. Make a list of different kinds of committees and discuss their function.

4. Which committees are usually present in most companies? How members are appointed?

4
CUSTOMER RELATIONS

Letters of Complaint

Positive Letters of
Adjustment

Negative Letters of
Adjustment

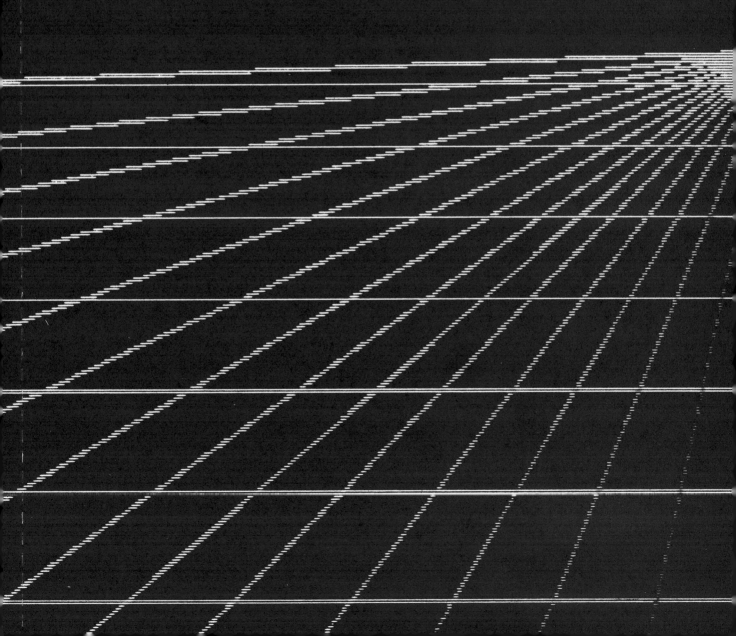

Objectives

1. Write letters
   of complaint.
2. Write concise sentences.
3. Use pronouns correctly.

Give the history
of the transaction.

Give the current
status of
the transaction.

Recommend the
action that will
best solve
the problem.

S.W. Briggs & Company Limited
9 Wembley Street, London NNE19 6BN

25 April 19..

Mr Edgar Fowler
Omnicomp International
17 Bunker Hill Road
Shrewsbury, MA   01545   USA

Dear Mr Fowler:

On 4 February we ordered an SP106 Interface to use with our
electrostatic plotter/printer. On 2 March we received the SQ106
Interface (Invoice 2502), a model obviously incompatible with
our EPP. We explained the mistake and returned the product,
confident that the SP106 would be delivered within a reasonable
period of time.

Yesterday, more than two months after placing our order, we
received another SQ106 Interface, accompanied by your letter of
apology.

Surely you can understand our concern. How would you feel
if you were in our place? We know that everyone makes
mistakes, but a further delay in the implementation of our
system will cause us great inconvenience. Please send us the
SP106 Interface before 15 May or refund our payment of
$5621,80

Sincerely yours,

Ian Stafford

Ian Stafford
Program Director

Purpose	People write letters of complaint, or claim letters, so that sellers of goods and services will know something has gone wrong and will take steps to correct the situation. These letters are an important part of doing business because the readers, though never glad to hear about their mistakes, want to correct their errors and satisfy their customers. Before you write a claim letter, however, you might try to resolve the situation by telephone. If the situation is a simple one and the solution is obvious, a phone call will probably bring the fastest results. If that fails, or if the problem is complex, a letter is the most effective response.
Preparation	Before you begin your letter, you should outline, at least in your mind, the business transaction in terms of its past, present, and future.
Organization	You will want to convince your reader of three main points. First, explain exactly what went wrong, from your point of view. You should not merely write "The right part did not arrive" or "The machine we ordered did not get here on time." The reader must learn from your letter every detail of your complaint. If you don't state exactly what happened, you will probably receive a reply asking for more information.

Next, explain how and why the reader is at fault. If parts arrived late, for example, be sure your order informed the seller that you needed them by a certain date. Most sellers will begin to correct a mistake as soon as they recognize their fault.

Finally, define the correction or adjustment that will resolve the situation. Perhaps you wish to exchange one product for another, with the seller paying the return cost. Or perhaps you want to have your money refunded. Some transactions will call for special considerations. Determining the loss caused by a delayed shipment of parts, for example, may require you to calculate the various extra expenses you suffered as a result of the delay. Whatever the adjustment, be fair and reasonable in your expectations. Try to appeal to your reader's sense of fairness.

Your opening paragraph, therefore, should clearly describe the particular goods or services that you requested. Then politely go on to state what went wrong. Include all the necessary details (names, dates, invoice numbers, dollar amounts, and so forth). Conclude your letter by describing the adjustment you want the reader to make and specifying the date by which you expect the reader to make the adjustment.

Your letter will be most effective if you write in a polite tone. Never insult the reader or accuse a company of being inefficient or stupid. A highly critical or angry letter will not help achieve your goal; it will only build resentment. The tone of your letter should involve the reader in your situation, and you should assume that he or she is sorry about the mistake and is anxious to correct it. Showing anger is not conducive to successful communication. If you are writing merely to express your anger and frustration, don't bother – it isn't worth the effort.

Follow-Up Letter	If your reader does not make the adjustment or respond to your request, write a second letter. This time address a senior officer of the company. Almost certainly, that person will review the situation and respond to the problem in a way that will bring results.

REVISING

Revise the following letters of complaint. Correct any errors in content, style, and structure.

Case A

Dear Mr. Ronald Nager:

In all my years of business, I have never seen such blatant stupidity and incompetence. What is wrong with you people?

On October 5, I placed an order for two cases of piston cups (#18625) and one case of Teflon seals (#6442). Twenty cases of die-cut gaskets and ten cases of urethane seals were received by us.

It is obvious that either you or someone in your shipping department is incapable of processing orders correctly. I want you to be aware that a corrective action must be taken by you within an immediate period of time.

Cordially yours,

Roscoe B. Tingley

REVISION A

Case B

Mr. Amu Karaba, President
East African Wildlife Company
Nairobi, Kenya

Dear Mr. Karaba:

For this intolerable situation, we demand that you return complete refund of our purchase price, with interest. If we have not received our refund by the first day of the month of August, it is our intent never to make a purchase of animals from you again.

Seven months ago, we sent you an order asking you to supply animals for our circus. Over a two-month period of eight weeks, you were to send us four full-grown elephants, one baby elephant, six mature tigers, three lions and one lioness.

Two of the elephants you sent were less than fully grown, and the baby has been seriously ill ever since the day of its arrival. One of the tigers is so old and full of arthritis it can barely move. All of the lions have contracted a skin disease that seems to be incurable, and the lioness is in a condition of being pregnant!

Sincerely yours,

Patricia T. Barnom
Associate Producer

REVISION B

_____

_____

_____

_____

_____

_____

_____

_____

_____

_____

_____

_____

CHECKLIST

Letter of Complaint

1. Determine what action would best satisfy your complaint. ☐

2. Describe the transaction chronologically (tell its past, give the present situation, and then state the future action to resolve the problem). ☐

3. Be specific. Provide all the necessary information – dates, invoices, shipping orders, and anything else that is available. ☐

4. Explain to the reader how and why he or she is at fault. ☐

5. Write in a courteous tone. Never insult or accuse your reader. ☐

6. Close by telling the reader the specific correction or adjustment that you want to be made. ☐

WRITING ASSIGNMENT

Prepare a letter of complaint for R. Welles, manager of Contemporary Office Equipment, 821 Sundown Avenue, Winnipeg, Manitoba 7M4. Address the letter to B. Wallace Foxx, Sales Manager, The Office Outlet, 150 Steelcase Road West, Markham, Ontario L3R 1B2. The letter is in response to the following situation:

Background

On April 5, you (R. Welles) ordered ten gray file cabinets and fifteen white file cabinets from The Office Outlet. You received fifteen gray file cabinets and ten white file cabinets. You sold all of the white cabinets and five of the gray cabinets.

Now you want to return five of the gray cabinets and exchange them for five of the white cabinets. You have advertised a sale, and if you don't receive the cabinets immediately, you will probably lose several customers.

Goal: _____

Audience: _____

FIRST DRAFT

_____

_____

_____

_____

_____

_____

Contemporary Office Equipment

821 Sundown Avenue   Winnipeg, Manitoba   7M4

STYLE AND STRUCTURE
Conciseness

A concise sentence contains no unnecessary words – it expresses its idea quickly and efficiently. Concise writing is easy to understand because the message doesn't have any useless words to hide behind. Unfortunately, concise writing requires constant care. Unnecessary words seem to sprout like weeds into a sentence, and if the writer isn't careful, the necessary words can get lost in the tangle. Consider the following sentence:

> I was wondering if a sufficient period of time has elapsed to allow the committee ample opportunity for the discussion and resolution of the issues raised by the recommendation submitted by the employees.

There is an an extremely overgrown sentence. If the writer had taken the time to weed out the useless words, he or she could have produced a concise sentence:

> Has the committee responded to the employees' recommendation yet?

Types of Wordiness

There are many types of wordiness. One is tautology, or the use of several words that say the same thing.

WORDY: We have begun to export our products to countries abroad.

CONCISE: We have begun to export our products.

WORDY: The machine was packed in a square-shaped carton.

CONCISE: The machine was packed in a square carton.

WORDY: There is another alternative that he can choose.

CONCISE: He has another alternative.

Another type of wordiness involves the use of phrases when one word will do.

WORDY: Mr. Johnson is of the opinion that we are not in a position to disclose information that is of a confidential nature.

CONCISE: Mr. Johnson thinks we cannot disclose confidential information.

WORDY: At this point in time, our production schedule is in conflict with our delivery date.

CONCISE: At this time, our production schedule conflicts with our delivery date.

WORDY: In the event that you speak to Wilbur in regard to production, ask him to give consideration to the delivery schedule.

CONCISE: If you speak to Wilbur about production, ask him to consider the delivery schedule.

Other problems arise from using unnecessarily formal language.

> WORDY: It is to be expected that your performance will improve in the coming year.
>
> CONCISE: We expect you will do better next year.

> WORDY: We are in receipt of your check in the amount of $10; pursuant to your request, we have sent the software manual under separate cover.
>
> CONCISE: We received your check for $10; as you requested, we have sent the software manual separately.

> WORDY: Ronald's proposal is one which we should do well to bear in mind.
>
> CONCISE: We should consider Ronald's proposal.

Still another affliction is the "Well, basically ..." syndrome. What is the "Well, basically ..." syndrome? Well, basically, it is the chronic use of useless words to introduce the meaningful part of a sentence.

> WORDY: Well, basically, the problem can be resolved.
>
> CONCISE: We can resolve the problem.

> WORDY: In response to your question, the answer is yes.
>
> CONCISE: Yes.

> WORDY: Please be advised that we have received your invoice.
>
> CONCISE: We have your received invoice.

Summary   Examine your sentences carefully. Ask yourself two questions: "What am I trying to say?" and "Have I said it clearly?" You can generally avoid wordiness by following these three rules:

---

1. Never use two words when one word will do.

2. Never use a long word when a short word will do.

3. If it is possible to eliminate a word, eliminate it.

Revise the sentences below to make them more concise.

Example 1. In my personal opinion, I think that the price we'll have to pay for the trucks is too expensive.
The trucks seem too expensive.
_____

2. Vacation days taken by your employees are to be reported monthly not later than the tenth day of each month.
_____

3. Acquisition of this product during the next year is necessary.
_____

4. The graph was round in shape and red in color.
_____

5. This machine has a tendency to be difficult to repair.
_____

6. We are asking that you take a good look at this report and notify us of any changes you want to make.
_____

7. The price we paid for the repairs was excessive.
_____

8. In this day and age, the skill of communicating effectively is an important skill to have in business.
_____
_____

WORDS IN ACTION

A Choose the best answer.

1. We received a _____ regarding our latest shipment to Clark Industries.
   a. resentment
   b. audit
   c. complaint
   d. result

2. I intend to _____ payment until the problem with the defective machine is resolved.
   a. withhold
   b. inform
   c. result
   d. defect

3. The pressure gauges that we received are _____ with the APCO Rotary Actuators we are using in our plant.
   - a. blatant
   - b. intolerable
   - c. reasonable
   - d. incompatible

4. If we don't receive the balance of our order within a _____ period of time, please cancel shipment and credit our account for the balance.
   - a. prohibitive
   - b. reasonable
   - c. defective
   - d. blatant

5. Please send a(n) _____ for the compressor that was damaged during shipment.
   - a. replacement
   - b. transaction
   - c. implementation
   - d. audit

6. I must _____ you that the ventilation system installed by your employees does not meet the standards specified in our contract.
   - a. credit
   - b. withhold
   - c. inform
   - d. complaint

7. The electronic alarm system you installed didn't operate properly. As a _____, we had to hire a security guard.
   - a. request
   - b. complaint
   - c. commitment
   - d. result

8. The _____ of our new system has been delayed because the software you promised has not been delivered.
   - a. implementation
   - b. resentment
   - c. transaction
   - d. inconvenience

9. Please correct the problem as soon as possible. The replacement parts are needed _____.
   - a. consistently
   - b. intolerably
   - c. immediately
   - d. incapably

10. Please modify the system so that it _____ to our original design.
    - a. defects
    - b. alters
    - c. withholds
    - d. conforms

B   Write the word that matches each definition: cancel, consideration, incapable, inefficient, reasonable.

1. invalidate; decide not to proceed with _____

2. incompetent; unable to perform adequately _____

3. thoughtful deliberation in forming a judgment or decision _____

4. not producing the expected result; wasteful

    _____

5. within the limits of common sense

    _____

GUIDELINES _____

Pronoun Case

Definition   Personal pronouns (*I, he, we,* etc.) change form, or case, depending on their function in the sentence. The subjective case is used when the pronoun is the subject of the verb or subject complement. The objective case is used when the pronoun is the object of the verb or preposition.

1. Use the subjective case (*I, he, she, we, they*) for pronouns used as subjects or predicate nominatives:

> Are you saying that *he* is more competent than *I* [am]?
> (*not* than *me*)
>
> There were only Casey and *I* left to tell the story.
> (*not* Casey and *me*)

2. Use the objective case (*me, her, him, us, them*) for objects:

> Between *you* and *me* (*not* between *you* and *I*), this isn't going to work.
>
> Some of *us* (*not* of *we*) readers disagree with your policies.
>
> What this company needs is a woman like *her* (*not* like *she*).
>
> He invited *her and me* (*not* she and I) to dinner.

3. Words connected by a form of the verb *be* must be in the same case:

> I wish the lucky winner had been *she.*
>
> If the culprit were *he,* Smith would surely have known it.

However, the subject of an infinitive is always in the objective case:

> Do you consider *him to be* more competent than Fowler?:

4. *Who* or *whom*? *Whoever* or *whomever*? In spoken and informal written English, *who* and *whoever* are frequently used for both the objective and the subjective cases. However *whom* and *whomever* are formally correct in the objective case.

> INFORMAL: *Who* do you plan to go with to the company picnic?
>
> FORMAL: With *whom* will you attend the conference next month?

If the relative pronoun is an object, in formal English use *whom* or *whoever:*

> You may hire *whomever you choose.*
>
> The person *whom you are discussing* is standing in the doorway.

4.2 POSITIVE LETTERS OF ADJUSTMENT

Objectives

1. Write positive letters of adjustment.
2. Correct inflated diction.
3. Write specific words that describe general terms.
4. Use the apostrophe correctly.

OMNICOMP INTERNATIONAL
17 BUNKER HILL ROAD, SHREWSBURY MA 01545

May 1, 19..

Mr. Ian Stafford, Program Director
S. W. Briggs & Company, Ltd.
9 Wembley Street
London NNE19 6BN

Dear Mr. Stafford:

Apologize and state the adjustment.

    I am very sorry for the many difficulties that you have endured in trying to buy an SP106 Interface. We have just shipped your SP106 via airmail, and you should receive it well before the fifteenth. In addition, we have enclosed our complete line of relevant software resources at no cost to you. Please accept this small gesture as an expression of our gratitude for your patience.

Tell what went wrong.

    We have finally discovered the source of your recurring problems. It seems that your customer account number was originally entered incorrectly into the computer at our warehouse. This error resulted in the incorrect shipments that you have received.

End in a positive tone.

    Please accept my sincere apology for the confusion. We value your business and hope to provide you with efficient service in the years to come.

Respectfully yours,

Edgar P. Fowler

Edgar Fowler
Account Correspondent

cc: Elvira Benway

Purpose
If you never make a mistake, you probably aren't working. Errors happen in the best of companies. When you receive a just complaint from a customer, don't be afraid to admit the mistake. Accept the responsibility for solving the problem. Act promptly, find out what went wrong, and then write the customer a thoughtful letter. The goal of your letter will be to restore the goodwill of the dissatisfied customer.

Preparation
Begin by putting yourself in the position of the customer. How does he or she feel? Is the requested adjustment reasonable? Examine the transaction carefully and fairly – don't let a claimant's anger interfere with your decision. Decide upon an adjustment that will satisfy your reader.

Start your letter with a polite apology. Keep it simple – too much regret tends to sound insincere. Then, if you are taking satisfactory steps to resolve the complaint, state the adjustment immediately. Customers appreciate a frank admission that the company is at fault and that you are trying to correct the problem.

In recognizing that the error has undoubtedly inconvenienced the customer, you might want to do something special for your reader as a compensation for his or her trouble. Such thoughtfulness demonstrates your sincerity and helps you to regain the customer's goodwill.

Organization
In your first paragraph, state your apology, the corrective action, and the special compensation. This will surely please your reader and reduce his or her hostility. Now that you've got your reader in a cheerful mood, write a second paragraph that explains how the error occurred. Your reader deserves an explanation of what went wrong, but he or she is not concerned with the particular details – only a speedy correction. Explain the mistake honestly, but do so as briefly as possible.

Conclude your letter with a short third paragraph. Begin by briefly restating your apology. This reminds the reader of the satisfaction he or she received in the first paragraph and it emphasizes your concern that such a mistake could have occurred. End with a positive, confident sentence that reaffirms your business relationship with the reader. Some writers use the closing to promote new sales, but this should be done only with extreme care. You risk obscuring the sincerity of your apology and minimizing the seriousness of the mistake.

Prepare your positive adjustment letters carefully. They give you the opportunity to transform justifiably unhappy customers into reliable clients who are pleased with the personal attention they have received.

REVISING

Revise the following adjustment letters.

Case A

Mr. Amin Nasrudin
P.O. Box 242
Abu Dhabi UAE

Dear Mr. Nasrudin:

I am heartily sorry that you received the wrong book. Please forgive us for this grievous error. We beg your forgiveness and plead with you to allow us to correct our inexcusable mistake. I humbly enclose the book that you originally ordered, along by a copy of our most popular printed product, the English Diccionary. Please accept this humble gift as a token of our disgrace.

A careless, foolish mistake was the cause of this disaster! A clerk transcribed your order's title number as 017117 instead as 017171. Now he must live with the shame of his error.

Please forgive us for this one moment of weakness. Give us another chance to redeem ourselves. We will not fail you again!

Regretfully yours,

Paul Benker

REVISION A

Case B

Ms. Ida Byrne, Resident Manager
Hadesville Condominiums
212 Baker Street, Apartment 1
Hadesville, SC 42122

Dear Ms. Byrne:

Well, it seems that you were right about not receiving the twenty-six air conditioners that you ordered in May. We never shipped them. But instead of refunding your payment, I've decided to send your order immediately by air parcel post. The air conditioners will arrive by December 1.

Let me tell you what happened to your order. Your order was received by a temporary employee who worked here last spring (the guy was a real chump). One day Sam, our mailboy, knocked over this guy's in-box. Some of the papers fell behind a heavy file cabinet, and the guy didn't even try to get them out. About a month ago, our office was being remodeled and somebody moved the file cabinet. There was your order, covered with about three inches of dust. What a joke! We couldn't believe such a thing could have happened.

Just to show you how nice we are here at Frostheave Appliance Company, I've sent you an extra air conditioner absolutely free! We try, but mistakes often happen to the best of us. I've also enclosed a brochure describing our new portable heaters. Why not order yours today?

Your friend,

Alfred R. Petersen

REVISION B

_____

_____

_____

_____

_____

_____

_____

_____

_____

_____

_____

_____

CHECKLIST

Positive Adjustment Letters

1. Try to understand your customer's position. Examine the transaction calmly and fairly. ☐

2. Begin your letter with a simple, polite apology. ☐

3. Conclude your first paragraph by stating the action you are taking to resolve the claim. ☐

4. Use your second paragraph to explain what went wrong. Keep the explanation short and simple. ☐

5. Begin your third paragraph with a brief statement that reaffirms your future business relationship with your reader. ☐

WRITING ASSIGNMENT

Background

Q. Baldwin, manager of Fuzzy's Furniture Factory Outlet, has just received the complaint letter below. You (the assistant manager) have been asked to prepare an adjustment letter to satisfy the customer. Decide upon an action that will correct the situation, and write the letter. You have been asked to sign the letter in Q. Baldwin's name.

---

12 Royal Street
New Orleans, LA 62524

March 5, 19..

Fuzzy's Furniture Factory Outlet
44 Tchoupitoulas Street
New Orleans, LA   62552

Dear Manager:

On February 6, I bought a desk and three chairs at your store (receipt #4062). They were delivered last Tuesday. When your deliverymen unloaded the desk, they dropped it from the truck onto the street. The desk top was badly scratched, and the driver told me that an adjustor would contact me on the following day (February 28).

Nobody has contacted me about the problem, and I'm unhappy about the situation and the condition of the desk.

Please help me to resolve this problem. You should either repair the desk, deliver a new one, or give me back my purchase price of $368.50. I expect to hear from you soon.

Sincerely,

Simone LaGris

FUZZY'S FURNITURE FACTORY OUTLET

○○○○○○ 44 Tchoupitoulas Street ○○○○○○
New Orleans, LA 62552

STYLE AND STRUCTURE
Diction

Inflated Diction

Short, familiar words suit business writing well because they allow the writer to make his or her point economically. Write your sentences as you would speak them, then revise your draft. The reader will probably understand you easily. Don't use long words without good reason; words used this way are called *inflated diction*.

> INFLATED: We *finalized* plans for the *modification*.
> SIMPLE: We *completed* plans for the *change*.

> INFLATED: *Subsequent to your compliance* with our request...
> SIMPLE: *After you comply* with our request...

As a rule, use specific rather than general words because they tell your reader exactly what you mean. General terms describe a category, while specific words name a particular item. But words do not fall merely into one category or the other; many degrees exist between the most general and the most specific.

GENERAL	SPECIFIC	MORE SPECIFIC
Corporate executive	Vice president	Ms. Ramirez
Office machine	Word processor	Verbex S-24
Vehicle	Truck	Kenbuilt 88

PRACTICE A

Substitute short, familiar words for the long and inflated ones in the following sentences.

Example

1. They embarked on a comprehensive audit.
   They began a thorough audit.

2. She will ascertain the prioritization of the steps.

3. The company discontinued utilizing the service.

4. He demonstrated the machine's malfunction.

5. The project will be finalized in April.

PRACTICE B

For each of the following general terms, write three specific words that provide examples of the type.

Example   1. an office machine   *typewriter, word processor, copier*

2. a container   _____

3. a communication   _____

4. a company position   _____

5. a method of shipment   _____

6. a part of speech   _____

7. a structure   _____

8. a motor vehicle   _____

WORDS IN ACTION

A   Choose the best answer.

1. Our new _____ explains the product and contains several illustrations.
   - a. client
   - b. brochure
   - c. method
   - d. situation

2. I appreciated Larry's frank _____ of his mistake.
   - a. admission
   - b. compensation
   - c. situation
   - d. accordance

3. Mr. Snipe's clear _____ allowed everyone to understand how the company's data processing system works.
   - a. admission
   - b. situation
   - c. compensation
   - d. explanation

4. In _____ with corporate regulations, all employees must receive a copy of the annual report.
   - a. degree
   - b. admission
   - c. accordance
   - d. opportunity

5. We must find an acceptable way to _____ the problem.
   a. resolve   c. provide
   b. receive   d. inflate

6. Several of our customers were _____ with the new products.
   a. inflated   c. resolved
   b. received   d. dissatisfied

7. Actually, it might be more efficient to send the product by _____ than by surface freight.
   a. parcel   c. airmail
   b. degree   d. ship

8. DECO manufactures a _____ drill press that eliminates the need for a nearby power source.
   a. relevant   c. familiar
   b. portable   d. comprehensive

9. Miss Handell is not _____ with international shipping procedures.
   a. relevant   c. familiar
   b. particular   d. inexcusable

10. We _____ an important message from Mrs. Snark.
    a. inflated   c. endured
    b. resolved   d. received

B Write the word that matches each definition: comply, endure, portable, recurring, relevant.

1. happening repeatedly; returning to one's memory   _____

2. agree with another; obey   _____

3. continue despite hardships   _____

4. in accordance with the matter at hand; pertinent   _____

5. easily transported   _____

GUIDELINES

The Apostrophe

Apostrophes are used to indicate possession, to indicate missing letters in contractions, and to form the plurals of certain initials, abbreviations, and numbers.

1. The apostrophe and *s* are used to show the possession of singular nouns and of plural nouns that don't end in *s:*

> Mr. Oda's letter   a year's work
> the company's profits   one dollar's worth
> Mr. Robert's report   The *Daily Press's* editorial

2. To show the possession of plural nouns that end in *s*, use only the apostrophe:

> the employees' suggestions   twenty dollars' worth
> four months' work   the students' reports

3. Apostrophes are used for contractions:

> isn't, they'll, I've, there's, wouldn't, o'clock, let's

4. Apostrophes indicate the plural of abbreviations with periods, lower case letters used as nouns, and capital letters:

> three Ph.D.'s, two A's, two SST's

5. Apostrophes are not used with possessive pronouns:

> its purpose   their report
> your idea   a briefcase of hers

4.3 NEGATIVE LETTERS OF ADJUSTMENT

Objectives

1. Write negative letters of adjustment.
2. Use proper tone.
3. Use capital letters correctly.

Thank the reader for writing and express your regret about the problem.

Explain the transaction from your point of view.

Sympathize with the reader and show that you look forward to more successful transactions in the future.

OMNICOMP INTERNATIONAL
17 BUNKER HILL ROAD, SHREWSBURY MA 01545

May 15, 19..

Mr. Ernst Lunde
Sardien Industrier A/S
Munkedamsvein 42
Oslo 2 NORWAY

Dear Mr. Lunde:

Thank you for your letter of April 28. I was sorry to hear of the difficulties you were having with your Omni Microcomp V. I immediately called Ilse Jaarlsberg, our service representative in your area, and asked her to contact you.

Ms. Jaarlsberg informed me that your hardware is in perfect working condition, but that defective application programs have caused some problems. She explained that since you contracted these programs from an outside firm rather than from an Omnicomp consultant, we cannot assume responsibility for the programs or for the resulting downtime.

We understand that the transition to an electronic data base can be a difficult process for any firm, and we are happy to provide instructional material and the services of our consultants to help make the transition as smooth as possible. I've asked Ms. Jaarlsberg to call on you again and explain the many options that we offer. Please let me know if I can be of any further help.

Sincerely yours,

Edgar P. Fowler

Edgar P. Fowler
Account Correspondent

cc: Ilse Jaarlsberg
Elvira Benway

Purpose   As we all know, the customer is not always right. When you are investigating a complaint, however, it is best to begin by assuming that the customer is right. You don't want to compound an error that your company might have made by denying it, nor do you want to delay the resolution of a just complaint. Sometimes, however, you may decide that your company is not at fault and that the customer is not entitled to the adjustment that he or she requested.

In such instances, you'll have to write a negative adjustment letter. The goal of a negative letter is to refuse the customer's request while maintaining his or her goodwill. To do this, you'll have to courteously convince the reader that you aren't at fault. Explain specifically why you can't make the adjustment and, if possible, find a way to make a small concession or gesture of goodwill.

Organization   Begin your letter by thanking the reader for writing and expressing your regret that the transaction did not work out entirely to his or her satisfaction. Use an apologetic tone of voice, even with the most ridiculous, totally unreasonable complaints. Let your reader know that you have looked into the problem carefully and objectively.

In your second paragraph, explain the situation in a way that clearly shows why you are not at fault. This does not mean proving that the customer is at fault. Simply establish your own innocence – never write an accusing sentence as such, "The product was ruined because of your carelessness and stupidity." Just point out that you cannot be responsible for something beyond your control. Give enough details so the reader knows the complaint has been carefully investigated, then close this paragraph by politely refusing the claim.

In the third paragraph, let your reader know that you feel bad about the situation. If you can make a concession or a lesser adjustment, state it at this time. Remember that you want your reader to deal with your company again, so make him or her believe that he or she has been treated fairly and sympathetically. Close with a sentence that shows that you look forward to future dealings with the reader.

In many ways, negative messages are the most difficult to convey successfully. Nobody likes to bring bad news, and nobody likes to receive it. Nevertheless, you should try to make it as easy as possible for the reader to accept the negative message. Pay close attention to the tone of the letter and to the way you explain the transaction. Giving successful negative messages is like telling the reader to go jump in a cold lake – while making him or her look forward to the swim.

REVISING

Revise the following negative adjustment letters.

Case A

The Beautiful Soup Corporation Ltd.
57 Campbell Crescent
Tadworth, Surrey KT20 6TD

28 June 19..

Mr Oliver Zagnutt, Manager
The Kookaburra Cafe
12 Argus Street
Cheltenham, Melbourne, Victoria 3192

Mr Zagnutt:

So, you were not entirely satisfied with our soup, were you? Well, let me say that your crudely composed complaint letter was the first negative comment that I, personally, have ever received concerning Beautiful Soup's soup. Obviously, your personal tastes and peculiarities are not shared by your fellow consumers.

I could certainly understand if, after testing the contents of a single can, you asked for a refund because you did not like the soup. But why did you find it necessary to consume three cases of our product before expressing your dissatisfaction and asking for a refund?

You, sir, shall receive nothing from us. Normally, we would send a case of soup as an expression of our goodwill, but in your case, I feel that you don't deserve it.

Sincerely

D. Tweedle

REVISION A

_____

_____

_____

_____

_____

_____

_____

_____

_____

_____

_____

_____

_____

_____

Case B

Ms. Eva Kneivell
43 Oakley Road
Kokomo, IN   46902

Dear Ms. Kneivell:

You cannot blame us at United Motors for your accident and
injury. When your car needed service, you didn't ask us to do
the work, nor did you ask us to recommend a factory-approved
mechanic. You made the foolish mistake of hiring an
incompetent "mechanic" to adjust your brakes. Your warranty
specifies that you must have your car repaired by an approved
dealership in order to keep the warrranty in effect. Apparently,
you feel that you can have your car serviced in the cheapest
possible manner, and then come crying to us if the job isn't
done well. Why don't you go back to Claude's Garage and ask
them for a new car? You certainly aren't going to get one from
us. If you do decide to buy a new car, I hope you'll buy it here
at United Motors. We offer low prices and a comprehensive
warranty.

Cordially yours

Hammond Egger
Service Manager

REVISION B

CHECKLIST

Negative Adjustment Letters

1. Be sure that you've examined the complaint carefully and that your company is not at fault. ☐

2. Remember that while you are refusing a claim, you still want to maintain the customer's goodwill. Try to find a way to make a small concession or compromise. ☐

3. Start your letter by thanking your reader for writing. Express your regret that the reader has had problems with the transaction. Let the reader know that the matter has been carefully investigated. ☐

4. Use the second paragraph to explain the transaction from your point of view. Don't try to prove that the reader is wrong – just try to convince him or her that you are not at fault. Give details when necessary. ☐

5. Use your closing paragraph to sympathize with your reader's problem and, if possible, to make a concession or gesture of goodwill. Close by expressing your hope that future transactions will be more successful. ☐

WRITING ASSIGNMENT

Background B. Bennet is the customer service manager for the Rodgers Casement Window Company. A few days ago, the following letter arrived from a dissatisfied customer:

> P.O. Box 538
> Oshawa, Ontario L1H 7L7
> February 2, 19..
>
> Rodgers Casement Window Company
> 1260 Clarendon Avenue
> Welland, Ontario L3B 5S2
>
> Dear Manager:
>
> On 4 September I purchased thirty-five Rodgers Insul-pane windows for the house that I was then building. Your sales representative told me that these windows would allow me to save money on my heating fuel bill. This wasn't true.
>
> When it is windy outside, I can feel cold air coming in through several of my windows. My heating bill is high, and I haven't noticed any savings.
>
> Please refund my purchase price of $3157 or replace every window in my house. I hope to hear from you quickly.
>
> Sincerely,
>
> R. Rhodes

Prepare a negative adjustment letter based on the following information:

On February 8, you (B. Bennett) sent a company representative to Rhodes's home in order to evaluate the situation. The representative reported that the windows had not been installed according to the company's directions. These directions state that the space between the rough opening and the window frame must be filled with fiber glass insulation. The person who installed the windows did not do this, and that is why cold air is entering the house. Rodgers' guarantee specifically states that the company cannot be held responsible for windows that aren't installed according to directions.

Goal: _____

Audience: _____

FIRST DRAFT

_____

_____

_____

_____

_____

_____

_____

_____

_____

_____

_____

_____

_____

_____

_____

_____

_____

_____

_____

_____

_____

_____

Rodgers Casement Window Company

1260 Clarendon Avenue   Welland, Ontario L3B 5S2

STYLE AND STRUCTURE
Tone

The tone of your writing reveals your attitude toward your subject and toward your reader. There are as many different tones as there are human feelings. The way you form your sentences can convey one or more types attitudes in any letter or memo you write:

indifferent, uninterested	overbearing, obnoxious
friendly, cordial	concerned, sympathetic
enthusiastic, hopeful	respectful, modest
rude, angry	demanding, arrogant
cool, formal	polite, tactful

You can easily see which of these types of attitudes best suit most business writing, and you can probably think of other tones, some of which are appropriate to business and some of which are not. As a general rule, write in a cordial, tactful tone (although on some occasions you may want to express your anger in a cool and formal tone). The most common weakness in business writing, however, is an impersonal, dull tone.

Some of the faults discussed elsewhere in this book help create an impersonal tone. The passive voice tends to prevent the use of personal pronouns (*I, we, you, she, he, they*) that make a letter sound as if a concerned person wrote it. Inflated diction and wordiness make letters sound pompous and overly formal.

IMPERSONAL: The program will be initiated.

PERSONAL: We will start the program.

Use of the active voice, uninflated diction, and concise wording will help you to achieve a friendly, lively touch. Another tool is the "personal" sentence, which adds a conversational flavor to your writing. Personal sentences can include questions, exclamations, quoted remarks, or informal structures. They take the place of the voice modulations that accompany the spoken word, but disappear on the written page. Look at the difference between the following:

Your suggestion was received and found reasonable.

and

We received your suggestion and liked it!

Try to create a positive feeling about your subject, even if it has negative aspects. Readers will usually respond in terms similar to those in which they are addressed. Therefore, every business letter represents a chance to create a satisfied reader.

NEGATIVE: Your loan cannot be granted because the amount you requested is unreasonable.

POSITIVE: We can lend you a sum smaller than you requested.

We often speak tactfully in a face-to-face situation because we do not want to see the frown that a brusque statement produces. When we write, the potential frown is invisible, and it is easy to be careless about tact. Try to consider the way your reader will receive your message.

TACTLESS: We return the enclosed document because of your failure to complete item 14.

TACTFUL: Please complete item 14 on the enclosed document.

Always choose the manner of "speech" that will produce the least resistance.

PRACTICE A

Choose the one sentence that best changes the impersonal tone to a personal tone.

Example
1. Transistors are made in our Kyoto factory. ___*b*___
   a. Transistors are manufactured in our Kyoto factory.
   b. We make transistors in our Kyoto factory.
   c. The Kyoto factory produces transistors.

2. It is regrettable that a meeting between us could not be arranged. _____
   a. I'm sorry that we weren't able to meet.
   b. I regret that a meeting between us could not be arranged.
   c. It is regrettable that we could not arrange a meeting.

3. With your concurrence, the memo will be issued. _____
   a. If you agree, I will send the memo.
   b. The memo will be issued with your agreement.
   c. If agreement is reached, the memo will be sent.

4. If assistance is required, call the undersigned. _____
   a. The undersigned should be called, if assistance is required.
   b. Call the undersigned for assistance.
   c. If you need help, call me.

5. The new salary plan will be implemented by the end of the month. _____
   a. We will begin the new salary plan by the end of the month.
   b. The new salary plan will have begun by the end of the month.
   c. The implementation of the new salary plan will have begun by the end of the month.

PRACTICE B

Rewrite each sentence to make it more tactful or positive.

Example
1. We can't help you because we are completely out of the item you ordered.
   Although we do not have the item you ordered, we expect to have it next
   month.

2. You misunderstood our request.

_____

_____

3. If your company does not cooperate, the experiment will fail.

_____

_____

4. You have left half the job undone, as you may be unaware.

_____

_____

5. You have insufficient income to receive credit at this time.

_____

_____

WORDS IN ACTION

A   Choose the best answer.

1. The clients were quite impressed by the _____ manner with which Ms. Yamada greeted them.
   a. successful   c. electronic
   b. cordial   d. comprehensive

2. Our insurance company will send an adjustor to _____ the matter and determine liability.
   a. investigate   c. cooperate
   b. compound   d. install

3. All department managers must _____ if the new program is to be successful.
   a. gesture   c. compound
   b. option   d. cooperate

4. Four employees were injured this afternoon because of a(n) _____ in the assembly room.
   a. attitude   c. option
   b. accident   d. company

5. The _____ has been caused by software problems.
   a. resolution   c. downtime
   b. transition   d. success

6. In order to reach an agreement, each of us must make a few _____.
   a. accidents   c. modulations
   b. consultants   d. concessions

7. Mr. Chumway has been acting as a _____ to our company for more than ten years.
   a. consultant   c. modulation
   b. gesture   d. concession

8. There are four _____ from which to choose.
   a. electronics   c. accidents
   b. options   d. downtimes

9. Although Ms. Dipster seemed _____ to our problem, she refused to make the adjustment we asked for.
   a. cordial   c. successful
   b. courteous   d. sympathetic

10. If our claim is not adjusted adequately, we shall purchase our future supplies _____.
   a. elsewhere   c. difficulty
   b. indifferently   d. incompetently

B   Write the word that matches each definition: comprehensive, downtime, enthusiastic, install, insufficient.

1. not enough; inadequate   _____

2. demonstrating an intense feeling or excitement   _____

3. an inactive period for a factory or equipment   _____

4. establish; place or adjust; put in position for use   _____

5. broad in content; exhibiting extensive understanding   _____

GUIDELINES

Capitalization

In addition to the first word of any sentence, capital letters are used in the following situations:

1. Capitalize all proper nouns, including months, days of the week, companies, cities, countries, nationalities, and the pronoun *I:*

> On Wednesday, March 4, I will meet with Mr. Todd, the president of our Australian subsidiary.

2. Capitalize the first letter of all the words in a title except coordinate conjunctions (*and, for, or, nor, but, yet*), articles (*a, an, the*), and prepositions. Capitalize even these exceptions if they are the first or last word in the title:

> Mr. Meeps published an article called "Marketing in the European Community."
>
> *In Search of Better Software,* a film, will be shown in the boardroom at 3:00.

3. Capitalize the names of streets, directions, subjects, and professional titles only when they are used as part of a proper noun:

> I happened to meet Professor Boer, the South African scholar, as I was walking down Fleet Street.

4. Capitalize the first letter of a direct quote:

> Then Mrs. Fuller asked, "Where can we best cut expenses?"

5. Capitalize official names of specific organizations and use lower case for unofficial names or generic terms:

> the Springfield Chamber of Commerce
> BUT: the local chamber of commerce
>
> The Ohio State University
> BUT: the state university in Ohio
>
> Heathrow International Airport
> BUT: the airport

6. Capitalize the names of distinct regions of a country and of the world:

> the West Coast   the Middle West, the Midwest
> The Eastern Hemisphere   the Middle East
> the East, the Orient   North Africa

Use lower case for directions and geographic terms used in a general or directional sense:

> northern Africa, western Europe
> along the Atlantic coast
> polar regions

7. Capitalize the following common geographic expressions:

> Arctic, Antarctic   New World, Old World
> Arctic Circle   North Pole, South Pole
> Earth (the planet)   International Date Line
>
> BUT: equator, prime meridian, tropic of Cancer/Capricorn

COMMUNICATION WORKSHOP

Telephone Techniques

Courtesy

Talking on the telephone differs from other types of communication discussed in this book because in telephoning, your voice and mode of expression are your sole means of getting your message across.

A telephone conversation is often the first experience a customer has with a company, so make it a pleasant one. Here are some guidelines for telephone courtesy:

1. Greet the person pleasantly and identify yourself immediately.

2. Be ready to give and receive information. If you're the caller and your message is complex, have clear, detailed notes to help you organize conversation time most efficiently. If you're on the receiving end, summarize the caller's message verbally to confirm your comprehension.

   If you're answering the phone for someone else, record the date and time, caller's name, telephone number, message, and further action requested.

3. To screen a caller for someone else, tactfully ask for the caller's name and reason for calling.

4. Keep the caller informed if you must hold or transfer the call. If the caller is on hold, check periodically to see if he or she wants to wait. Apologize for errors or delays. If the caller decides not to hold, suggest a good time to call back. If you transfer the call, give the caller the extension number in case you are disconnected.

5. Generally, the caller should terminate the call. If the receiver of the call must end the conversation first, he or she should make a polite excuse.

Here are some additional suggestions for long-distance calls:
- Be aware of time differences and call at an appropriate time.
- Find out if direct dial is possible, and note differences of dial tones and other telephone audio indicators.
- When talking with those for whom English is a second language, avoid slang and idiomatic expressions that may be unfamiliar. Speak slowly and clearly.

Taking Orders by Phone

When you take orders for merchandise by phone, be prepared. Here are some suggestions:
- Keep sales forms handy, as well as having price lists, catalogues, and advertisements available for possible use.
- Be sure to record the customer's name, address, and account number accurately.
- After printing the descriptions and prices of merchandise, delivery instructions, and method of payment, repeat the order to the customer for verification.
- Finally, end the conversation politely.

Greeting and Screening Visitors

To create good will for your company, it's important to greet all visitors promptly and politely. If you're talking to someone else when a visitor comes in, acknowledge the visitor and conclude or interrupt your conversation as soon as possible. When visitors come without appointments, you can screen and direct them to the most appropriate person. If your supervisor is very busy, you may be able to recommend someone else in the company who can help.

When visitors arrive for scheduled appointments, announce them by phone or in person. You may need to guide new visitors to the correct office. Sometimes delays are unavoidable. Keep visitors who are waiting informed about delays and, if it becomes absolutely necessary, suggest rescheduling the appointment.

DISCUSSION ACTIVITIES

1. Call four local businesses to request such information as the name of the personnel manager, the price of a product, or the hours the business is open. Report on the information received and evaluate the telephone manners of the person with whom you spoke.
2. Practice telephoning the message of any of the letters of complaint in the Revising section of this chapter. The caller does not follow the guidelines for tactfully expressing a complaint, and the receiver follow's the guidelines for giving a positive or negative adjustment response. Observers should evaluate the speakers' performances in terms of adhering to the guidelines.
3. You are taking Ms. Benway's calls. She has told you that she's not to be disturbed. A caller insists on speaking to her because he's leaving town and won't return for four months. Choose one of the answers below, or make up your own, and explain why.
   a. "Ms. Benway can't be disturbed."
   b. "Ms. Benway will be in a meeting all day, but let me talk with her secretary again."
   c. "I'll see if she can work you in."
   d. "I'm sorry, but Ms. Benway isn't seeing anyone this morning."
4. Practice handling unpleasant situations on the phone.
   a. Dickey Manufacturing Company has called to place another big order with your company, but the company hasn't paid for the last order yet. You can't extend credit until payment is received.
   b. A representative from Bilgestone Builders has called to see if you've chosen a contractor to build a new wing on your plant. Your committee accepted a bid yesterday – but it was a competitor's. You have to let the representative know your decision.
5. A very important client has called while you're preparing last-minute notes for a presentation. The client insists on telling you all the good and bad things about a computer just received from your company. You have to get off the phone as quickly as possible while retaining good will.
6. A visitor walks up to your desk and asks to see your supervisor immediately. Your supervisor is busy and the visitor has no appointment. But if you can find out what the visitor wants, you may be able to direct him or her to someone else. The visitor will not give the reason for the call, and your goal is to politely help the visitor without disturbing your supervisor.

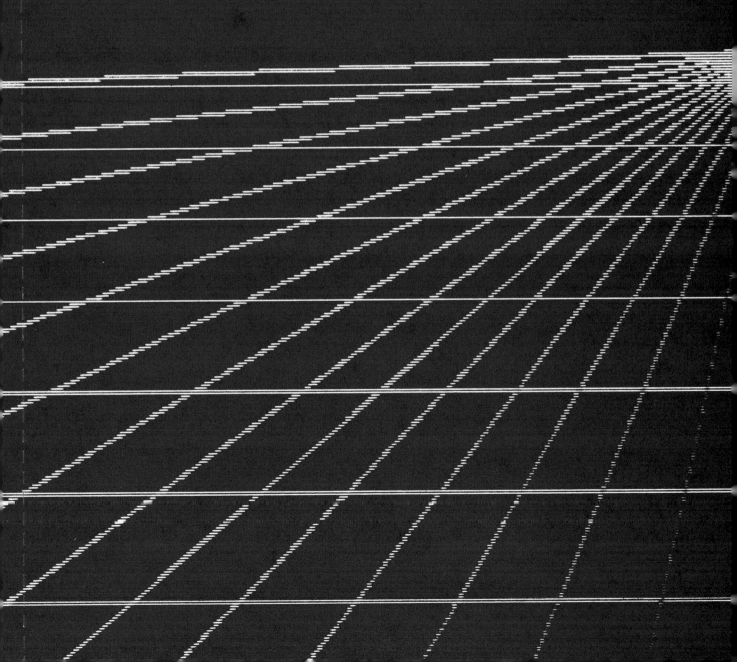

5

THE SALES SEQUENCE

Sales Letters

Promotions and
Press Releases

Orders and Invoices

5.1 SALES LETTERS

Objectives

1. Write sales letters.
2. Revise sentences to make them logical.
3. Avoid slang.
4. Avoid clichés.

OMNICOMP INTERNATIONAL
17 BUNKER HILL ROAD, SHREWSBURY MA 01545

May 27, 19..

Ms. Yokiko Miyamoto
Yoda Biiru KK
679 Yamate-cho
Naka-ku
Yokohama 231 JAPAN

Dear Ms. Miyamoto:

Begin with a strong opening statement that attracts the reader's attention.

As an owner of the Omni Microcomp 4, you will be very excited to learn about our recently developed SPELLGRAMM software package. This revolutionary new software concept not only verifies the spelling of more than 70 000 English words but also corrects many of the most common mistakes in grammar and sentence construction.

Identify your product's features in a positive way.

Spellgramm's unique ability to locate misplaced modifiers, incorrect tense sequences, superfluous punctuation, and other grammatical problems makes it the most advanced word processing software available. Spellgramm requires a memory allocation of only 128K, and it is available in either British or American English. In addition to its standard word base, Spellgramm allows you to enter industry-specific terminology and the proper names of your clients.

End confidently, and encourage your reader to respond.

After you read the enclosed brochure, I'm sure you will agree that Omnicomp's Spellgramm offers unprecedented practicality, flexibility, and speed. Simply return the enclosed order form and let Spellgramm improve the efficiency of your company's English language communications.

Sincerely,

Edgar P. Fowler

Edgar P. Fowler
Account Correspondent

Enclosure

Purpose   The goal of a sales letter is to create interest in your product or service, and you should try to do this from the start. Always begin with a strong, compelling statement that will somehow erode or bypass your reader's natural resistance to sales messages. If your sales letter doesn't intrigue, invite, or involve your reader from the opening sentence, there's a good chance that it will be quickly filed in the reader's wastebasket.

Pay close attention to the tone of your sales letter. It should sound positive and convincing. The sales letter presents an opportunity that must be seized early and then developed convincingly so you must create the initial desire for your product, and then provide the logical reasons for your customer to satisfy that desire.

Your sales letter should convince the reader that your product excels in every respect, that it has benefits surpassing all competition. Make the product *sound* good. Don't exaggerate or make false claims, but describe your product as if there were no alternative. Emphasize the strengths of your product.

Preparation   To write an effective sales letter, it is important that you prepare yourself by following three steps. First, you must know your product. Second, you should learn as much about your customers as possible. Finally, you'll need to learn about your competitors' products.

Know your product completely. If you aren't thoroughly familiar with your product's strengths and weaknesses, you aren't prepared to write a convincing sales letter. Ask yourself the questions that your reader will ask. How does your product differ from the competition? Why is it better? What are its special features? What are its weaknesses (what do your competitors regard as its weaknesses)? In order for your sentences to convey a tone of conviction and assurance, all of these questions must be answered. If you don't believe in your product, your customers won't believe in you.

Know your audience. While this is true for all business writing, it is particularly important in sales letters. Of course, you won't always have personal information about your customer, but you can begin by assuming that the customer needs your product and by presuming that he or she will suffer without it. Then use whatever bit of background information you can find to personalize your sales letter. If, for example, Jonathan Jeepers originally is from Brisbane, you might point out that the STX-30 component of your new minicomputer is manufactured near his home town. Personal comments like these often do more than several pages of descriptive copy in making a sale.

Know your competitor. In order to properly respond to a customer, it may be necessary to identify a competitor's strengths and weaknesses. Potential customers may already be aware of a competitor's strong points, so it's wise to treat them directly and without denigration. Not all strong points will be counterbalanced with weaknesses. Pick another point and deal with a weakness. Remember that you are in control of the discussion. Write persuasively, as if the benefits of your product are so obvious that they hardly need pointing out (nevertheless, do so!). If the competitor's product has more-than-adequate voltage, compression, or power, imply that it has too much. Why is it necessary for them to have that much resolution, capacity, or compatibility? Remember that benefits cost money and add to the price, especially if they are the competitor's.

Always close the sales letter on a positive note. "When may I expect to hear from you?" Make sure that you have made it as easy as possible for the reader to take action as soon as possible.

REVISING

Revise the following sales letters. Use the guidelines in the "Style and Structure" section on page 136.

Case A

Dear Mr. Williams:

Perhaps you might be interested in our new product. Our new product is a handy, easy-to-use device called the Speedo Wonder Tool. The Speedo Wonder Tool is the hottest new thing to come down the pike in many a moon. It's fantastic! It's incredible. It's cheap! The Speedo Wonder Tool can perform the tasks of a hammer, a screwdriver, a saw, and an adjustable wrench—all in one!

Whatever the job, you'll be ready for it with your Speedo Wonder Tool. It comes in an attractive plastic carrying case that easily fits into your car's glove compartment or into a large pocket. The case contains the Wonder-Grip handle and four interchangeable Wonder Tool attachments. These precision instruments enable even a novice craftsman to undertake a project confident in his ability to really do a bang-up job.

Well, what do you say, pal? Can you afford to live without your very own Speedo Wonder Tool at the affordable price of $14.95? In spending this amount, you could probably only expect to buy one good hammer or wrench, but the Speedo Wonder Tool gives you more. Call me or write for a brochure and an order form so you can buy one.

Sincerely,

Ralph Phelps

REVISION A

Case B

Dear Ms. Jackson:

Our magazine comes out once a month, and it contains interesting articles and useful features that are of special interest to florists. We offer the latest news in horticultural techniques, greenhouse designs and operation, and what is new in flower arranging. Each month, we offer stimulating, full-page color photographs of beautiful, exciting flowers and bouquets.

By filling out the enclosed order form, you can have Professional Florist Today delivered to your home or place of business.

Since you are a member of the Florists Trade Association, you won't want to miss our new magazine, Professional Florist Today. Professional Florist Today keeps you up to date and in the know about current trends and growing complexities in the floral industry.

We are making a special offer to F.T.A. members—12 issues, sent to you each month for the annual price of $18. How can you pass up this swell one-shot deal to enter your subscription to our excellent periodical.

Sincerely,

Rose Astor
Circulation Manager

REVISION B

CHECKLIST

The Sales Letter

1. Be convincing and persuasive from the start. Open the letter with a strong statement. ☐

2. Use an assured and confident tone throughout the letter. ☐

3. Identify your product's features. Emphasize them while minimizing any weaknesses. ☐

4. Develop any information that you have about your reader's circumstances, tastes, and preferences. Try to learn as much about your reader as possible. ☐

5. Use information about a competitor's product's strengths and weaknesses. Make comparisons that favor your own product. Know how to graciously admit a competitor's strengths. ☐

6. Conclude with a positive statement. Encourage your reader to take prompt, positive action. ☐

WRITING ASSIGNMENT

Prepare a sales letter for M. Howard, manager of the Iry International Convention Center in Kingston, Jamaica. The letter is addressed to Arnold Ziffel, Chairman of the American Livestock Producers Organization, 1220 Morganfield Street, Chicago, Illinois. Use the following information to write the letter. Write your first draft on a separate sheet of paper.

Background   You (M. Howard) have learned that ALPO is planning to hold its annual conference in the West Indies next year, and you want them to use your convention center. Your center has 300 hotel rooms, five function rooms, a large exposition area, and complete restaurant facilities. It is located on a beautiful beach, and it offers a swimming pool, tennis courts, a golf course, and boating. You and your staff are fully prepared to plan and conduct an individualized conference. There are a number of options available, and you can offer a basic, five-day package, including meals, for $250 per person. Enclose a brochure that provides pictures and more detailed information.

Goal: _____

Audience: _____

STYLE AND STRUCTURE
Language Awareness

Clear meaning depends on the writer's accurate choice and arrangement of words. To be certain that you've selected exactly the right words, always read your first draft carefully. Make sure that there's a step-by-step logic in the way the words are arranged. The following sentence, for example, doesn't make any literal sense:

> The purpose of the information needed for the Engineering Department is essential to assure the fewest possible breakdowns.

The writer probably meant to say that the information was essential. By starting the sentence with the real subject and then following it with a strong verb, we can straighten out the sentence.

> The engineering department needs the information to assure the fewest possible breakdowns.

First Draft   Don't let your fear of mixing up words or sentences slow down the process of your writing; every writer makes mistakes. It's easier to correct your first draft than it is to write perfect sentences. Just remember to look for inexact or illogical phrases that may have come out in the first draft.

Slang   A few types of language should appear only on rare occasions in business writing. One is **slang**, which is inappropriate for typical business communications, although copywriters sometimes use it effectively in advertising. For most of your writing, however, a simple, informal style is best. You can't achieve that, of course, by combining slang with important-sounding terms, as this writer did:

> Goal-setting is not a one-shot deal but an iterative process.

Each extreme sounds silly.

Clichés   **Clichés,** which are overused phrases and metaphors, don't suit business writing either. They suggest that the writer can't find a plain straightforward phrase:

> CLICHÉ: The sales managers stuck to their guns at the meeting.

> CLEAR: The sales managers maintained their position at the meeting.

Technical Terms   Write **technical terms** only to readers who will understand them easily. If your audience consists of both technical and nontechnical readers, use either the specialized or the general vocabulary throughout your writing. Then you can supply in parentheses either the explanation for the lay reader or the technical term for the specialist.

Jargon   Every business and profession develops its own **jargon**, a specialized vocabulary used by people who work in a common field. Jargon is useful within the boundaries of the trade, but when people use jargon beyond the limits of their field, they corrupt meaning. The words are more technical than necessary and therefore inappropriate.

> JARGON: The committee will interface next week.
> CLEAR: The committee will meet next week.
>
> JARGON: Nova Scotia is beyond our shipping parameters.
> CLEAR: Nova Scotia is beyond our shipping boundaries.
> CLEARER: We don't ship to Nova Scotia.

PRACTICE A

Revise the following sentences to make them logical.

Example

1. Of the various faults in business-writing, clarity is the one that is most irritating.
   Lack of clarity irritates readers more than any other business-writing fault.

2. We have yet to hear of a computer that is not without downtime.

3. The capacity of the warehouse was exceeded and had to be stored outside.

4. Individuals who have not yet reported will be posted outside my office.

5. Guidelines have been prepared in which each department should charge materials.

6. We must consider one more step before using it as the starting point for the program.

7. Dissension and disagreement were displaced by four newly elected members of the committee.

8. Do not report days off that are managerial discretion.

_____

_____

PRACTICE B   Choose the best expression to replace the underlined slang.

Example   1. Frederick's new report stinks. ___c___
   a. smells   c. is of poor quality
   b. is creative   d. is wonderful

2. Our engineers must learn to be less picky. _____
   a. hasty   c. talkative
   b. selective   d. accurate

3. At the meeting last week the reported results were lousy. _____
   a. unfavorable   c. interesting
   b. accurate   d. inappropriate

4. Sidney has been our hottest salesperson. _____
   a. newest   c. worst
   b. warmest   d. most successful

5. Our new product is based on a really terrific concept. _____
   a. excellent   c. ordinary
   b. standard   d. new

PRACTICE C   Choose the one sentence that best changes the underlined cliché to an appropriate expression.

Example   1. The accountants' audit told the same old story. ___a___
   a. The accountants' audit revealed a familiar situation.
   b. The accountants' audit sang the same old tune.
   c. The accountants' audit included the new information.

2. The people in the personnel department are beating their heads against the wall. _____
   a. The people in the personnel department are making new decisions.
   b. The people in the personnel department are fighting with one another.
   c. The people in the personnel department are frustrated.

3. When our competitors see this, they will realize we have a tiger by the tail.

   a. When our competitors see this, they will see that they need to get on the stick.
   b. When our competitors see this, they will realize our product is hard to match.
   c. When our competitors see this, they will be worried.

4. We must beat them at their own game: price cutting. _____
   a. We must outdo them with their own tactic: price cutting.
   b. We must show them who's boss by cutting prices.
   c. We must challenge them by price cutting.

5. The research team reported they had gone up another blind alley. _____
   a. The research team reported a breakthrough.
   b. The research team reported the results of another expensive experiment.
   c. The research team reported another unsuccessful experiment.

WORDS IN ACTION ─────────────────────

A   Choose the best answer.

1. The salesperson must _____ the customer to buy the product.
   a. convince   c. convey
   b. excel   d. force

2. Mr. Hyman's arguments were very _____, and the board finally accepted his proposal.
   a. persuasive   c. inappropriate
   b. superfluous   d. obvious

3. Our _____ offers a product similar to ours, but it is much more expensive.
   a. alternative   c. competitor
   b. warehouse   d. subscription

4. The Perez Corporation was awarded the contract for the _____ of the new warehouse.
   a. resistance   c. allocation
   b. construction   d. subscription

5. The circulation department is hoping to increase _____ to the trade journal.
   a. alternatives   c. resistance
   b. subscriptions   d. allocation

6. The discount offered by the manufacturer makes the machines much more _____.
   a. superfluous   c. flexible
   b. logical   d. affordable

7. Materials that are shipped across international _____ must be approved by customs officers.
   a. guidelines   c. concepts
   b. warehouses   d. boundaries

8. Some unforeseen maintenance expenses will require an additional _____ of funds to the miscellaneous account.
   a. occasion
   c. subscription
   b. construction
   d. allocation

9. Please _____ my appreciation to Ms. Wiswell.
   a. convey
   c. misplace
   b. adjust
   d. condone

10. The _____ goal in a sales letter is to create desire for the product.
    a. superfluous
    c. initial
    b. persuasive
    d. inappropriate

B   Write the word that matches each definition: alternative, concept, guideline, specific, superfluous.

1. a choice between possibilities
   _____

2. a general idea or understanding
   _____

3. beyond what is expected, required, or needed
   _____

4. a policy statement or procedure
   _____

5. clearly set forth; definite
   _____

GUIDELINES

Pronoun Reference

1. Whenever you use a pronoun, make sure that the reader knows immediately what that pronoun refers to. The word, phrase, or clause referred to by the pronoun is known as the pronoun's antecedent. Be on the lookout for vague and unclear references in groups of sentences as well as within a single sentence:

> UNCLEAR: *Jones* picked *Dawson* to help him write the report because *he* knows a lot about law. (Who knows a lot about law, Jones or Dawson?)
>
> CLEAR: Jones picked *Dawson* to help him write the report because *Dawson* knows a lot about law.
>
> UNCLEAR: *Jocelyn* asked to be placed in *Stephanie's* department so she could help *her* with *her* report. (Is the report Jocelyn's or Stephanie's?)
>
> CLEAR: Jocelyn asked to be placed in Stephanie's department so she could help *Stephanie* with her report.

> UNCLEAR: He forgot his *plane tickets* and his *itinerary*. When he thought about *it*, he laughed. (What does *it* refer to?)
>
> CLEAR: He forgot his plane tickets and his itinerary. When he thought about *his forgetfulness*, he laughed.
>
> UNCLEAR: One of her responsibilities was to prepare travel vouchers for the sales department, *which* required a thorough knowledge of international travel regulations. (Does *which* refer to *preparing travel vouchers* or to the *sales department*?)
>
> CLEAR: One of her responsibilities was to prepare travel vouchers for the sales department, a *task requiring* a thorough knowledge of international travel regulations.

2. Never use possessive pronouns without a clear referent.

> UNCLEAR: The Carson newsletter became very popular, largely because of *her* witty commentary.
>
> CLEAR: The Carson newsletter became very popular, largely because of *the editor's* witty commentary.

3. *It* and *they* are often used without clear referents.

> UNCLEAR: Why do *they* design buildings to make so little use of sunlight?
>
> CLEAR: Why are *buildings* designed to make so little use of sunlight?
>
> UNCLEAR: *It* says in the charter that every shareholder must receive quarterly reports.
>
> CLEAR: *The charter* says that every shareholder must receive a quarterly report.

4. *This* is often used without a clear antecedent. Often a writer will begin a sentence or paragraph with *this,* referring to the general idea or argument or situation of the preceding sentence or paragraph. Always restate what *this* refers to.

> UNCLEAR: *This* was responsible for several misunderstandings.
>
> CLEAR: *This attitude of the supervisor* was responsible for several misunderstandings.

Objectives

1. Write promotion letters.
2. Write press releases.
3. Combine sets of choppy sentences.
4. Use quotation marks appropriately.
5. Eliminate inappropriate references to gender.

Use attention-getting devices early.

Highlight important features with headings.

List benefits.

Make it easy for the reader to respond.

OMNICOMP INTERNATIONAL
17 BUNKER HILL ROAD, SHREWSBURY MA 01545

April 1, 19..

Dear Distributor:

SUBJECT: OMNICOMP DEVELOPS THE SPELLGRAMM
ENGLISH SPELLING AND GRAMMAR VERIFICATION SOFTWARE
PACKAGE

Do your internashonal custamurs ever has problums with speling, sentense contruction adn typografical errors?

If so, their problums [query: problems?] are over with the new Omnicomp SPELLGRAMM—the first word processing software package that combines English spelling verification with English grammar verification.

70,000-WORD VOCABULARY—WITH ROOM FOR MORE
Since 70,000 words comprise 99.4 percent of our everyday vocabulary, the size of the database is not as important as which words are included. Our word-frequency research has created an immensely practical database. And we give the customer the opportunity to add user- and industry-specific terms—even proper names of individuals.

AUTOMATIC HYPHENATION, CAPITALIZATION, AND ABBREVIATION
SPELLGRAMM offers unique features that will automatically hyphenate words correctly whenever necessary. Proper nouns and the initial words in sentences are automatically capitalized, and correct abbreviations are available upon command.

TWENTY OF THE MOST COMMON GRAMMATICAL ERRORS AUTOMATICALLY ELIMINATED
Dangling participles, misplaced modifiers, incorrect pronoun referents, inconsistent tenses, and more—all are flagged for quick correction. SPELLGRAMM is the most advanced, efficient, and practical word processing adjunct ever developed. Your customers will no longer have to worry about grammar.

THE SOFTWARE OF THE FUTURE—AVAILABLE TODAY
The SPELLGRAMM program is efficient, requiring only 128K of RAM memory. It will enable your customers to easily produce attractive, readable copy. And, with Omnicomp's special introductory price, it is inexpensive as well.

For complete details, send us the enclosed reply form today, or call us at (617) 555-6600 (Teléx 940959; Cable OMNICOMP).

Sincerely yours,

Edgar P. Fowler

Edgar P. Fowler
Account Correspondent

Promotions	Another way to generate interest in a new product or service is to use a promotional mailing. Promotions differ from sales letters in format and are written not to individuals but to a wide range of potential customers. Like sales letters, promotions provide an opportunity to give maximum, focused exposure to a product. In addition, many of the principles of writing an effective sales letter are true for promotions as well. Write according to the ABCD rule of sales writing:

The ABCD Rule

A. Attract the reader's attention.
B. Build interest in the product.
C. Create desire for the product.
D. Define the action necessary to close the sale.

Format

The format of the promotion letter is less restrictive than other forms of business writing. Generally, a letterhead is used, followed by a salutation and a subject line. The body of the promotion letter is often broken up with headings, radical spacing, indentations, or anything else that might help to attract attention and hold interest. The use of paragraph headings, underlined or in capital letters (or both) allows you to highlight the major points of your sales message in a way that the reader cannot overlook. The promotion letter generally has a conventional closing and signature.

Audience

Promotion letters are usually sent to people on various mailing lists, so it is often difficult to accurately define your audience. Nevertheless, it is usually possible to determine a category for your readers and to assume that persons in that category have a common interest. Try to use these interests to help develop the content and tone of your message.

Organization

Since the promotion letter is not often specifically addressed to an individual, it runs an even greater risk than the sales letter of being routed directly to the wastebasket. To avoid this response, you'll need to devote considerable care to the attention-getting qualitites of your opening statement. Many standard openings can attract attention; they include special offers and gifts, questions, challenging or provocative statements, humor, and quotations. Your decision concerning which type of opening to use will depend upon your product and your audience, but never fear to be too creative or unusual.

The body of the promotion letter allows you to highlight and describe the main strengths of your product. It usually isn't possible to develop all the positive features of a product. Therefore, you'll need to choose the most important and attractive points to create the theme of your sales message. Your closing paragraph should, as in the sales letter, provide the details necessary for your reader to contact you easily, and it should encourage an immediate response.

Press Releases

The press release is another way to develop interest and awareness in a new and innovative product, and it is also used extensively for public relations purposes. While the promotion letter is used to provide the complete details of a new product, the press release can inform the general public about a wide range of company activities, personnel, and products. However, there is one question you'll need to answer positively before writing a press release. Why should the general public be interested? If your message isn't really news, then the press release is not the form to use. If it's simple advertising that you want, then you'll probably have to pay for it. Basically the press release is an opportunity to put the company's name or products before the general public in a dramatic and compelling way.

Format

Since the real purpose of a press release is to place information before the public, a successful release should answer the classic questions of a good news story: Who, What, When, Where, and Why? The press release format (see below) starts out with a company logo or letterhead, and often identifies the spokesperson responsible for the release or the person within the company who can be contacted for further details. Below the date line, you can state "FOR IMMEDIATE RELEASE," or "NOT TO BE RELEASED BEFORE MARCH 23." A headline follows, which concisely states the main point of the story: "OMNICOMP ANNOUNCES SPELLGRAMM." The first paragraph of the press release should state the basic facts of the story. Often newspapers will devote no more than that amount of space to the story. Try to limit the entire press release to a single page.

OMNICOMP INTERNATIONAL
17 BUNKER HILL ROAD, SHREWSBURY MA O1545

Contact: M. McLuhan
            Communications Director

April 1, 19..

FOR IMMEDIATE RELEASE

OMNICOMP ACQUIRES CONTECH

Shrewsbury—Omnicomp International, the Shrewsbury, Massachusetts computer firm, announced today that it has acquired Contech Industries, an influential software research and development group located in Beaverton, Oregon. George Landry, Omnicomp's chief executive officer, explained that the acquisition will allow Omnicomp "to enter the software market much more aggressively, particularly in the area of computer-assisted education."

Contech represents the first major acquisition for Omnicomp, and it indicates the firm's emergence as a leader in the computer industry. In making the announcement, Mr. Landry stated that while the Contech line will remain intact, the acquisition will allow Omnicomp to triple its software list for the popular Microcomp 4 personal computer within the next nine months.

Get your message across in the opening headline and in the first paragraph.

REVISING

Revise the following promotion letter. Improve the flow of information to the reader by making the sentences less choppy and by deleting unnecessary words.

Case A

PETE'S PUBLISHING COMPANY
85 Blackstone Street
Haymarket, Oklahoma

Dear Mr. Teacher:
SUBJECT: The promotion of our new audio cassettes

We have a new product. It is for children in grades 1 and 2. The product is called STORYTIME. STORYTIME is a set of audio cassettes. The cassettes are designed to help children develop language and reading skills through listening.

DO THE CHILDREN IN YOUR CLASS LIKE TO LISTEN TO STORIES?

DO YOU SPEND TIME READING TO THEM?

WOULD YOU LIKE TO SAVE TIME?

Well, STORYTIME presents delightful stories in a format that allows each student to work independently. They will have fun. They will learn, and they will be entertained at the same time. And each story has an accompanying worksheet with questions for children to answer.

EACH STORY HAS ITS OWN INDIVIDUALIZED WORKSHEET.

Your pupils can listen to each story and then answer challenging questions that build comprehension and listening skills. After children answer the questions, a narrator or character in the story gives the correct response.

EACH STORYTIME PACKAGE CONTAINS 12 CASSETTES, A TEACHER'S MANUAL, AND DUPLICATING MASTER WORKSHEETS.

STORYTIME is packaged in a full-color binder that's compact and easy to use. Each cassette has two 15-minute lessons on each side. THE LESSONS TEACH IMPORTANT SKILLS AND MAKE LEARNING TO READ EASIER. Why don't you get STORYTIME for your class? There are several ways to contact one of our representatives in your area.

Sincerely,

Mickey Thompson
Vice President, Sales

REVISION A

Revise the following press release. Improve the format and the sentence flow.

Case B

NEWS
from
The Cornuto Corporation
Apdo 4305
Río Piedras Station, PR 00928

Contact: Armando Zapata
Communications Director
(213) 555-2016

November 22, 19..
FOR IMMEDIATE RELEASE

CORNUTO CORPORATION APPOINTS DR. J. MARTINEZ
TO ITS BOARD OF DIRECTORS

RIO PIEDRAS—The Cornuto Corporation made an announcement today. It announced that a new member of its board of directors has been elected. The new board member is Dr. Jesús Martinez.

Joachim P. Murietta, chairman of the board, made the announcement. He spoke about Dr. Martinez. Mr. Murietta said, "Dr. Martinez is a respected scientist and honored member of our community. He will surely complement the many strengths of our board members and lead our company into the future."

Dr. Martinez is currently chairman of the National Committee on Public Safety and Health. Previously he served as dean of the Hope University Medical School in Caracas, Venezuela, for fifteen years. He had also held other jobs. He was a professor. He taught radiology. He taught it at Harvard University. He also taught at Tulane University.

He received a Bachelor of Science degree from M.I.T. in 1941. It was in biological science. He received his Doctor of Medicine degree from Harvard Medical School. This degree was awarded in 1946. Dr. Martinez is an author. He has written several textbooks. He has written many scientific articles for professional journals.

The Cornuto Corporation is a manufacturer of pharmaceuticals and medical supplies. Its headquarters is in Río Piedras. It has two other facilities. One is in Los Angeles. The other is in Lisbon.

REVISION B

CHECKLISTS

Promotions

1. Get the reader's attention early. ☐

2. Highlight the major points in your presentation by using all capital letters, underlining, and/or headings. The promotion letter is like a continual exclamation point. ☐

3. Develop each major product feature. ☐

4. List benefits. ☐

5. Open and close on attention-getting summaries about your product. ☐

Press Releases

1. Before writing, make sure your subject is newsworthy. If it isn't – or even if you're doubtful – the press probably won't be interested. ☐

2. State your basic message in the opening headline and in the first paragraph. If you don't, a busy news editor may not care to search further for the story. ☐

3. Present your release as a general-interest, newsworthy item, minimizing the commercial, private-interest aspect. ☐

WRITING ASSIGNMENT

Background Using the information about the Omnicomp Spellgramm program, prepare a press release that announces its development. Keep the press release short, and emphasize that the Spellgramm software is the first of its kind ever developed. Present the information in a way that will appeal to the general reader.

Write your first draft on a separate sheet of paper.

Goal: _____

Audience: _____

OMNICOMP INTERNATIONAL
17 BUNKER HILL ROAD, SHREWSBURY MA 01545

Press Release

Contact:

STYLE AND STRUCTURE
Sentence Flow

A series of short, choppy sentences makes it difficult for your reader to follow the flow of information in your writing. Furthermore, although each sentence is short, such writing is actually wordy: the sentences unnecessarily repeat certain words, usually the subject or object of the preceding sentence.

CHOPPY: Sandra wrote a memo. It was addressed to Chihoe. He manages the financial section.

BETTER: Sandra wrote a memo to Chihoe, the manager of the financial section.

CHOPPY: The division's budget has been cut. This means we must limit our international travel.

BETTER: We must limit our international travel because the division's budget has been cut.

CHOPPY: The purchasing department head has ordered new computers to expedite work in the billing department. The purchasing department head expects the computers to arrive next month.

BETTER: The purchasing department head expects the new computers, ordered to expedite work in the billing department, to arrive next month.

Choppy sentences often fail to show readers the connection between ideas. They also make it difficult to determine which, among several facts, is the most important. They hinder the writer's goal of delivering the message as clearly as possible.

PRACTICE
Combine each of the following sets of choppy sentences into one sentence, subordinating statements or adding words to express connections when necessary.

Example
1. Successful goal-setting cannot be done all at once. It is a process in which we continually evaluate our objectives.
   In successful goal-setting, we continually evaluate our objectives.

2. The press release will be discussed on October 6. The meeting is for middle management.

   _____

   _____

3. In this section of the manual you will have a chance to review some of the commands you have learned. At the same time you will learn a new way to enter them.

   _____

   _____

   _____

   _____

4. At the present time there are three diskettes. This is one year after we bought the first.

_____

_____

5. I have worked for Omnicomp for the past year. During that time I have conducted numerous demonstrations of computer hardware.

_____

_____

6. Enclosed you will find our latest semiconductor catalog. This will provide additional information to aid you in acquiring new business.

_____

_____

7. You have been entering each Super-Sort command individually. This is done by pressing **RETURN** at the end of the command. But commands do not have to be entered separately.

_____

_____

_____

8. The following people have expressed interest in attending the seminar. Please submit the requested information for each person to me by September 20. Your people will not be registered until this information is received.

_____

_____

_____

9. Please make the adjustments needed to match the analysis entries. The change should be implemented by November 15.

_____

_____

WORDS IN ACTION _____

A   Choose the best answer.

1. The committee will need more time to _____ the proposal.
   a. abbreviate   c. evaluate
   b. encourage   d. expedite

2. Their company's _____ is in Osaka, but it has a branch office in New York.
   a. data base
   b. headquarters
   c. implements
   d. highlights

3. We have made _____ visits to the regional sales office.
   a. conventional
   b. maximum
   c. numerous
   d. route

4. Mr. Christenson thinks that the new advertising campaign will _____ new sales.
   a. verify
   b. query
   c. evaluate
   d. generate

5. A number of customers' orders were _____ by our special discount offer.
   a. attracted
   b. evaluated
   c. expedited
   d. received

6. The management committee is _____ by the interest in our new model.
   a. acquired
   b. encouraged
   c. expedited
   d. practical

7. Our hotel offers _____ rates to organizations that hold meetings here.
   a. comprehension
   b. highlight
   c. adjunct
   d. special

8. We _____ our customers to test drive our newest line of trucks.
   a. attract
   b. acquire
   c. route
   d. encourage

9. Ms. Ashley left _____ instructions on how to handle the Morton account.
   a. comprehension
   b. specific
   c. promotional
   d. adjunct

10. The main office sent a marketing consultant, who offered _____ advice on how to increase our distribution.
    a. practical
    b. maximum
    c. various
    d. abbreviated

B   Write the word that matches each definition: expedite, highlight, innovative, query, verify.

1. inquire; question   _____

2. new   _____

3. perform quickly; facilitate   _____

4. determine or test the validity of
   something; confirm   _____

5. feature   _____

GUIDELINES

Quotation Marks

Quotation marks always appear in pairs – opening quotes and closing quotes.

1. Use quotation marks to indicate a direct quotation (dialogue or quoted material):

   > "Now tell me where you sent the letter," said the manager.

2. Use quotation marks to set off words defining or explaining another word:

   > The word *design* means "a plan or project," "a particular purpose," and "an artistic work."

3. Use quotation marks to set off chapter titles and titles of articles, short stories, poems, and songs:

   > The article "What's Happening in the Middle East?" appeared in *Foreign Affairs*.

4. Do not use quotation marks to set off a very brief response, such as *yes* or *no*, that can easily be distinguished from the rest of the sentence:

   > WRONG: For each statement her answer was "yes."
   >
   > RIGHT: For each statement her answer was yes.

5. Place closing quotation marks after a comma or period:

   > "Turn right," he said, "and go four blocks."

Gender

Avoid using the pronoun *he* to refer to both sexes. Because the excessive use of *he or she* often seems awkward, revise the sentence to avoid the problem. Here are some guidelines you can follow to avoid inappropriate use of gender in your writing.

1. Use the plural form of the noun:

   AVOID: If an *employee* is late, ask *him* to explain his tardiness.

   BETTER: Ask *employees* to explain *their* tardiness.

2. Repeat the noun if style and sound permit:

   AVOID: When a *programmer* comes up with a solution, ask *her* to write the steps on the chalkboard.

   BETTER: When a *programmer* comes up with a solution, ask *him or her* to write the steps on the chalkboard.

   BEST: When a *programmer* comes up with a solution, ask *that programmer* to write the steps on the chalkboard.

3. Many readers are sensitive to the use of masculine terms applied to people of both sexes. Instead of *man* or *mankind,* try to use *human beings, people, the human race.* Rephrase sentences to avoid expressions like *the common man, the man in the street,* and *every man.*

4. Use nonsexist occupational labels. Here are some other terms to avoid, with possible substitutes:

   steward / stewardess — flight attendant
   chairman — chairperson
   businessman — business person
   salesman — salesperson
   mailman — mail carrier, letter carrier
   policeman — police officer
   fireman — firefighter

You may not be able to find a simple substitute. Sometimes you will need to rephrase an entire sentence in a way appropriate to the context.

5.3 ORDERS AND INVOICES

1. Write orders.
2. Write invoices.
3. Use numbers correctly.

Give detailed information.

Companie Générale Logistique
4 rue de Fromage
92400 Courbevoie FRANCE

2 June 19..

Mr Edgar Fowler
Omnicomp International
17 Bunker Hill Road
Shrewsbury, MA   01545

Dear Mr Fowler:

Please send me the following items listed in your current
catalogue:

144	24766-X	Spellgramm British English Verification Programs (8" Drive) @$69,50 ea.	$10 008,00
20	10778-2	Space Apocalypse (Tape) @$15.50 ea.	310,00
1	PR774-4	ODO Analog Input Module	280,00
		Subtotal	10 598,00
		Less 25% discount	− 2 649,50
		Total	$ 7 948,50

Indicate how the product must be shipped.

Please apply this amount to our account, and ship the order via
surface freight. Thank you very much.

Sincerely yours,

Robert deCoteau

156

Orders   Order letters are a common form of correspondence for obtaining equipment, services, and supplies. Because the typical company offers a great number of items for sale, you must give specific, detailed information in the order letter. Start out with a "Please send..." sentence, and then give details about the following matters:

1. Model and catalog number, size, color, and physical description. Be sure all numbers are in correct order. One wrong number can bring an incorrect product or none at all.
2. Quantity – how many?
3. What is the price per item? What is the total price?
4. How will it be shipped? Be specific!
5. Where will it be shipped? If it's going to a branch office, be sure that's stated. If there is any special delivery information, make sure that it is given.
6. Is there any requirement for special handling? Refrigeration? Insurance? Special packaging?
7. How will payment be made? What's the specific payment procedure?

The order letter spells out in considerable detail what exactly is being ordered. Accompanying it may be a purchase order, which is simply a condensed and quite explicit version of the order letter. The purchase order gives all of the information found in the order letter, but without the more formal structure and format of the letter.

Invoices   The invoice is similar to the purchase order, but it originates with the seller rather than the buyer. In most sales transactions, the last paperwork the seller sends to the buyer is an invoice, or bill, for the goods sold or the services rendered. The invoice, too, is a condensed form of the order letter, and it often repeats the purchase order or order letter information precisely and completely. Quantity, unit price, totals, and credit information are particularly critical on the invoice form.

Sometimes the invoice will accompany the shipment of goods. It might even be attached to the shipment in the case of bulky items. In still other cases, the invoice follows the shipment within a few days. If the seller services or installs a product, the invoice is customarily sent after the completion of the service. Ongoing work may necessitate several partial invoices, with the amount specified for the final service or installation being withheld until the service is performed.

The invoice should be as detailed as the nature of the business requires. Data-processing equipment differs in essential respects from machine tools, for instance. Sometimes weights or dimensions are critically required, sometimes not. Summarize the basic elements of the transaction: catalog numbers and descriptions, dates, quantities, unit prices, hourly charges, credit arrangements, installation charges (if appropriate), and so on. If you have doubts concerning any details in the invoice, ask yourself if *you* would be satisified if you were to receive it. It's better to include an unnecessary specification than to leave the customer puzzled. A completely satisfied customer is one who has been informed right up to – and including – the closing of the transaction.

CHECKLISTS

The Order Letter

1. Start out with a "Please send.." sentence, and then give specifics of the model, catalogue number, size, color, and any other relevant information about the particular product. ☐

2. Specify the quantity, price per unit, and total amount of the order. ☐

3. Indicate how or by what method the product is to be shipped. ☐

4. Carefully indicate the product's destination if it is different from the return address. ☐

Invoices

1. Be specific about the details, including price, quantity, shipping information, and terms. ☐

2. Give information in a condensed but comprehensive form, leaving no questions unanswered or information unspecified. ☐

OMNICOMP INTERNATIONAL
17 BUNKER HILL ROAD, SHREWSBURY MA 01545

ORIGINAL INVOICE

AN EQUAL OPPORTUNITY EMPLOYER

BRANCH

PENDING ORDER NUMBER

INVOICE DATE

INVOICE TOTAL

Terms Net 30 Days—We assume no responsibility for safe delivery of shipments by mail unless insured. All claims for allowance for shortage, etc. must be made immediately upon receipt of goods and invoice.

SOLD TO

SHIP TO

PLEASE REFER TO THIS NUMBER ON ALL CUSTOMER SERVICE CORRESPONDENCE

PLEASE REFER TO THIS ACCOUNT NUMBER INVOICE NUMBER AND DATE ON ALL REMITTANCES

ACCOUNT NO.	INVOICE NO.	INVOICE DATE	PURCHASE ORDER NO.

PLEASE RETURN TOP SECTION OF THIS INVOICE WITH REMITTANCE. DETACH HERE

ITEM NO.	QUANTITY	DESCRIPTION	LIST PRICE	UNIT NET	NET PRICE

ACCOUNT NO	INVOICE NO.	DATE

ABBREVIATIONS
O.I. - OUT OF STOCK (INDEFINITELY) ORDER CANCELLED
SUB. - SUBSTITUTION
C.P. - CONTRACT PRICE
I.P. - IN PROCESS OF BEING SHIPPED
N.P. - NOT YET AVAILABLE, BACKORDERED
O.S. - OUT OF STOCK, BACKORDERED

SUB-TOTAL
TAXES
TRANS.
TOTAL
LESS CASH RECEIVED

WRITING ASSIGNMENT

Background   The following is an excerpt from the Omnicomp Software Catalog. Choose four items and prepare an order letter for them. You are the sales manager of The Computer Discount Center, 1040 Scenic Road, Westwood, New Jersey, 07974. The prices listed in the catalogue are list prices. You are entitled to a 15-percent discount. Ask Omnicomp to send your order by air parcel post, and enclose a check for the net price.

TITLE/DESC.	ORDERING NUMBER	LIST PRICE
Asteroid Destruction	61241-8409	$ 9.95
Atomic Structure	84212-9899	15.50
Automated Chart Service	12031-0092	25.95
Automatic Test Scoring/ Administrative Tracking Module	84413-22X	260.00
Averages	84205-5790	30.00
Bar Tab	68666-9229	10.95
Bar Graphs	82120-8872	20.50
Baseball Fever!	90981-1147	15.95
BASIC Instructional Package	81882-2240	25.50
BASIC Systems Command	81883-2251	25.50
BASIC Test File Commands	81883-2284	25.50
BASIC/FORTH Translation Program	62421-8401	9.95
Battle of Waterloo	64401-4044	9.95
Battle of the Sea Monkeys	62122-4051	29.50

Goal: _____

Audience: _____

FIRST DRAFT

_____
_____
_____
_____
_____
_____

◻◆◼ The Computer Discount Center ◼◆◻
1040 Scenic Road
Westwood, NJ 07974

GUIDELINES

Numbers

In business writing, numbers are usually written as figures rather than words. Writers often feel figures stand out better and enable the reader to find them easily on the page. Here are a few guidelines that may help you avoid inconsistencies in your writing.

1. When a number begins a sentence, spell it out. If necessary, revise the sentence:

> AWKWARD: *One hundred and six* sales representatives from our company attended the conference.
>
> BETTER: Attending the conference were 106 sales representatives from our company.
>
> ACCEPTABLE: *Sixteen* sales representatives from our company attended the conference.
>
> BUT: 1976 was a good year for business.

2. Generally, spell out numbers from zero to ninety-nine when used singly or with other numbers. Use numerals for numbers of 100 or more. Treat all numbers consistently when two or more in the same category appear in one sentence:

> The business manager bought *twenty-two* trucks and *fifteen* cars.
>
> The business manager ordered 22 chairs, 15 wastebaskets, and 125 file folders.

3. Use figures for dates, times, measurements, page numbers, addresses, percents, decimals, and mixed numbers:

> May 9, 19..   5:40 A.M.   100.22 mm $30 a share   76 tons
> page 2   19 Park Avenue   1-1/2 gallons   5 percent

4. Spell out ordinal numbers in most contexts. Ordinals in business addresses are easier to read if spelled out, but abbreviations are also acceptable:

> the eighteenth century   our tenth anniversary
>
> 123 Fifth Avenue   123 5th Avenue

COMMUNICATION WORKSHOP
Direct Mail Marketing

Many businesses use the postal system to persuade the customer to buy the product directly with the enclosed mail-order form or to buy it elsewhere.

The effectiveness of advertising by direct mail depends mainly on the mailing's appeal to its audience. To enhance their success, businesses usually purchase selective mailing lists that give names and addresses of people in specific geographic locations, age groups, income brackets, educational and occupational backgrounds, or interests groups.

Direct mail marketing allows a business to locate and sell to its customers without having any personal contact with them. In addition, direct mail can support advertising in other media, cover any location, and test such factors as price, copy, and product appeal. Finally, it gives the advertiser the advantage of an almost immediate response.

Components

A typical direct mail package includes a letter, an advertising brochure, and an order form (self-mailing or with a business-reply envelope). It may also include a "special bonus offer" or another attention-getting device.

The letter outlines the sales offer, the features of the product, and the benefits to the buyer. The brochure, through descriptive copy and art (preferably in color), illustrates the product in detail.

Optional enclosures such as the bonus gift offer provide additional incentives to buy the product described in the brochure and the letter. The special bonus offer describes a free or inexpensive gift that accompanies the main purchase. Another device is the involvement piece, which requires the reader to take an action, such as placing a stamp on the return form.

The order form gives the price and terms of payment, and requests the buyer to submit information. The postage may be prepaid on the return envelope.

The outside envelope can be as important as its enclosure in attracting the reader's attention with copy and art. All pieces in a mailing should be coordinated in theme, art, typeface, and color.

Distributor/Manufacturer Direct Mail Campaigns

Although it's common for companies to conduct their own direct mail campaigns, another way to sell is through a distributor. Distributors, such as credit or charge card companies, often run their own direct mail campaigns to expand sales. The distributor usually incurs part or all of the costs for promoting the products in exchange for a commission.

The Travel Division of the American Express Travel Related Services Company, Inc., for example, enters into agreements with manufacturers of business products, collectibles, clothing and accessories, electronics, and general merchandise to advertise and sell their products. A large diversified travel and financial service company with offices throughout the world, American Express encourages charge cardmembers to use their cards to purchase a variety of products by direct mail. Before embarking on a major direct mail campaign, American Express sends billing inserts and special mailings to a sample of its customers to test the effectiveness of the package. Then American Express sends the revised package to as many of its fourteen million charge cardmembers in the United States as seems appropriate. The firm uses product inserts with the five million monthly bills it sends to cardmembers.

Xerox is one of the manufacturers some of whose products American Express advertises. Xerox manufactures a wide variety of equipment for the reproduction, reduction, and transmission of printed material. American Express is a good distributor for Xerox because many of its charge cardmembers are interested in and can afford office machines.

©1984, American Express Travel Related Services Inc.

The American Express Direct Mail Package

The letter on pages 164 and 165 and other enclosures from American Express describing Xerox's products follow the *ABCD* Rule of Sales Writing discussed earlier in the chapter.

A. It attracts the reader's attention by its format and by the color photographs, charts, and reduced letter samples.

B. The mailing builds the reader's interest through a repetitive description of product features and buyer benefits. The letter outlines these features and benefits, and the brochures develop them in greater detail.

C. American Express creates desire for the product by the description of features and benefits as mentioned above and by additional incentives: the free fifteen-day trial, the "never-lower" price, and the bonus gift.

D. American Express completes the sale in the order form. To overcome the prospective customer's last-minute hesitations, the order form offers a choice of several different payment plans.

ROBERT L. MEYERS
SENIOR VICE PRESIDENT
COMMUNICATIONS DIVISION

Discover State-Of-The-Art Xerox, Take The Opportunity to Save $179.00
And Receive A Randix Super Cube Radio and Quasar 10" Color TV
As Free Gifts With Your Purchases.

Dear Cardmember:

American Express has the pleasure of making an outstanding offer of two exceptional products from Xerox. They are: (1) the remarkable 1020 Marathon Desktop Copier, the most advanced, compact Xerox copier in history; and (2) the affordable Xerox 610 self-correcting, automated electronic typewriter that eliminates the most time-consuming typing procedures.

We greet the availability of these innovative, productive and cost-efficient products with great enthusiasm, and we are pleased to offer these superb Xerox products with special Cardmember benefits.

For example, when you purchase the Xerox 610 Memorywriter you will receive a Randix Super Cube AM/FM radio and cassette player, with a host of entertainment features in an amazingly compact 6-inch cube. Purchase the Xerox Marathon Copier and you will receive an exciting Quasar 10-inch color portable TV.

And, if you purchase the Xerox 610 Memorywriter and the Xerox 1020 Copier you will enjoy an impressive savings of $179.00. In addition, Xerox will make its complete line of Memorywriter products available through this offer.

American Express, with its pledge to bring you total satisfaction, and Xerox, esteemed for providing products to help you run a more successful business, have combined their efforts to bring you this unique gift and savings opportunity on the Xerox 1020 Copier and the Xerox 610 Memorywriter. As a Cardmember you will enjoy a risk-free examination of these Xerox products, and the exclusive Cardmember advantage of monthly payments with no down payment and no finance charge.

The Xerox 1020 Marathon Copier -- The ultimate compact copier, the Xerox 1020 is an advanced state-of-the-art member of the new Xerox Marathon Copier family. Small enough -- just 17" x 17" x 11" -- to sit on a desk, yet it's big enough to perform many of the most-wanted copier capabilities. It goes beyond everyday copying needs to produce quality black and white duplicates from linework, colors, three-dimensional objects and pages in bound volumes.

And the Xerox 1020 is fast. The first copy takes just seven seconds and the reproduction process continues at a steady rate of 11 copies per minute. Each copy, 5½" x 8½" all the way to 8½" x 14", is always clean, clear and professional-looking.

The Xerox 1020 has five contrast controls. "Friendly", easy-to-use control panel lights tell you how to solve a problem or show you what's going on. There are also a host of other electronic features to make copying precise, fast, and cost-effective.

The Xerox 1020 is for those who depend on true quality copies from originals. It fits beautifully in any office, or as a satellite copier in a conference room, executive suite, construction trailer -- anywhere a standard electrical outlet is available.

Ahead in performance, efficiency and technology, the Xerox 1020 is backed by Xerox reliability, service and versatility. There's never been a compact Xerox copier like it. And, the plain-paper Xerox 1020 is being offered to you at no increase from the lowest introductory copier price in Xerox history.

continued . . .

And there's further cause for celebration.

The Xerox 610 Memorywriter -- Fully automated. Self-correcting. A memory storage system that does away with retyping your most frequently used words, paragraphs and phrases. These are just a few of the many compelling features of the Xerox 610 Memorywriter, an automated electronic typewriter that is way ahead of electrics -- even self-correcting electrics!

The Xerox 610 Memorywriter erases up to 180 characters with the touch of one key. It automatically centers, underlines, bolds, returns the carriage, erases, sets up complex formats and columns, flushes right, organizes statistics -- and much, much more. It stores up to 1150 characters in memory to type automatically everything from dates, addresses, and titles to frequently used sentences and short paragraphs.

Advanced daisy wheel letter -- quality printing is faster and quieter than "golf-ball" elements. Easier to insert and remove, the daisy wheel has 98 characters (instead of the usual 88) and is available in a wide range of type fonts and 10, 12, 15 pitch or proportional spacing.

With all of these outstanding capabilities, the Xerox 610 is simple to use and provides a pleasant, productive and reliable way to achieve professional typing results.

Furthermore, your Xerox 610, can expand as your needs grow. Its add-on capabilities -- a visual display, more automation, more memory -- can be increased by Xerox right in your office for an additional fee. However, if your current requirements demand more display and memory, you many order, through this offer, a Xerox Memorywriter with more capabilities. Just call our Xerox representative toll-free -- 1-800-828-9090 for details.

An invitation to you from American Express -- Words and photographs cannot fully capture the wide-ranging capabilities and potential benefits of either the Xerox 1020 Copier or the Xerox 610 Memorywriter. Each is a remarkable Xerox product backed up by the integrity of Xerox quality, design and service.

To appreciate their excellence, American Express invites you to enjoy a 15-day risk-free trial examination of the Xerox 1020 Copier and/or the Xerox 610 Memorywriter. We firmly believe that this will convince you that these Xerox products are truly extraordinary.

Most importantly, as a Cardmember you will enjoy a meaningful advantage should you decide to keep the Xerox 1020, the Xerox 610 -- or both at a $179.00 savings. For you may charge your Copier or Memorywriter purchase to your American Express® Card Account and take 12 months to pay for the Xerox 610; 15 months to pay for the Xerox 1020; or 20 months to pay for both with no down payment and no finance charge.

Right now, we suggest you read more about these remarkable Xerox products in the accompanying brochure, and that you call us or use the enclosed Reservation Form for a risk-free trial examination of these fine products.

We are excited to be able to offer these truly great Xerox products and the Free gifts of a Quasar 10" color TV and Randix AM/FM cube radio and we look forward to hearing from you soon.

Sincerely,

Robert L. Meyers
Senior Vice President

© 1984 American Express Travel Related Services

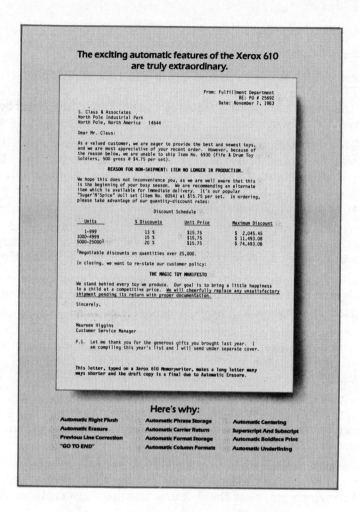

© 1984 American Express Travel Related Services Inc.

Discussion Activities

1. Compare the letters from American Express to the checklists for writing negative letters of adjustments in Chapter 4 and promotion and sales letters in this chapter. Do you consider the letters effective? Why or why not?

2. Advertisers and other people working in communications have long found Maslow's Needs Hierarchy a useful tool. According to this theory, everyone has certain needs that must be fulfilled before other needs can be considered. First on the list are physical needs, such as food and shelter. When these are met, safety and security become primary. Then a person becomes concerned about group identity. Next, personal recognition takes on importance. The later needs include fulfilling one's potential and helping others.

   Advertisers appeal to different needs for different products. For example, an advertisement for a burglar alarm would probably appeal to the need for security.

   What needs does the American Express package appeal to? Is it successful?

3. Discuss examples of good and bad direct mail campaigns. Explain why you feel they are or are not effective.

6
CREDIT INQUIRIES

Requests for
Credit Reference

Letters of Acceptance
and Refusal

6.1 REQUESTS FOR CREDIT REFERENCES

Objectives

1. Write requests for credit references.
2. Write topic sentences.
3. Write developing sentences.
4. Organize developing sentences.
5. Use hyphens correctly.

OMNICOMP INTERNATIONAL
17 BUNKER HILL ROAD, SHREWSBURY MA 01545

July 11, 19..

Ms. Marie Laveau, Credit Manager
Paracelsus Digital Equipment, Ltd.
P.O. Box 2, Woden
Canberra ACT 2606, AUSTRALIA

Dear Ms. Laveau:

SUBJECT: CREDIT INQUIRY CONCERNING SOSEKI K.K. OF
        OSAKA, MANUFACTURER OF GRAPHIC ELECTRODES

Use a subject line.

   Would you please send me a summary of your credit experience with Soseki K.K.? I assure you that your response will be kept completely confidential.

Make your request in the opening sentence.

   In applying for a credit account for our firm, Soseki K.K. gave your name as a reference. We'd like to hear about your credit experiences with the company, its credit limit, terms, and paying habits.

Give background information and describe the details of your request.

   We greatly appreciate your help in this matter, and we'll be happy to assist you in a similar manner whenever we can. Thank you for your time and consideration.

Thank the reader and express your appreciation.

Sincerely yours,

Edgar P. Fowler

Edgar P. Fowler
Account Correspondent

Purpose	Credit is a standard part of doing business, and it is standard procedure to obtain credit references from individuals or companies planning to establish an account with you. To do this, it is often necessary to write a letter of inquiry asking for credit information about a proposed client. The handling of this information, however, requires tact and diplomacy. Most requests for credit information should, therefore, be considered confidential. The entire objective of the letter to secure credit references is to accomplish that end promptly by gaining the information needed to extend credit quickly and with minimal discomfort. Once credit references are secured, promptly notify the potential customer.

Credit References

How does a credit manager determine a potential customer's risk? There is a specific procedure that will not unduly embarrass the customer. The most important single credit reference is a list of the banks and financial institutions with which the customer does business. These institutions will supply a time-line of association with the potential customer and will help to establish a history of reliability in financial transactions.

A second important reference is the company's latest financial statement, either a quarterly or an annual statement. Since the annual statement is audited and publicly filed, its information can be regarded as reliable. Unlike bank credit references, the annual report almost always permits comparisons with previous years and projects a multidimensional picture of the company's efforts.

Another source for obtaining a credit rating on American or multinational companies is that company's Dun and Bradstreet rating. The D & B rating is a widely accepted evaluation that provides an approximate gauge of a customer's financial strength.

When a potential customer submits credit references in support of an order, there is certain information you want to obtain from those references. Basically, you want to obtain data about the "Three C's" of credit: Character, Capital, and Capacity. As you contact credit references, keep the three C's in mind.

A long history of successful business relationships clearly helps to establish the *character* of a company. Therefore, ask such questions as:

How long have you known Standard Industrial Castings Corporation?
How long have you done business with them?

As far as the company's *capital,* assets, liquidity, and actual growth are concerned, the annual report is the best source of information. If a company is not publicly owned, it will probably expect you to ask for its income statement and balance sheet as evidence of its financial stability and capital.

Will Standard Industrial Castings Corporation have the *capacity* to remain in business in the years ahead?

While this may seem to be a subjective judgment, there are concrete sources of information. This evaluation involves studying a combination of data, including credit references, financial statements, and financial ratings. It is up to your credit manager to put together all the appropriate information.

Most companies will quickly respond to a credit inquiry because they expect a similar courtesy from other companies in return. Nevertheless, you should make it as easy as possible for your reader to respond. A subject line is often useful in this instance because it allows the reader to determine the nature of the request immediately. Begin by directly and politely asking for the information you want. If there are any unusual circumstances or there is special information that you want, define it in the second paragraph. Conclude by thanking your reader.

REVISING

Revise the following credit inquiry. Look for errors in punctuation and grammar as well as in content and style.

HOSER'S DEPARTMENT STORE
3 Mackenzie Road South
Mount Albert, Ontario LOG 1M0

February 19, 19..

Rizzuto E-Z Finance Corp.
1540 Lexington Avenue
New York, NY 10011

Dear Sir or Ms.;

SUBJECT: Credit

Thank you for responding to our request. If we can be of help to you in the future, please don't hesitate to call.

Ms. Welch has applied for credit from us. She told us that she used to owe money to you. Did she pay? How much did you lend her?

Ms. Yolanda Welch, will you please send us credit information about her. She recently moved to Mount Albert from 469 7th Ave., New York.

She is hoping to open a charge account at our store. We'd like to know a little bit about her for our files.

Sincerely

Grace Whitenorth
Credit Manager

REVISION

CHECKLIST

The Credit Reference

1. Determine a potential customer's credit reference with as much tact and diplomacy as possible. ☐

2. Send requests for credit information to banks and financial institutions that do business with the customer. Obtain other credit information from published financial statements and other publicly available data. ☐

3. Verify the company's character through its successful business association with other firms. ☐

4. Establish the company's capital soundness through its annual report and financial statements. ☐

5. Use a subject line to make it easy for your reader to respond to your request. ☐

6. Ask for the information you want in the first sentence. Do so directly and politely. Then follow the guidelines listed on page 44. ☐

WRITING ASSIGNMENT

Prepare a credit inquiry to be sent by J. García, Sales Manager of Alembic Metallurgical Supply Company. Continue your first draft on a separate sheet.

Background   Your (J. García's) company has just received a very large order from the Boa Mining Corporation of Buenos Aires, Argentina. The order was accompanied by a corporate annual statement and a listing for its parent company, Vipercorp. They listed as a credit reference the Borges Chemical Corporation, Avenida Guevara 68, Bahía Blanca, Argentina. Write to the Credit Department of the Borges Corporation and ask for information about the Boa Mining Corporation.

Goal: _____

Audience: _____

FIRST DRAFT

_____

_____

_____

_____

_____

Alembic Metallurgical Supply Company

8 Towerstone Square   Palmerston, New Zealand

STYLE AND STRUCTURE
Topic Sentences

The paragraph, you'll remember, is a group of sentences related to a single topic or idea. Normally, a paragraph has a beginning sentence and a closing sentence, with several developing sentences filling in the middle. Those middle sentences develop the topic, which should have been introduced in the first sentence. Let's look at the following paragraph:

> Our wholesalers in the Midwest have complained that they are not receiving deliveries when promised. I checked with the shipping department last week and verified that the products went out on time. The fault must be that of our carrier, National Parcel Company. I have, therefore, begun an investigation of its performance, and I'll let you know what I find.

Every sentence in the paragraph should relate to the topic sentence; if one doesn't, it doesn't belong in that paragraph.

Because the topic sentence states the main idea of the paragraph ("wholesalers... not receiving deliveries"), the writer usually helps the reader by putting it first. This lets the reader know where the paragraph is going. By its nature, the topic sentence needs further development to complete the thought it is introducing.

As so often happens, writers who help their readers help themselves. When you begin the paragraph with the topic sentence, you force yourself to consider what belongs in the paragraph and what does not. You shouldn't allow your developing ideas to slip into the first sentence. They will only confuse the clear, concise statement of the subject on which the reader can easily focus.

PRACTICE

For each of the following paragraphs, write a topic sentence that states the main idea of the passage.

1. Be sure to check the cost of the Multex software because their shipping will be fastest and least expensive. Get quotes from Formpro and KPM, too, because they have supplied us well in the past. Have the figures ready for me not later than the first of next month.

   _____

   _____

2. We discovered instances of-less-than satisfactory workmanship. As a result of our initial findings, we began a comprehensive audit to determine the seriousness of the problem. Where we found problems, we kept looking until we were certain no further deficiencies existed.

   _____

   _____

Developing Sentences

Developing sentences expand on the topic we introduce in the paragraph's first sentence. They usually state facts or ideas that enlarge the reader's awareness of the subject. When you write more than one developing sentence, try to arrange the sentences in their best logical order. As a general rule, don't write more than three developing sentences because your reader may have trouble following your line of reasoning. After three developing sentences, write a conclusion about your development of the main idea to that point. Then you can begin the next paragraph from your new perspective of the topic. Let's take another look at our sample paragraph.

You can see that there are two developing sentences. In the first, the writer relates an action that was taken in response to the customers' complaints, showing that the action did not locate the cause of the problem. In the second, the writer suggests another possible cause of the problem, one made likely because the first possibility has been eliminated. The final sentence completes the development by stating what the writer is presently doing ("I have, therefore, begun an investigation...") and looks ahead to the future (I'll let you know what I find").

We might summarize the writer's procedure this way:

TOPIC SENTENCE: statement of problem

DEVELOPING FACT: past action

DEVELOPING IDEA: likely cause of problem

CONCLUSION: present action

Developing sentences frequently follow this pattern because so much of our business writing deals with problem-solving, and also because the natural order of events is chronological.

PRACTICE A

For each of the following topic sentences, write two developing sentences in their best logical order:

Example

1. We enclose our research and development division's report on the design of new mainframes.
   Please examine it carefully. After you have done so, call us to arrange a meeting about the design.

2. On the basis of the figures shown, I recommend that we open our new office in Sweden.

_____

_____

_____

_____

3. The president's message to the technology section contains two points of great importance to all of us.

_____

_____

_____

_____

4. Here is the brochure describing the latest discoveries about solid state transistors.

_____

_____

_____

_____

5. Under separate cover, we are mailing you the Asteroid 78 replacement parts.

_____

_____

_____

_____

PRACTICE B

Using the following topic sentences, develop the main ideas into complete paragraphs.

Example

1. The best site for our new distribution center in Australia is Melbourne.
   The best site for our new distribution center in Australia is Melbourne. The city is a central shipping point, and we can lease convenient warehouse space there. Furthermore, the labor force available in Melbourne matches our needs. We considered other cities, but none suits us as well as Melbourne.

2. I recommend that Mrs. Onosato be promoted to the position of senior laboratory technician.

_____

_____

_____

_____

_____

_____

3. You asked why the January sales figures were late arriving from our finance department.

_____

_____

_____

_____

_____

4. Please send me a memo on the prospects for buying transistor parts from a distributor located near our Glasgow factory.

_____

_____

_____

_____

_____

5. Workers may be shifted to a more profitable division within the company.

_____

_____

_____

_____

_____

WORDS IN ACTION

A   Choose the best answer.

1. According to its glowing financial statement, the Snark Corporation had a
   _____ year.
   a. technological   c. financial
   b. profitable   d. minimal

2. We solved the problem easily by making a _____ change in the system's
   design.
   a. minimal   c. reliable
   b. chronological   d. financial

3. Mr. Yamada did not attend last week's meeting, so please send him a _____ of what we accomplished.
   a. carrier
   b. deficiency
   c. possibility
   d. summary

4. Please _____ your report before five o'clock tomorrow.
   a. approximate
   b. submit
   c. credit
   d. notify

5. If there is any problem with the machine, _____ Mr. Beevis in the maintenance department.
   a. elaborate
   b. concern
   c. submit
   d. notify

6. We'll begin an _____ to find the cause of the problem.
   a. approximation
   b. investigation
   c. elaboration
   d. establishment

7. I don't need the exact total right now; an _____ figure will suffice.
   a. approximate
   b. elaborate
   c. accomplished
   d. initialed

8. Although the market is small, our research shows great _____.
   a. credit
   b. deficiency
   c. potential
   d. possibility

9. There is a _____ that their plant will close next year.
   a. possibility
   b. potential
   c. consideration
   d. investigation

10. If I can help you with the project, don't _____ to call.
    a. concern
    b. hesitate
    c. notify
    d. submit

B Write the word that matches each definition: accomplish, clientele, elaborate, stability, wholesaler.

1. succeed in doing; achieve   _____

2. a person who sells goods in bulk   _____

3. work out with detail; expand on   _____

4. constancy of purpose; reliability   _____

5. a group of customers or patrons   _____

GUIDELINES
Hyphens

1. Hyphenate an adjective made up of two or more words when it precedes the noun that it modifies; otherwise the hyphen is not required:

   > a well-planned campaign
   >
   > BUT: the campaign was well planned

   Exception: Do not hyphenate when the first element is an adverb ending in *ly:*

   > a carefully planned campaign
   >
   > a slowly descending elevator

   Exception: Do not hyphenate when the first element of the compound is modified:

   > a very well known person
   >
   > BUT: a well-known person

2. When two or more compound adjectives have a common base, use a hyphen after each first element and punctuate normally:

   > first-, second-, and third-class mail

3. Use hyphens in spelled-out numbers:

   > seventy-two, twenty-three and ninety-six hundredths

4. Do not hyphenate spelled-out fractions unless the fractions are used as adjectives:

   > a majority of two thirds, a two-thirds majority

5. Most common prefixes are joined to the following word without a hyphen. The following list of prefixes do not ordinarily require a hyphen:

   > anti, bi, co or con, extr, in, inter, intra, mid, non, over, post, pre, pro, radio, re, semi, sub, super, supra, trans, ultra, un, under

   Exception: Use a hyphen following the prefixes *all-*, *ex-* and *self-:*

   > ex-president, self-starting, all-powerful, all-important

   Exception: Use a hyphen when the word following the prefix is capitalized:

   > non-Roman languages

   Exception: Use a hyphen in order to avoid an awkward combination of vowels:

   > non-overlapping, intra-atomic, re-use
   >
   > BUT: cooperate, coordinate, reestablish, preeminent

6.2 LETTERS OF ACCEPTANCE AND REFUSAL

Objectives

1. Write letters of acceptance.
2. Write letters of refusal.
3. Recognize concluding sentences.
4. Use parentheses correctly.

Give the positive message in the first paragraph.

State billing procedures and credit terms.

Close with an offer of further assistance.

Acceptance:

Dear Mr. Taketomi:

Omnicomp International will be happy to establish a credit account for Soseki K.K. I hope that this will be the beginning of a long and mutually beneficial relationship between our two companies.

On the fifteenth day of each month, we will send you a statement listing your purchases made through the last day of the preceding month. In addition to your standard discount, you can receive another 2 percent off on items paid within thirty days from the invoice date.

Again, let me welcome you as a new customer. I have taken the liberty of asking our agent in Osaka, Mr. Taro Tanaka, to visit you and describe the many services that Omnicomp offers. If I can be of further help, please contact me.

Sincerely yours,

Edgar P. Fowler

Edgar P. Fowler
Account Correspondent

State the reason for the refusal tactfully.

Try to persuade the reader to do business on a cash basis.

Close with a confident tone.

Refusal:

Dear Mr. Grappa:

Thank you for your order of Omnicomp Software. Since your business has been in operation for only three months, we haven't been able to locate enough information about it on which to base a credit approval. Therefore, we cannot establish a credit account for your firm at this time.

Would you allow us to ship your order C.O.D.? As a cash customer, you would receive a liberal discount and efficient service. Our excellent line of products and attractive promotional display material would surely contribute to sales in your store.

We wish you every success in your new business, and we look forward to a long and pleasant association.

Sincerely yours,

Edgar P. Fowler

Edgar P. Fowler
Account Correspondent

After you have determined the credit rating of a potential customer, you'll have to write a letter of response. This letter will be either a positive letter of acceptance or a negative letter of refusal. As always, the positive message is the easier one to write.

Letter of Acceptance

Let's imagine that your credit inquiries have been completed, and that the potential customer has passed the test admirably. Now you have the pleasant task of announcing the good news.

Your letter doesn't have to elaborate on the procedure that you went through to establish the customer's credit. Instead, enthusiastically welcome the reader to your "family of satisfied customers." Briefly outline the credit terms and define your company's billing procedures. That's it.

Three short paragraphs should do it. The first extends credit as if there had never been any doubt about it. A second paragraph describes the specifics of billing, discounts, and long-term credit. In a final paragraph, you might want to point out any special services that you are prepared to offer the customer. Perhaps you have a branch location that will make it especially convenient for sales and service in the future.

Sometimes a company will send out a pre-printed "Welcome" card. Even such a standard acceptance of credit often spells out benefits and gives a sales message. If there is a big sale on your new 2000-lines-per-minute printer, let your new customer in on the news. The point is to leave the reader with a pleasant glow at the conclusion of the letter.

Letter of Refusal

The negative letter of refusal, however, is much more difficult to write. No one likes to bring bad news. In addition, the refusal has to be transformed, somehow, into an invitation that will bring a positive response.

Begin the letter by thanking your reader for the interest he or she has shown in your company. Then give the reason for your refusal clearly and tactfully. Be honest, but remember that the poor credit risk of today may be the valued customer of tomorrow. If there are any favorable aspects of the reader's financial situation, refer to them. This shows that you have considered all the information and take a personal interest in the improvement of the reader's credit standing. Anything positive can be used to soften the tone of the rejection.

Unlike other negative messages, it is probably best to state the credit refusal in the opening paragraph. This will allow you to devote the rest of your letter to developing the goodwill of your reader. You might want to refer to some future (and undefined) time when your reader's improved situation will require reconsideration. Then, if possible, you should try to persuade the reader to do business with you on a cash basis. If you can offer any incentive for your reader to buy from you, do so.

End your letter with a positive, confident tone. Never underestimate the value of anyone's goodwill, and never irrevocably alienate a reader. Convey your negative message as positively and as pleasantly as possible.

REVISING

Revise the following letter of acceptance. Especially consider the tone.

Case A

SHEARSON'S DEPARTMENT STORE
9 Shropshire Street
Sydney NSW 2001

6 June 19..

Mr Archibald Leech
100 Swann Way
Sydney NSW 2001

Dear Mr Leech:

We have received your request for credit at Shearson's. We have carefully investigated your background. We have written to your bank and to the references listed on your application.

As you probably know, our credit customers receive special benefits, such as advanced notification of our sales and specials. They receive statements each month that list their credit transactions and the amounts they owe.

Let me take this opportunity to announce a special sale for our credit customers on 4 July. All television sets and stereo systems will be discounted by 35 percent. You, Mr. Leech, will be able to participate in this sale because we've decided to accept you as a credit customer.

Congratulations,

Abigail Adams
Customer Service Manager

REVISION A

_____

_____

_____

_____

_____

_____

_____

_____

_____

_____

_____

Revise the following letter of refusal, making it more tactful.

Case B

Ms. Barbara Skink
Sedgewick & Sedgewick, Ltd.
94 Trumptop Place
Greelway Close, London N4 2EZ

Dear Ms. Skink:

A company that extends credit to everyone who asks for it will soon find itself deeply in debt. Therefore, we take every precaution to weed out the undesirable customers from the many applications we receive. Those with an unsavory character, an unsound financial standing, or a limited capacity to repay their debts are quickly and summarily denied credit.

We have received your order for stationery and your application for a credit account. We will not extend credit to your company. We will fill your order only after you send payment in full.

Surely you will agree that your financial circumstances will be healthier without incurring another debt to us. I am happy to have been able to help you in this matter.

Faithfully yours,

Ezra Jarndyce

REVISION B

CHECKLISTS

Credit Acceptance

1. In the first paragraph, enthusiastically welcome the credit applicant to your company's select group of preferred customers. ☐

2. In the next paragraph, give the specifics about your credit terms, billing, and any special terms. The information should be presented as if it were given for most favored status. ☐

3. Close with a special invitation to take advantage of a sale or service. ☐

Credit Refusal

1. Begin by thanking the reader for considering your company. Then state your refusal. Be tactful but firm in rejecting a credit application. Without exaggeration or emphasis, give the specific reasons for the refusal. ☐

2. Demonstrate a personal interest in the applicant's financial situation. ☐

3. Point out any benefits in the customer's current financial circumstances. ☐

4. Retain the customer's goodwill by offering special cash and discount arrangements. ☐

WRITING ASSIGNMENT

Background   On January 6, the Carbone Specialty Steel and Alloy Company received a large order from Bend-o-Matic Corporation (BMC), 240 Weldham Road East, Markham, Ontario L3R 253. Accompanying the order was a request for credit, signed by Owen Flasser, Bend-o-Matic's business manager.

You were required to determine Bend-o-Matic's credit reliability. Its financial statement seemed sound, and a bank gave BMC a good reference. But three companies to which you sent credit inquiries responded by saying that BMC was very slow in paying its bills. Since the Carbone Specialty Steel and Alloy Company is a small organization with a limited operating budget, you have decided to deny credit. You would like very much to fill the order on a cash basis, and you can offer BMC a 15-percent discount if BMC orders the Nickel Alloy 204 that it wanted C.O.D. Prepare an appropriate response.

Goal: _____

Audience: _____

Carbone Specialty
Steel and Alloy
Company

240 Weldham Road East
Markham   Ontario L3R 253

STYLE AND STRUCTURE

Concluding Sentences

Importance

The final sentence of your paragraph should conclude the development of the topic introduced in the first sentence, and it can lead into the next paragraph by a transition, which may consist simply of mentioning the next topic. In the paragraph below, for example, the first sentence introduces the topic by stating a problem. The next two sentences analyze the problem and begin to develop a solution, and the final sentence suggests a conclusion but mentions a new point (budget restrictions). The writer probably plans to discuss this point in detail in a following paragraph.

> It appears that the people who work in the Technology Division do not read the newsletter we publish for them. Certainly its format is unattractive; some pictures would enliven it, and the writing style is pretentiously wordy. We should consider giving the newsletter a new look, allowing for the restrictions that our budget imposes.

If the writer of the above paragraph went on to discuss "budget restrictions" without beginning a new paragraph, he or she would risk confusing the reader. The topic here is "people don't read the newsletter"; budget limitations are not directly responsible for the problem. When you are writing about a complex topic, present different aspects of the situation one at a time, that is, one per paragraph. If you organize your writing into these "building blocks," you will not only help your reader follow your argument but you will help yourself construct it.

A weak concluding sentence in a paragraph leaves the reader hanging, wondering what the writer's point is. Had the paragraph above stopped after "pretentiously wordy," the reader couldn't tell what steps, if any, the writer had planned in order to solve the problem. Draw together your development at the end of every paragraph so that each paragraph closes at a resting point, however tentative that point may be in the context of your complete message.

PRACTICE

Restructure each of the following paragraphs so the sentences are in the most logical order. Make sure the paragraph closes with the concluding sentence.

Example

1. The meeting will take place Friday, October 17. Please let me know whether you will come. We would like you to be one of the experts on a panel that will discuss the new reporting procedures.

   We would like you to be one of the experts on a panel that will discuss

   the new reporting procedures. The meeting will take place Friday, October

   17. Please let me know whether you will come.

2. They arrived last week along with the regular shipment. We have installed them, and the equipment is now working well. Thank you for sending the replacement parts.

   _____

   _____

3. I enclose a résumé giving the details of my education and experience. Most recently I have been a programmer trainee in the records department at the Export Bank. I would like to explore the prospect of obtaining a position with your firm.

4. These results reflect our continuing efforts to improve the margins on our product lines. The fourth quarter was especially strong, with net earnings of 83¢ per share, versus 69¢ last year. Earnings were up nearly 27 percent over last year.

5. But Solvitol still has not developed an outstanding over-the-counter drug. Its plan to acquire an ethical drug manufacturer should improve its ethical drug position substantially. Solvitol has increased its research budget and has expanded its international marketing.

6. Because no comprehensive review has been made, some sections are now obsolete. John Smith points out other problem areas in his letter (attached). The bylaws have been partly revised several times in the past decade, either in response to FCC requirements or to an internal need.

WORDS IN ACTION

A   Choose the best answer.

1. As a(n) _____ to our salespeople, we have increased their commission on our new model.
   a. limitation
   b. debt
   c. incentive
   d. precaution

2. The corporation has recently _____ a new subsidiary.
   a. acquired
   b. contributed
   c. discounted
   d. suggested

3. Because of a large staff, we'll have to increase our operating _____ for next year.
   a. budget
   b. debt
   c. discount
   d. limitation

4. All of our representatives _____ in an annual training seminar.
   a. reconsider
   b. hesitate
   c. contribute
   d. participate

5. Our credit department has _____ firm guidelines for evaluating credit reliability.
   a. reconsidered
   b. incurred
   c. discounted
   d. established

6. Because of Webster's financial situation, we've decided not to _____ his credit application.
   a. discount
   b. incur
   c. acquire
   d. approve

7. Our inquiries have revealed that the Hodge Corporation is deeply in _____.
   a. budget
   b. character
   c. debt
   d. discount

8. Our distributors received a standard _____ of 40 percent.
   a. budget
   b. discount
   c. debt
   d. capacity

9. We simply cannot _____ an additional debt.
   a. alienate
   b. contribute
   c. incur
   d. reconsider

10. It is not _____ to take credit for somebody else's work.
    a. tentative
    b. mutual
    c. irrevocable
    d. ethical

B   Write the word that matches each definition: beneficial, hesitant, irrevocable, substantial, tentative.

1. solidly built; of considerable importance   _____

2. encouraging a favorable result; advantageous   _____

3. uncertain; conditional   _____

4. exhibiting indecisiveness; faltering   _____

5. incapable of being undone; irreversible   _____

GUIDELINES
Parentheses

1. Parentheses are used to enclose supplementary information, as well as to set off numbers or letters used to list items in a sentence:

> An Omnicomp ICE (in-circuit emulator) is essential for efficient system maintenance.
>
> Our goal is to (a) locate the problem, (b) consider alternatives, and (c) suggest a solution.

2. When parentheses are contained within a sentence, any punctuation mark is placed after the closing parenthesis:

> Because of their outstanding balance ($4625), we cannot ship them additional equipment.

3. When parentheses are used to enclose an independent sentence, the final punctuation mark is placed inside the closing parenthesis:

> To connect the Model III to any of these printers, you'll need the optional Model III Printer Cable. (For more information, see Chapter 5, "Connecting Cables.")

Parenthetical Matter

Parenthetical matter is any element within a sentence that amplifies, digresses from, or otherwise interrupts the flow of the sentence. It should be set off from the rest of the sentence with some form of punctuation. Try to limit interruptive elements. This construction is effective when used sparingly, but distracting when used repeatedly.

1. If the parenthetical material is a phrase or clause closely related in meaning to the rest of the sentence, set it off with commas:

> There are many reasons, some of which were discussed earlier, for these negative results.

2. If the parenthetical material indicates a sudden break or change in continuity, set it off with dashes:

> In business writing, save the dash—hoard it, we might say—for occasions needing a change of pace or a bit of color.

3. If the parenthetical material already has commas in it, set it off with dashes or parentheses:

> Industrial accidents—and there are, as you know, too many—can be decreased if precautions are taken.
>
> Mr. Sullivan waited for the article on banking in *Business Journal* (although it was, to his dismay, very late in appearing) before he decided to borrow money to expand his new business.

COMMUNICATION WORKSHOP
The Credit Process

A company can only afford to give credit to customers who are good credit risks. The credit process is the method by which a company gathers and evaluates the information needed to decide whether or not a customer is a good credit risk. Since so many transactions, both large and small, are based on credit, this process is an important part of doing business.

Most businesses must provide credit services to their customers in order to develop and maintain a significant market share. Although a company's credit services may occasionally create financial difficulties and cash-flow problems, offering credit enables a larger number of people to buy its products or services. The types of credit services a company offers depend upon the company's financial status, its potential market, the type of product or service it sells, and the type of credit services its competitors offer.

For many transactions, however, customers finance the cost of their purchases with loans from commercial banks, insurance companies, pension funds, credit unions, and other financial institutions. These loans can be either short-term loans or long-term loans. Short-term loans must be repaid within one year, and they are usually easier to obtain than long-term loans. This is because the shorter repayment period reduces the risk of nonpayment, and also because there is usually an existing working relationship between the short-term borrower and the lender. In most cases, the borrower will have established a line of credit with the lender. This means that the lender has approved a short-term loan, up to a specific amount, before the loan is actually needed. Since the credit process has already been completed, the borrower can obtain the money as soon as it is needed and without any delay.

Long-term business loans usually have a repayment period of three to seven years. In such cases, the borrower must sign a term-loan agreement, a promissory note that contractually requires the borrower to repay the loan in specified installments. Long-term lenders usually require some type of collateral, such as real estate, machinery, or equipment. If the borrower fails to repay the loan according to the term-loan agreement, the lender can take possession of the collateral. The repayment terms and the interest rates for both long- and short-terms loans vary, and borrowers should always compare the rates offered by competing financial institutions.

Applications for credit from financial institutions usually begin with the borrower completing a pre-printed form. This application form asks the borrower to provide the information necessary to begin the credit process, such as credit references from banks and business associates. The application form is usually accompanied by financial statements that show the borrower's assets, liabilities, and equity. The lender uses this information to analyze the potential borrower's ability to repay the loan. By examining financial statements and balance sheets for different years, lenders can conduct different types of analyses. A *trend analysis* determines the direction of a company's growth over a given period. A *comparative analysis* compares a company's financial situation and stability to its competitors. *Ratio analyses* mathematically determine relationships between separate items in the financial statement. The lender will contact the banks and companies listed as credit references to learn how the applicant is handling its existing credit relationships. To enhance this information, the lender will consult Dun and Bradstreet or Standard and Poor to determine the company's credit rating.

However, the credit process is simply a study conducted by people, based on information provided by other people. There is no magic, no precise formula, and no computer program that decides who gets credit and who doesn't. Of course, borrowers must remember that the more closely their credit information conforms to the lender's credit policy, the more likely their application will generate a positive response.

COMMERCIAL CREDIT APPLICATION

Date ___March 18, 19.._____

Full Name of Organization
Neville Brothers Precision Instruments, Inc.

Address 2122 Beaver Street		Telephone Number and Contact (904) 555-2024	
City Jacksonville	County Duvall	State Florida	Zip Code 33213

Type of Business Entity: ___X___ Corporation _____ Partnership _____ Individual

How Long in Business ___18 years___ Line of Business ___Manufacturer of Medical Supplies___

Bank References:

Name Townbank	Address or Branch Atlanta, GA	Acct. Officer Lance Bertino	Telephone Number (404) 555-8018
Name Manhattan Central	Address or Branch New York, NY	Acct. Officer James Flint	Telephone Number (212) 555-1240

Trade References:

Name National Steel Corp.	Address 414 Skidd Road, Pittsburg, Pennsylvania	Telephone Number (215) 555-1213
Name Zipco Industries	Address 1220 Foster St., Fargo, Georgia	Telephone Number (912) 555-2986

Other Credit References — Preferably Outstanding or Paid Debt Obligations

Company Commercial Funding Assoc.	Address 44 Moosedrop Rd., Hibbing, Minnesota	Tel. # (218) 555-3232	Amount $45,000	Paid X Open
Company Suarez Investment Corp.	Address 913 Toot Street, Miami, Florida	Tel. # (305) 555-8108	Amount $25,000	Paid Open X

Vendor Name & Address	Quantity	New (N) Used (U)	Description (attach brochures or detailed configuration if available)	Cost
Omnicomp International 17 Bunker Hill Rd. Shrewsbury, MA	1	N	Minicomp 7 Computer	$325,000

Total Equipment Cost $ _325,000_
Term Requested __7 yrs._
Lease _____ Financing __X___
Rate Quoted __15%___
Down Payment or # Advance Rentals _____

Delivery Date __May 15, 19.._
Payments M ___ Q _X_ S ___ A ___ OTHER
ITC (check one) Retained _____ Pass _X_
Purchase Option (check one) Stated_____ FMV_____
Renewal Option _____

PLEASE PROVIDE INFORMATION AS TO USE OF EQUIPMENT, ITS REVENUE GENERATING OR EXPENSE SAVING CAPACITY, AND WHETHER ITS AN ADDITION OR REPLACEMENT, ON THE REVERSE OF THIS APPLICATION.

APPLICANT'S SIGNATURE _____

Discussion Questions

1. What are your experiences with the credit process?
2. What are some of the differences between consumer credit and commercial credit? What are some similarities?
3. How might a company's credit policy affect the sales of its products? Why might a business operate on a strict cash-only basis? Why would a retailer encourage its customers to establish credit accounts? Does a company's credit policy influence the price of its products? Why or why not?
4. What are some of the different financial institutions that extend credit? What types of credit transactions could be done at a local bank? What type of institutions might finance the construction of a forty-story office building?

7

THE COLLECTION SERIES

Collection Letters

Follow-up Collection
Letters

Objectives

1. Write collection letters.
2. Use transitional words and phrases effectively.
3. Use prepositions correctly.

OMNICOMP INTERNATIONAL
17 BUNKER HILL ROAD, SHREWSBURY MA O1545

October 20, 19..

Mr. Noburo Taketomi, Business Manager
Soseki K.K.
21–29 Nozaki-cho
Kita-ku Osaka-shi
Osaka, JAPAN

Dear Mr. Taketomi:

I hope that your new Omni Minicomp 7 system is performing according to your expectations. If you have any questions or concern about the implementation of the system, please contact either me or Omnicomp's local representative.

Refer to the product for which payment is due.

As you can see from the enclosed statement, we have not yet received payment for the shipment listed on Invoice Number 2412. The balance due is $12,476.

State the current status of the overdue account.

I've also enclosed a brochure that describes our new Omniscript high-speed printer, along with a listing of our newest software. Please call me if you have any questions about these products or your account.

Conclude by indicating your faith in the customer's continued business.

Sincerely yours,

Edgar P. Fowler

Edgar P. Fowler
Account Correspondent

Purpose   A company that extends credit to its customers must recognize that collecting payment on overdue accounts is a common part of the credit process. The majority of customers may be occasionally late with a payment, and temporary difficulties, problems, and errors often occur. Therefore, a missed payment should not be a cause for great concern.

A common procedure in this instance is simply to reissue the bill, along with a reminder that payment is overdue. The message should suggest that perhaps the customer has overlooked the previous bill. This procedure is often a standard part of the billing process, with uniform messages sent to all customers routinely.

For companies like Omnicomp, much of their business is with established dealers and wholesalers. They must always be careful in the tone of their collection procedures, or they might lose a valuable customer. It is often a matter of the credit department's policy to send at least two reminders before the first collection letter. Another matter of policy is that each customer is regarded as unique, and that individual circumstances determine not only how many reminders will be sent but exactly how the first collection letter will be worded.

If these standard reminders don't bring a response from the customer, the next step is to write a more personalized collection letter. This letter is basically a polite inquiry. You should have two objectives in mind while conducting a collection: (1) to obtain payment and (2) to retain the customer's goodwill and future business. If the customer, because of a temporary financial difficulty, is unable to pay the bill, then you should expect an explanation so that you can agree upon an alternative schedule of payment. If your personal collection letter does not bring payment, it should at least bring a response.

At this stage of the collection process, it is best to assume that the customer has a reasonable explanation for why the payment is late. In some cases, the customer may be dissatisfied with a product or service. Then the problem becomes one of adjustment rather than collection. Although your collection letter should indicate a concern over the late payment, you should maintain a polite and helpful tone.

Format   For an initial collection letter write three paragraphs. In the first, refer to the product or service that your reader purchased. Express your hope that the reader is satisfied with the transaction. In the second paragraph, briefly state the current status of the reader's account. You may also wish to refer to the reminder that was sent earlier, asking why the account was overlooked. The third paragraph should emphasize your faith in the customer and in the continuation of your business relationship. You might mention your reluctance to bring the matter of the debt to his or her attention and your assumption that you will be hearing from the customer shortly.

Another strategy is to conclude your letter with a sales message or a reference to a new product or event. This closing implies that the customer's continued business and goodwill are not in doubt and softens the tone of the reminder.

REVISING

Revise the following collection letters. Use transitional words and phrases as discussed in the "Style and Structure" section on page 200.

Case A

Ms. Wanda Hoover
Owings Pipe Company
44 Dunnings Road
Homeway, IL 60430

Ms. Hoover:

I am trying to control my impatience and anger over your delay in paying your account. You owe us $754, and we want it now. The amount is three months past due. We have sent you two reminders. You failed to respond. Your behavior in this matter has been most annoying. Perhaps you forgot to send your payment. We all make mistakes.

Is there a reason why you haven't paid? Please tell us, and maybe we can help. Perhaps you think that you can avoid paying your bills. Well, let me tell you that we will not allow you to cheat us out of the money we deserve. So pay up, before we take more unpleasant actions. We delivered 100 ten-foot lengths of cast iron drainpipe without any problems, so why don't you deliver our money?

You'd better communicate with this office immediately.

Sincerely,

Mary H. Lambert
Account Correspondent

REVISION A

Case B

Thornton Broadstreet & Sons Ltd.
8 Fotheringay Mews
Ruddersfield HO5 PJS, Great Britain

5 November 19..

Mr Ramon Velcro, Business Manager
Solomon Bivar et Fils
4 Rue de Vallee
74000 Annecy, FRANCE

Dear Mr Velcro:

You have received the six drafting tables we shipped last March? You are pleased with them? We are proud of every table we manufacture.

We also offer other architectural supplies. Our newest product, a portable drafting table that comes in an attractive case. It is useful. It is reasonably priced.

Speaking of prices, the price of the drafting tables was £684.

Respectfully yours,

Elmore Jones
Account Supervisor

REVISION B

CHECKLIST

Initial Credit Reminder

1. Before writing a collection letter, reissue the bill with a short reminder. ☐

2. Remember the two objectives of the collection process: collect the debt and retain the customer's goodwill. ☐

3. Begin by referring to the product or service for which payment is due. ☐

4. In the second paragraph, briefly state the current status of the overdue account. ☐

5. Conclude with a polite reminder. You can also use a sales message to indicate your faith in the customer's future business. ☐

6. Treat each delinquent account individually. You should at least receive a response, if not a partial payment, from the first collection letter. ☐

WRITING ASSIGNMENT

Background

You (T. Murray) are the business manager of DeMento Brothers, Inc., a large paint contracting firm. The Kearney Construction Corporation, of 1414 Preston Street, Houston, TX 77002, is one of your best customers. In the past, Kearney Construction has always paid its bills within thirty days of receiving them. On March 28, DeMento Brothers sent Kearney a bill for painting five houses in Kearney's Pinehurst development. The amount of the bill was $14,850.

It is now July 2. Kearney has received three monthly statements indicating that the payment is past due, but Kearney has not responded. Prepare an initial credit reminder. Address it to Mrs. Irma Dillow, the accounts payable supervisor at Kearney Construction. Continue your first draft on a separate sheet.

Goal: _____

Audience: _____

FIRST DRAFT

_____

_____

_____

_____

DeMento Brothers, Inc.

44 Mezcal Boulevard   Nacogdoches, TX 75961

STYLE AND STRUCTURE
Transitional Words and Phrases

Throughout your writing, it is important that you clearly show the relationship between the ideas expressed in your sentences and paragraphs. You can help your reader follow the progress of your ideas by using transitional words and phrases. They act as signs to tell the reader where you are going.

You can use the following guidelines to show the relationship between ideas.

To introduce a topic in a sentence, use:

in addition	further	besides
and	again	first, second, . . . , last
a second point	moreover	another

The weekly department meeting has been postponed because of employee illness. **In addition,** the senior staff meeting has been rescheduled for Wednesday of next week.

To continue or refer to a topic, use:

that, this	he, she, it, they	who, whom
these, those	few, many, most	

Your collection letter is eloquent. **That**'s the best one you have written.

To restate a point, use:

to put it	in other words	to summarize
another way	in conclusion	that is

Our financial situation is grim. **In other words,** unless we collect more of our outstanding debts, we won't be able to launch our new product.

Present a contrast with:

nevertheless	but, yet, however	on the contrary

The company's sales were declining. **Nevertheless,** he increased his inventory.

To concede a point, use:

of course	although	certainly
no doubt	even though	surely
granted that	obviously	

We are sorry that your shipment didn't arrive on time. **Of course,** with the strike, you can understand our situation.

To show cause and effect:

accordingly	thus	so that
because	as a result	therefore
consequently	hence	

We have added three new credit managers in the Bombay area; **consequently,** revenue should increase.

To make a comparison, use:

similarly   likewise   in the same way

We try to fill our orders as quickly as possible, Ms. Duggan; **similarly,** we trust that our customers will send payment promptly.

To account for time, use:

previously	since	next
now	eventually	before
earlier	then	after
later	finally	such as

Last year we were working with a rented computer system. **Previously,** we had no system at all.

To indicate examples or details, use:

for example	namely	the following
for instance	in particular	to illustrate
including	specifically	

The following is a rough draft of my answer to Mr. Taketomi's letter.

When you make your readers follow a series of sentences without transitions, they may have trouble finding the relationship between the important points in your message.

WITHOUT TRANSITIONS: Last Friday our European office suffered a power failure. The computers were down all day. The weekly sales report was delayed. Our estimated sales figure proved correct.

WITH TRANSITIONS: Last Friday our European office suffered a power failure. **As a result,** the computers were down all day, and, **consequently,** the weekly sales report was delayed. **However,** our estimated sales figure proved to be correct.

PRACTICE A

Complete the paragraphs with transitional words or phrases.

1. Many managers feel that supervisors should show subordinates their evaluations. _____ when evaluations are poor, some supervisors resist sharing evaluations with their subordinates.

_____ employees can put them on the defensive.

_____ confrontations between outspoken employees and supervisors can occur. _____ when the supervisor can demonstrate that the employee has been carefully evaluated and can point out specific areas for improvement, the supervisor can use the evaluation as an instructional tool.

2. _____ there are times when management tries to get a relative evaluation of several employees for possible promotion. If the supervisor does not have to account for the entire evaluation, the employee may receive a more impartial view. _____ it might be better to have a group evaluation;

_____ an evaluation from an immediate supervisor, the department head, and a representative from the personnel department.

PRACTICE B   Improve each of the following groups of sentences by adding transitional words or phrases.

Example   1. The bylaws have been revised a little at a time. No comprehensive review has taken place. Certain sections are now obsolete.
The bylaws have been revised a little at a time, but because no
_____
comprehensive review has taken place, certain sections are now obsolete.
_____

2. In 1983 the company opened an office in Sweden. It had been the practice to rely on a single sales representative.

_____

_____

3. For six months the semiconductors were unavailable. They came on the market again.

_____

_____

4. The report has a number of weaknesses. It does have some strengths.

_____

_____

5. The sale of transistors declined 10 percent. Net profits from their sales rose 5 percent.

_____

_____

PRACTICE C   Write four sentences or sets of sentences in which you use four transitional words or phrases you did not use in your answers to the exercises in *A*.

1. _____

_____

2. _____

_____

3. _____

_____

4. _____

_____

WORDS IN ACTION

A Write the best answer.

1. The _____ submitted an excellent design for our new facility.
   a. net
   b. routine
   c. architect
   d. policy

2. Although our budget will not allow us to hire a full-time auditor, we have been able to employ one on a _____ basis.
   a. transitional
   b. temporary
   c. unique
   d. initial

3. I've tried to make an appointment with Mr. Hyde, but he's been _____ all week.
   a. routine
   b. difficult
   c. obsolete
   d. unavailable

4. It is important to _____ the customer's goodwill during the collection process.
   a. rely
   b. concede
   c. retain
   d. decline

5. Although our sales remained constant, lower production costs resulted in a higher _____ profit.
   a. net
   b. behavior
   c. architect
   d. policy

6. Because of research and innovations during the past few years, the system we bought in 1975 is now _____.
   a. unique
   b. obsolete
   c. temporary
   d. transitional

7. Problems such as this are not unusual; they are a(n) _____ part of doing business.
   a. useless
   b. routine
   c. net
   d. unavailable

8. We can _____ on Miss Stakes to locate the problem and solve it.
   a. initial
   b. retain
   c. rely
   d. concede

9. Although the plan received some _____ resistance from the advisory committee, we expect that the plan will gain approval.
   a. great   c. obsolete
   b. initial   d. unique

10. One of our trucks was involved in an accident this morning. _____, the delivery will be delayed.
    a. However   c. Previously
    b. Eventually   d. Consequently

B   Write the word that matches each definition: accordingly, impatience, previous, unavailable, unique.

1. consequently; correspondingly   _____

2. a feeling of being unable to wait   _____

3. occurring before something else   _____

4. being one of a kind; without rival   _____

5. incapable of being obtained or used   _____

GUIDELINES

Prepositions

Definition   Prepositions are words that show the relationship between a noun or pronoun and another word in the sentence. The noun that follows the preposition is called the object of the preposition. Together, the preposition and its object make up a prepositional phrase. Prepositional phrases can modify nouns, verbs, adverbs, or adjectives.

Examples

> Mr. Maxwell traveled extensively **in** Asia. (The preposition *in* shows a relationship between its object, *Asia,* and the verb *traveled*.)
>
> Ronald's report **of** the international conference was quite interesting. (The preposition *of* shows a relationship between its object, *conference,* and the noun *report*.)
>
> The choice for promotion was **between** him and me. (The preposition *between* shows a relationship between its objects, *him* and *me*, and the noun *choice*.)

Phrasal Verbs   Verbs and prepositions may be combined, giving new meaning to the pair of words. This combination has many names (phrasal verbs, two-word verbs, verb-preposition combination). There are countless pairings of verbs and prepositions, all with distinct meanings. Below is a list of some phrasal verbs and their uses.

Examples

Agree on or **upon**—come to an understanding on a course of action: Mr. Shetler and Mr. Branch do not agree on the final analysis.

agree to—consent to plans or conditions: If you agree to the last condition in the contract, please sign.

agree with—be of one opinion with a person: I don't agree with you.

account for—explain something: The Christmas party costs account for the high entertainment expenses in December.

apply for—request something: Although she is inexperienced, she will apply for the position of credit manager.

apply to—request assistance of someone: Employees have the right to apply to the grievance committee with specific complaints.

argue about—quarrel about plans or conditions: The members of the finance committee argued about the five-year plan.

argue for—speak forcefully in favor of something: The discouraged employee argued for a pay raise.

argue with—dispute with someone: The credit manager shouldn't argue with his clients.

succeed in—accomplish something intentionally: She succeeded in making a good impression.

succeed to—replace someone in a position: Jones succeeded to the vice presidency.

Objectives

1. Write follow-up credit letters.
2. Combine sentences by using parallel structure.
3. Correct sentences with faulty parallel structure.
4. Revise paragraphs by using parallel structure.
5. Recognize appositive phrases.
6. Combine sentences by using appositive phrases.

OMNICOMP INTERNATIONAL
17 BUNKER HILL ROAD, SHREWSBURY MA 01545

December 20, 19..

Mr. Noburo Taketomi, Business Manager
Sosekei K.K.
21–29 Nozaki-cho
Kita-ku, Osaka-shi
Osaka, JAPAN

Dear Mr. Taketomi:

Summarize the status of the overdue account.

As you can see from the enclosed statement, we have received no payment on your account for the merchandise that we sent to you on July 24. Moreover, we have not received acknowledgement of the reminders and letters that we have sent to you since then.

Ask for an explanation.

Are there any unusual circumstances that have prevented you from making payment on your account? If so, we would be glad to discuss them with you and arrange an alternative schedule of payments.

Demand payment or an explanation by a certain date.

We feel certain that you will want to settle this account without any further difficulty. Unless we hear from you, we expect to receive full payment of $12,476 by January 15.

Sincerely yours,

Edgar P. Fowler

Edgar P. Fowler
Account Correspondent

Purpose   When your first personal collection letter goes unacknowledged, it becomes necessary to take another step, but one that still attempts to maintain a positive relationship with the delinquent customer. Although an individual debtor's circumstances have to be taken into account, most companies have a certain collection procedure and a given time sequence in which they operate. Each follow-up letter takes a slightly different approach. While your first letter assumed the accidental or inadvertent nature of the credit problem, your second letter should adopt an attitude of increased concern.

In fact, the second collection letter should turn from the possibility of a mere overlooking of a due date to a concern about what may have caused the problem. You can ask such a question directly, and you might even suggest that the customer call your office in an effort to come to some settlement.

However, your second collection letter should also appeal to the customer's sense of obligation and the desirability of maintaining a good credit rating. If you are writing to a company, rather than to an individual account, you should assume that any current financial difficulties can be straightened out and that a healthy credit relationship can be restored. However, you have already sent a sequence of reminders (two or more) and an initial collection letter. This may be your fourth effort to get some kind of response from the customer that indicates payment will be coming. Obviously, a stronger form of reminder is called for.

Format   Therefore, begin your letter by directly stating the history and the current status of the overdue account. Your tone should be polite but firm. Then use your second paragraph to inquire about the reason for the long delay in payment. You can also offer your assistance in resolving any problem as easily as possible. In the final paragraph, write a direct demand for payment or for a reasonable explanation, and let your reader know that you expect a reply before a certain date.

Final Letter   If this letter brings no response, you are obviously dealing with a customer to whom you shouldn't have given credit in the first place, and you will have to take some type of action to resolve the account. The type of action depends upon the company's policy, and the delinquent customer is usually notified in a final letter.

The final letter, then, is a notification of that action. Each succeeding letter has been, in some sense, a sales letter, emphasizing that selling, rather than penalizing, constitutes the main business of your company. Now, however, the customer has left you no alternative but to take stronger steps to settle the account. For example, you have no choice but to turn the account over to your attorneys for collection unless you receive a positive response within a given period. Always give the customer one last chance. The final collection letter respresents the possible severing of what once might have been a productive business relationship, but always consider the happy possibility that the customer will remit payment. Consequently, the wording and tone of the final collection letter should still be somewhat placating and helpful.

REVISING

Revise the following collection letters. Correct grammatical errors, if any, and improve the tone.

Case A

Roberto Fazulo, S.P.A.
Via Polenta 49
1-20135 Milano
Tel. [02] 5640323

2 November, 19..

Mr. Oliver Trout
Acme Import Co.
260 Mott Street
New York, NY   00104

Dear Trout:

We want an explanation of why you will not pay your bill. Before December 10, please.

　As you probably know, we have not received payment for the items listed on Invoice #2001. These items, they were shipped by us on May 4. Our many reminders and monthly bills have been without response from you. You owe us $1,492.

Is there a reason for this unfortunate delay? If not, the balance of your debt is $1,492. I know that you will want to resolve this matter immediately, if not sooner.

Very truly yours,

Donato Anatra
Credit Manager

REVISION A

Case B

ALLIANCE NOVELTY CORP.
4 Cottonwood Road
Zephyr Cove, NV 89448

April 1, 19..

Richard W. DeBruin
5344 Shakedown Street
Beaver, WI 54105

Dear Mr. DeBruin:

We have tried and tried to reason with you. We've sent bills, reminders, and letters to you. The item that you ordered from us last December 27 was delivered. We sent you the bill for $59.95. You sent us nothing.

Pay up, Mr. DeBruin, before it's too late.

Sincerely,

Loretta Wynn
Sales Director

REVISION B

_____

_____

_____

_____

_____

_____

_____

_____

_____

_____

_____

_____

CHECKLIST

Follow-up Collection Letters

1. In the first paragraph, summarize the status of the overdue account. ☐

2. Use the second paragraph to ask if there is a reason why the account has not been settled. Suggest that the customer contact you if there is a problem. ☐

3. Close with a third paragraph that makes a direct demand for payment or for an explanation by a given date. ☐

4. If this letter brings no response, prepare a final collection letter. This letter simply gives an ultimatum that further action will be taken if payment isn't received immediately. ☐

5. Maintain a polite and helpful tone throughout the collection process, and always leave open the possibility that a once-successful business relationship can be re-established. ☐

WRITING ASSIGNMENT

Background

It is now August 4, more than a month since T. Murray sent an initial collection letter to the Kearney Construction Corporation (see page 198). Kearney has not responded to the letter.

You (T. Murray) have become quite concerned over the situation, particularly because Kearney had been such a reliable customer in the past. Nevertheless, if the matter of the outstanding balance of $14,850 isn't cleared up quickly, your company will not accept any new contracts from Kearney.

Prepare another collection letter. Insist that the account be paid before August 20, but remember that you still hope to do business with Kearney in the future. Address your letter as follows:

Mrs. Irma Dillow, Accounts Payable Supervisor
Kearney Construction Corporation
1414 Preston Street
Houston, TX 77002

Write your first draft on a separate sheet of paper.

Goal: _____

Audience: _____

DeMento Brothers, Inc.

44 Mezcal Boulevard   Nacogdoches, TX 75961

STYLE AND STRUCTURE
Parallel Structure

Importance The idea of parallel structure within a sentence is simple: when you repeat a part of speech, you establish a pattern. And patterns make it easy for your reader to understand your message. Here are some examples.

NOUN PATTERN: We need **accountants, lawyers,** and **engineers.**

INFINITIVE PATTERN: The company tries **to increase** its profit margin and **to improve** its image.

VERB PATTERN: Their new product **seals** the joint and **prevents** corrosion.

ADVERB PATTERN She worked **hard, often,** and **well.**

GERUND PATTERN Our department needs some extra help with **typing, proofreading,** and **filing** this week.

Faulty Parallelism On the other hand, careless construction of parallels can confound and confuse your reader. If you break up a pattern, the result is faulty parallelism.

FAULTY PARALLEL: We need **accountants, lawyers,** and **to hire** some engineers.

CORRECT: We need **to hire** accountants, lawyers, and some engineers.

The following rules will help you avoid faulty parallels:

1. Do not mix infinitives and gerunds in the same sentence:

> INCORRECT: The company tried **to increase** its profit margin, and **maintaining** its image was also important.

2. Do not mix active and passive voice:

> INCORRECT: Their new product **seals** the joints and corrosion **will be prevented.**

3. Do not switch from adverbs to verbs:

> INCORRECT: She worked **hard, often,** and **did well.**

Constructing parallels on a larger scale is often a good way to explain a series of steps or to present a comparison. Let's suppose, for instance, that you have to write a memo defining your company's vacation-reporting procedures. Rather than stating your points in an ordinary, narrative paragraph, you can list the points in a numbered series, beginning each item with a parallel part of speech (usually a verb).

1. Submit to me, not later than the tenth of each month, a report of vacation days that the employees in your section have taken during the previous month.

2. Omit "compensation" days because they are subject to managerial discretion.

3. Make sure your department managers agree with the content of your report.

4. Use the report forms available from your division administrator.

Always look for opportunities to use parallels in your work. Their symmetry helps you organize your material and helps your readers understand it.

PRACTICE A

Correct faulty parallel structure in each of the following sentences.

Example

1. You may enter the command either by pressing the RETURN key or simply touch the SORT button.
   You may enter the command either by pressing the RETURN key or by

   touching the SORT button.

2. A basic knowledge of computers will help you get a job and doing good work.

   _____

   _____

3. Being close to headquarters and with ample space are the major advantages of the new giant warehouse.

   _____

   _____

4. Our research people found instructive your ideas about color fidelity, print-processing, and in the area of negatives.

   _____

   _____

5. They had expected Mr. Crawley to arrive not by train but flying.

   _____

   _____

6. First the motor must be started; then remove the supercoating.

_____

_____

7. The reduction of overhead, elimination of shipping surcharges, and a whole new model being produced are our main goals for the coming year.

_____

_____

PRACTICE B

Revise the following paragraphs, using parallel structure. Reorganize material and use numbered lists.

1. Over the next six months the work group will look at the consistency of population counts and the accuracy of demographic and tracking data recorded on the system. The group will identify data-quality problems and recommend steps toward their resolution. Recommendations will be shared with the User Committee and others.

   Over the next six months, the work group will do the following:

   _____

   _____

   _____

   _____

   _____

2. Dividing the span of the existing beams by providing new girders will reduce the stress due to the concentrated loads to an acceptable level. Increasing the stiffness of the existing slab by removal of the concrete overlay will increase the load-carrying capacity to correspond with the actual loads and to protect the existing beams from further corrosion. This work is shown on the attached sketch.

   _____

   _____

   _____

   _____

   _____

   _____

   _____

   _____

3. Both companies have been increasing their research budgets each year (AMCO considerably more than Vesey). Both are becoming more aggressive in acquisitions and expanding their positions in international markets. Vesey has a lot of catching up to do in international markets, but appears to be doing it well in carefully designed stages, relying on worldwide sales of its antacids as the keystone of its plans. Recent acquisition of a Japanese company will strengthen its ethical drug research capability. AMCO has a longer product list than does Vesey and a broader marketing and promotion effort. Yet in its long history it has not come up with a new, "winning" drug. In the past AMCO has relied too much on known ingredients to design its drugs. Recent moves to "license in" products, and plans to acquire an ethical drug manufacturer may improve AMCO's situation in the ethical drug market.

_____

_____

_____

_____

_____

_____

_____

_____

_____

_____

_____

WORDS IN ACTION

A   Choose the best answer.

1. Bundix Corporation announced today the _____ of Wallis Industries.
   a. acquisition   c. margin
   b. comparison   d. acknowledgment

2. At our meeting earlier this month, Mr. Kawabata did not _____ that he would approve the plan.
   a. indicate   c. arrange
   b. issue   d. remit

3. In _____, Eastern Electric Company is much more profitable than Spleenco Industries.
   a. comparison   c. parallel
   b. obligation   d. margin

4. Please _____ payment in full before the fifteenth of this month.
   a. remit   c. prevent
   b. license   d. indicate

5. Thanks to the _____ work of our sales department, this has been the most successful year in our company's history.
   a. acceptable   c. outstanding
   b. ethical   d. unfortunate

6. Ms. Pierce decided that our estimate was _____ and asked us to begin work as soon as possible.
   a. unfortunate   c. managerial
   b. acceptable   d. delinquent

7. Call Mr. Amir and try to _____ a meeting for early next week.
   a. remit   c. cancel
   b. arrange   d. correspond

8. Although I have never actually met Mr. Porker, we have _____ frequently during the past year.
   a. indicated   c. corresponded
   b. issued   d. placated

9. Because of the confidential nature of the material, I was _____ to discuss it with him in detail.
   a. arranged   c. prevented
   b. happy   d. reluctant

10. The directors plan to _____ a formal statement early next week.
    a. issue   c. anticipate
    b. pacify   d. license

B   Write the word that matches each definition: compensate, debtor, delinquent, placate, recommend.

1. commend another as being worthy; endorse   _____

2. appease; pacify   _____

3. a person who owes something   _____

4. make up for; counterbalance   _____

5. failure to do what is required   _____

GUIDELINES

Appositives

An appositive is a noun or noun phrase that explains or defines another noun or pronoun. The appositive must always be next to the noun that it identifies, either before or after it. The appositive is usually set off by commas or dashes.

> Mr. Henderson, **our European distributor**, is responsible for the Cartier account.
>
> Our European distributor, **Mr. Henderson**, is responsible for the Cartier account.
>
> The president's son, **Michael,** was the first to speak.

Appositives are often used to replace certain relative clauses, thus helping to make the sentence more concise.

> RELATIVE CLAUSE: Mr. Henderson, **who is our European distributor,** is responsible for the Cartier account.

Words or phrases in apposition are frequently introduced by *or*. The punctuation marks are important for clarity because they signal that you're discussing one thing, not two.

> A "zinc," or line engraving, will be made from the sketch. (A "zinc" and a line engraving are the same thing.)
>
> A painting or line drawing will be made from the sketch. (A painting and a line drawing are two different things.)

Punctuation Although commas are the most frequent punctuation for appositives, parentheses may be interchanged on most occasions, and dashes may be used whenever they would make the meaning and construction more quickly understood.

> Mr. Henderson (our European distributor) is responsible for the Cartier account.
>
> Our research and development department has determined the stimulus—an electric current—that would be just adequate to waken a sleeper.
>
> All members of the production department—supervisors and clerical staff—attended the meeting.

COMMUNICATION WORKSHOP
Product Announcements

The computer revolution, barely half-a-century old, has turned the modern office into a marvel of electronic communication. *Input* into early computers was entered by paper tape or punched cards. The *Central Processing Unit*, or CPU, was often a transistor. There was so little storage capacity, or *memory*, that even the electronic typewriters of today have more. Finally, *output* was like early television, with poor, feeble signals flickering on tiny screens. Hard copy printouts were equally poor in quality and exasperatingly slow in speed.

In fifty years both the *hardware* (the machines themselves) and the *software* (the programs that constitute the *input*) have changed enormously. Computer designers and engineers went to work on the size, shrinking everything from the external frame to the silicon wafer in the CPU. Systems analysts and computer programmers developed more sophisticated software. What did business want? It wanted to sell its product or service by effectively communicating with customers. The average office, awash in a sea of paperwork, was desperately searching for a way to efficiently process its correspondence.

Today a typical word processing operator takes dictation recorded earlier and transfers the material into one of three kinds of devices: a stand-alone text editor, a shared-logic system, or a communicating typewriter. Typing time was thereby reduced by a staggering 70 percent because the operator could quickly correct, delete, or move words, sentences, and entire paragraphs in a fraction of a second. Identical letters can be sent, "individualized" by the word processor with a different name, address, or other information, to thousands of customers.

Some office managers could not conceive of an office without a computer. Who would process the messaging, spreadsheets, direct mail, payroll, inventory control, and the boss's complicated itinerary? What would they do without the desktop computers, the point-of-sales (POS) terminals, the data base management programs, and the instant updating of sales information? Although word processing may be the single most important function of the computer in the modern office, such tasks as payroll, billing, inventory management, and sales projection are also routinely performed. But even with the advent of the fully automated office, a need still persisted to put as much power as possible into the smallest-possible package.

Case Study: The *DATA GENERAL/One*™

The first portable computer appeared as recently as 1981. Data General, a Massachusetts computer manufacturer, went to work in 1983 with its Japanese subsidiary, Nippon/Data General, and two development teams in North Carolina and Massachusetts to create a full-size LCD (liquid crystal display) panel that could operate for up to eight hours on a one-pound rechargeable battery. They wanted to make it fully compatible with the IBM Personal computer in order to take advantage of the thousands of available software programs. Finally they wanted to place these features in a package smaller and lighter than a thirty-pound sewing machine. For Data General, the need was there. Salespeople, managers, executives, and engineers wanted to carry their computers anywhere they have a need for information retrieval, manipulation, or preservation of all kinds of data.

The result was the *DATA GENERAL/One,* a fully functional portable computer weighing less than ten pounds. How did Data General go about marketing the *One?* The availability of applications software was terribly important. Prototype units were sent from Nippon/Data General to the United States to test software late in 1983. Major software vendors were approached in February of 1984 to determine the compatability of their application packages with the new 3.5-inch diskettes of the *DATA GENERAL/One.* Agreements were eventually reached with thirty of the most popular applications vendors. Data General was ready to go.

Used by permission of Data General Corporation.

Promoting the *One*   Business has many tools for promoting a product, especially in a highly competitive field. There are cash refunds, rebates, coupons, even sampling (the most expensive promotion, but especially effective with new products). There are all kinds of incentives, such as premiums, trading stamps, even gifts. Data General chose a media and promotional campaign. Applications-oriented photographs were made of users in realistic, non-office settings. News and press releases were produced for specific audiences and for specific purposes. A product brief, a four-page advertising "insert," and promotional brochures were written. Articles were sent to the most popular and influential trade periodicals. Advertisements announced the product in periodicals and newspapers. A promotional booklet was developed and distributed to 1500 member of the press, analysts, consultants, and customers at a product announcement party in New York City in the early fall of 1984. The *DATA GENERAL/One* portable had arrived.

Used by permission of Data General Corporation.

1. Research other products which have had promotional campaigns similar to the *DATA GENERAL/One* campaign. Find out as much as possible about the product's development, features, competitors, and any unique advertising or promotional efforts.

2. You are the Vice President in charge of promotion and public relations for a company that has developed a new product. Design a sales promotion campaign for your product, using as many media as possible. Describe the various kinds of announcements, purposes, audiences, and so forth.

3. As the chief engineer in a computer firm, you can choose a course of development for a new feature such as portability, expanded memory, processing speed, or ease of use. Describe the benefits of whatever feature you decide to develop in terms of public relations.

4. Discuss why many companies change their procedure when promoting their products abroad. Discuss cultural differences that might influence such changes.

DATA GENERAL/ONE is a trademark of Data General Corporation.

8
REPORTS

Reports

Graphs and Charts

8.1 REPORTS

Objectives

1. Write reports.
2. Use adverbial conjunctions.
3. Use commas correctly.

OMNICOMP INTERNATIONAL   **Memorandum**
17 BUNKER HILL ROAD, SHREWSBURY MA   O1545

TO: Larry Fine   DATE: June 11, 19..
FROM: Richard Trainer
SUBJECT: Product Development Report

Here is a copy of my report, "The Interactive Videodisc: Its Role in the Classroom."

Do you think we can market such a product effectively?

I look forward to your response.

Enclosures

State the
report's purpose.

Summary

Because the use of microcomputers in classrooms is growing at such a fantastic rate, Omnicomp should not decide if it should enter the educational hardware market, but determine where. This report suggests that one possibility for entering this market lies in developing an interactive videodisc system.

The growth of CAI (Computer-Assisted Instruction) in the schools is rapid but unorganized. No clear consensus of preferred hardware or software currently exists, and there has been no systematic study to determine the long-term educational benefits of CAI.

The best educational software is limited to mathematics and to subjects requiring developed reading skills. Little of value has been done for the many students with limited reading ability, either those in the early grades or those with learning disabilities. However, by developing a system that incorporates the Omni Microcomp 4 with a random access videodisc player, along with related software, Omnicomp could enter this vast segment of the educational market with a distinct advantage.

This report, therefore, recommends the following initial procedures:

1. Adapt the video interface currently available for the Minicomp 7 for compatability with the Microcomp 4, the JFB videodisc player, and a light-interrupt touch screen.

Summarize conclusions
and recommendations.

2. Conduct a marketing survey to resolve questions concerning pricing, licensing, and distribution.
3. Consult an educational publisher to explore the possibilities of jointly producing software and distributing the product.

Introduction

There is no need to expound in great detail the benefits of using computers in the educational environment. Computers can reach each student at his or her own level and accurately monitor progress. They provide a nonthreatening learning situation that can be adapted to a variety of educational uses and they are highly motivational.

Similarly, video-assisted instructional (VAI) programs, particularly in the area of language, seem to be particularly effective in the classroom as well. Both VAI and CAI have proven successful within limited areas, but these areas could be vastly expanded by combining the two. The result would be a system that could interact with the student both visually and verbally.

We can achieve such a breakthrough by perfecting the hardware necessary to interface the Microcomp 4 with a random-access, industrial-quality videodisc player, preferably the JFB Model 53. This system offers a fast, economical, and feasible way to store and present audio/visual (AV) data.

Data

Give pertinent facts.

The optical videodisc allows the random access of 55 000 frames of AV data in less than four seconds, and accessing segments within a program will require only a fraction of a second. The optical disc can present both still and motion pictures with a minimum of wear, a factor that rules out the use of contact discs.

Industrial videodisc players can be directed to search out any scene and operate in any of several modes by computer control. The computer programs used to direct the videodisc can be stored on floppy disks or cassettes, or they can be stored directly on the videodisc during mastering. Computer-generated text or graphics can either be superimposed over the images emitting from the videodisc or be superimposed onto a separate cathode ray tube (CRT). The microcomputer can then be programmed to process the student's responses to the information presented.

The course software should be designed to effectively teach, and it should be based on research available from other interactive systems. Basically, CAI can be categorized into two types of control models: systems control and learner control. Each model can be used with videodiscs. With systems control, the courseware leads students through the course content in a planned sequence determined by system algorithms. The system decides what the students will see, based on their individual past performances. However, pacing is usually under the students' control.

With the learner-control approach, the courseware provides orienting information, as well as options for presentation modes, options for difficulty level, and options for sequence. Another option is to design one part of the program to function under learner control and another to provide systems control.

For example, an integrated system designed for very young children might begin by presenting an audio instruction and a related video image on the television screen. The child can then respond by touching a certain part of the screen. A light-interrupt touch panel indicates which area of the screen the child has touched and transmits that information to the microcomputer. The program then evaluates the response. If the response is correct, the computer sends a signal to the videodisc player. This signal references a segment on the videodisc that provides an audio/visual reinforcement (a video segment). Other possibilities are an incorrect response, a nearly correct response, or a nonresponse. The nonresponse can be signalled after a specified period of time has elapsed without a response. Recorded segments are available on the disc for all possible response conditions, as well as for a variety of positive reinforcements that vary in length and type. There are also remediation segments that can be accessed when appropriate. Parameters can be set for each lesson to determine the branching sequence to reinforcement and remedial sequences.

Analysis

Analyze the facts.

An initial consideration, or course, is cost. Although videodisc players designed for the consumer are available for $400, industrial models with the ability to be driven by a micro-computer now sell for $2000. When we add the net prices of the Microcomp 4, a color television monitor, and the hardware interface, this cost will be more than doubled.

However, the steady cost reductions in the electronics industry should eventually work in our favor. Furthermore, we should consider the efficiency value of the proposed product compared with the cost of the uncoordinated slide, film, and tape hardware that it will eventually replace.

The success of the project hinges on the development of effective software. To be cost-effective, the software must be produced in great quantity; thus we cannot afford to produce ineffective or unpopular software. Therefore, I suggest that we explore the possibilities of co-producing software programs with an educational publisher, thereby making use of its courseware expertise and marketing network.

Conclusions

State your conclusions.

Clearly, the technical capabilities for the Microcomp-Videodisc interface are already in place. Our research department has developed a prototype, and an interface for the Minicomp 7 is available for the industrial market. To apply this research and experience to the microcomputer for educational purposes is a small step. Our remaining problems lie elsewhere—in cost, software development, and in marketing.

Recommendations

Give your recommendations.

Our first step should be to contract a market research survey from a reputable consultant. The survey should determine the current status of CAI and VAI in each of our regional territories. The results of this study will indicate which hardware is in place, what the user response has been to these systems, and what plans exist to incorporate new systems. Our marketing department should begin to determine the approximate cost of advertising, commissions, and sampling to distributors. Based upon the results of these preliminary investigations, we could prepare a cost analysis of production expenses and complete a profit summary projection for the proposed system.

Next, we'll need to produce a video interface for the Microcomp 4. Our research department has developed a prototype for such a product, and a video interface for the Minicomp 7 has been marketed successfully for several years. Preliminary studies indicate that the JFB Model 53 optical videodisc player is best for our purposes. It offers the greatest flexibility at the lowest cost. We might obtain further cost reductions through a licensing agreement with the JFB Corporation of Japan.

Finally, we need to explore the availability of quality video software. We might wish to consult an educational publisher about the possibilities of jointly producing programs based on popular textbooks. In addition, several independent groups operating on research grants have designed interactive video programs. One such group, directed by Dr. Milton Boyle at Pibb University, has already approached Omnicomp with its systems design.

The potential for this project is enormous—such a system could vastly influence CAI and AV practices and place Omnicomp in the forefront of educational systems developers. Surely such possibilities warrant further exploration and market research.

Purpose   In business writing, the noun *report* describes a number of communications. Basically, a report presents information too complex to be transmitted in a standard letter or memo. Reports can be long or short, formal or informal, spoken or written. They may simply report facts; or they may present arguments, analyze information, and make recommendations. Whatever the type or topic of your report, you'll have to gather and analyze the information that you're going to present.

Reports that only convey information are easy to organize. Simply begin by stating why you have gathered certain facts; then present them in a logical arrangement. When you are expected to go beyond informing, however, organizing the substance of your report requires more planning. In such cases, you should think of your report as a solution to a problem.

As with all types of business communications, begin by defining your goal. If your report responds to a specific problem, you can define your goal by defining the problem the report will address. Next, you'll have to determine the scope of your work. How big is the problem? Where can you find the information? The answers to these questions will determine how you schedule your research and gather the appropriate facts.

Once you have gathered all the relevant information (and have made sure that the information is accurate), analyze it in terms of its usefulness. Then decide how you can best present it to your readers. It is often helpful to first write your facts on separate index cards and then organize the cards into a logical order. When all these steps are completed, you'll be ready to organize your report and write your first draft.

When you're trying to solve a problem, remember that defining the problem is perhaps the most important step. After all, it isn't very difficult to be aware that something is wrong somewhere. It's another matter, however, to state exactly what is wrong and why. If you can locate the specific problem, it will be easier for you to see the steps necessary to solve it.

Format   Therefore, begin your report by defining the problem in the most specific, concise terms possible. Stating the problem clearly will help your reader to accept your definition of it. Once this is done, your reader will be more likely to accept your recommendations toward a solution. Suppose, for example, you are asked to decide which of three computer models should be purchased for your office. You have decided that the most important feature of a computer is the percentage of time it functions properly. You would not state the problem in general terms ("Should we buy A, B, or C?"), but specifically ("Among A, B, and C, which is likely to have the least downtime?").

Of course, you may not always be able to write a clear definition of the problem until you have gathered some facts and analyzed them. Nevertheless, begin with a tentative statement of the problem. You can go back and revise that trial definition as you learn more about the subject. In your first draft of the report, set apart your definition of the problem under just such a heading: "Definition of the Problem." You may decide, depending on your audience and the occasion, to remove that heading in your final version.

Your next sections should be entitled "Data" (or "Facts") and "Analysis." You can combine these sections if the amount of data is small, but your reasoning will stand out most clearly if each one is given a section by itself. Set apart "Conclusions," too, so that your reader can easily see the basis for your recommendations. Your conclusions are the final results of your analysis. Your final section, "Recommendations," refers to your conclusions but looks forward to a necessary action, or at least presents specific advice.

Although you arrive at "Recommendations" last, it is a good idea to mention your recommendations at the beginning of the report so the reader knows where you are going, and can evaluate your information in terms of your recommendation. If you wait until the end to state your recommendations, your reader may find it necessary to re-read the earlier parts of your report.

For a long report, state your conclusions and recommendations in a summary placed at the beginning of the report. The summary is important because it allows your reader to learn quickly the essentials of your report; in some cases, it is the only part of your report that will be read. Begin the summary by stating the purpose of your report. Then give your conclusions and recommendations. All that follows will then support this synopsis of the situation.

Many companies have a prescribed format for long reports, and employees are often expected to use printed forms that the company supplies. In this way, all reports have a uniform structure. Such a format will usually have three basic parts: preliminary information, the body of the report, and supplementary material.

In addition to the summary described above, the preliminary information can include a letter (or memo) of transmittal, a title page, a table of contents, and an abstract. The abstract is a short, objective statement of the points discussed in the report. If you have written a concise summary, you usually don't need an abstract.

The body of the long report usually begins with an introduction. The introduction provides some background information on the problem while leading toward the report's conclusion. The introduction can also describe the method used to gather information or to obtain results when applicable. This section is followed by the Facts, Analysis, Conclusion, and Recommendations sections that we discussed earlier. The supplementary material at the end of the report includes any appendix, bibliography, or index that you use.

For short reports, go right to the main information and eliminate the preliminary information and the supplementary material. Begin by stating the problem and your recommendations for solving it. Then give the facts, present your analysis, and draw your conclusions. Be direct, concise, and clear in your presentation.

As we said at the beginning of the lesson, there are many types of reports: technical reports, sales reports, marketing reports, feasibility reports, progress reports, credit reports, annual reports, quarterly reports—it would require a lengthy report on reports to address them all. Nevertheless, they all share the same purpose: to present complex information or ideas in a way that allows the reader to understand them easily. Although the format of the report may vary with the situation, clarity should be a constant consideration.

Style

All the writing strategies presented in this book should be applied to your report writing. Use concrete words and avoid jargon. Use topic sentences, concluding sentences, and transitional phrases to help your reader follow your argument. Consider your reader and choose an appropriate tone. Keep your sentences fairly short and vary their structure.

Headings call attention to the information that follows and help the reader understand your method of organization. Headings are a particularly effective feature in report writing. Itemized lists are also an effective tool. Both headings and itemized lists do the following:

1. call attention to important points,

2. foster concise, parallel phrasing, and

3. allow the reader to grasp related points easily.

Use headings and lists selectively, however. Too many headings can break up the continuity of your argument into unrelated fragments that the reader will be forced to assemble.

Title   Finally, let's consider the title of the report. It should be concise, easy to understand, and it should tell the reader something about the nature and conclusions of the report. If possible, include an active verb.

Try to keep your title short. If it is longer than seven words, it is probably too long. Let's imagine that we have written our formal report on the many types of reports used in business, and we have chosen a title: "A Study of the Many Current Uses of the Report in Business Today." Such a title is totally ineffective.

To begin with, phrases such as "A Study of. . .," "A Report on. . .," or "Some Concise Observations of. . ." are useless and should be eliminated on sight. This would leave "The Many Current Uses of the Report in Business Today." *Current* and *Today* are redundant, and they add nothing to the title. Now we are left with "The Many Uses of the Report in Business"–functional but boring. "The Report: Its Uses in Business" is a bit better, but it gives no hint of our conclusion. A verb might help: "Report Writing Prospers in Business."

Although the title is a small part of your report, it is important. It is usually the first thing your reader sees, and if he or she isn't attracted by it, it might also be the last thing your reader sees.

REVISING

The following summary of a report contains a number of typographical errors, misspellings, capitalization errors, and punctuation errors. Read the report carefully and correct any such mistakes that you find.

The most difficult challenge confronting Zeppco's Management is to estalbish effective corporate direction and control over hte local retail profit centers; without destroying their local autonomy and character. Even though the concept is a Corporate one, ultimate succes lies with the succesful execution of local broker performance.

It is important to emphasize, that most of the basic recmmendations that follow are not new in fact, most have been discussed and even tried in the past. The critical difference is that they are being recommended as a total program—oen that will establish a commitment to a revised operating philosophy.

Asuming that top management agrees with the Corporate/Local "Charter" and the basic responsabilities of each

---

(see next section) then the highest priority is to establesh operating procedures adn guidelines that will simply, directly, profitably and effectively lead to better management control and direction over the Corporate enterprise.

This can best be done by first identifying those basic areas of the busness that most directly affect volume and profit. Its my feeling that there are four such key areas?

(1) Revenues
(2) Expenses
(4) Relatioships With Curent Principals
(4) New Business

I intend to deal directly and in detail with these four areas. In summary I am recomending:

(1) Revenues—That the initial fiscal year revenue budget be revised Quarterly, using a simplified key Principal format. Further, that revisions to the budget, continually look twelve, month forward. This documint would be the base of a flexible bugdet system and becom a key communication tool for both local and Corporate management.
(2) Expenses—Expenses would be budgeted anually and reported monthly via the current financial statements. A variance/exception report would be required when and if expenses exceed certain pre-set limits
(3) Establised Business—To establish ways and means of efficiently tracking curent business and communicating those problems or opportunities that require corporate orlocal action.
(4) New Business—The creation of a complete new businss stategy—the selection and tracking of target acounts and the creation of new business presentations.

If these four key areas are to be monitored and managed profesionally; then a device is required to ensure that the four areas are constantly under review and revision.

I feel that the answer lied in pre-planned Quarterly meetings between Corporate and Local. Both Corporate and Local managment would commit themselves to attendance. The agenda for each meeting would always be the same.

(1) Revenues—Actual and Projected
(2) Expenses
(3) Status fo Current Business by Principal
(4) New Business Activity and Progress Against Agreed Targets
(5) General Discussion/Status of Projects/Management

In summery, the Quarterly meeting, with its fixed agenda, will, in my opinion, establish productive, communication, and load to more effective, results-oriented, management of the business. better control and direction can be acheived with less day-to-day corporate involvement

CHECKLIST

Reports

1. Before you begin writing a report, complete the following series of preliminary steps:
   a. Define the problem. ☐

   b. Determine the scope of your work. ☐

   c. Schedule your research. ☐

   d. Gather the necessary facts. ☐

   e. Analyze the facts. ☐

   f. Draw your conclusions. ☐

   After completing these steps, you'll be ready to organize and write your report.

2. Prepare a summary that concisely states the problem and purpose of the report, as well as your conclusions and recommendations. Sometimes it is easier to write the summary after you have finished writing the report. ☐

3. Write an introduction. The introduction should give the purpose of the report, the necessary background information, and the method used to gather information (if applicable). It may also foreshadow your recommendations. ☐

4. Present your data, or facts. You can present the facts together with your analysis of them, or you can present your analysis separately. ☐

5. State your conclusions, based on your analysis of the facts. ☐

6. Give your recommendations, based on your conclusions. ☐

7. Prepare any preliminary or supplementary information needed for your report, and choose a title that in some way indicates your findings. ☐

8. Don't forget to use a transmittal letter or memo with your report (see Chapter 3) ☐

WRITING ASSIGNMENT

Background

The United Broadcasting System (UBS), a cable-transmitted television network, is trying to improve its dismal share of the potential viewing audience. During the past season, the Friday programs from 9:00–10:00 P.M. (two 30-minute comedies) have been disasters. The first, *Lucky Logan*, cost $100 000 per show to produce. The second, *The Great Baboons of Boston*, cost $140 000, but because each drew only 13 percent of the viewing audience, UBS was able to charge for only commercial advertising time at a rate bringing in $195 000 per hour.

Advertisers will pay a substantially higher fee for commercial time only if the program draws at least 20 percent of the viewing audience. In addition, surveys show that young adults and middle-aged people spend far more money than children and people who are retired or near retirement; programs demonstrating appeal to these "big spenders" command higher fees than do other programs.

The competing networks screen relatively successful shows on Fridays from 9:00–10:00. The three most popular competitors are *Friday Night Baseball, Murder à la Mode*, and *Video Rock'n Roll*. Each show's audience has two basic types of viewers: (a) the person who is committed to that type of program, and (b) the person who is not particularly interested in that type of program. A one-hour program nearly always costs less to produce than do two half-hour programs.

Three new hour-long programs emerge as possibilities:

a) *The Chick Cole Hour* features a popular bandleader and guest entertainers. Production cost will vary according to the salaries of the entertainers who are invited, but it will apparently average $180 000. The pilot program projects an initial audience of 23 percent.

b) *The Colonel and Spouse* is about a female officer who runs a Judge-Advocate unit; her husband is a retired sewerage worker. The show appears to be funny, and it would supposedly attract 29 percent of the viewing audience. The Colonel is played by the famous comedienne Stella Blue. This show would cost $210 000.

c) *Exclusive Residence for Sale* concerns four British real estate brokers, two women and two men, who become involved in a number of humorous situations. Though the pilot indicates only a 21 percent viewer rating, the show's cast is little known and production would cost only $120 000 per episode.

The president of UBS asks you, as vice president in charge of programming, to write him a short report indicating what you plan to do about Friday's 9:00–10:00 P.M. programs. Keep your report short, and do not repeat the descriptions of each show – refer only to titles, costs, and percentages. State the problem and your solution, give the facts and your analysis, and present your conclusion.

Write your first draft on a separate sheet of paper.

Problem: _____

Audience: _____

UBS United Broadcasting System

STYLE AND STRUCTURE

Adverbial Conjunctions

You can use adverbial conjunctions to build logical bridges from one main clause to another. They provide transitions that help the reader follow your meaning. It's important to distinguish between adverbial conjunctions and the common conjunctions that simply join words, phrases or clauses without referring to their relationship. Adverbial conjunctions indicate a relationship between two clauses, and they join ideas together in a stronger, more emphatic way.

COORDINATING CONJUNCTION: We wrote to them a month ago, **and** they have not replied yet.

ADVERBIAL CONJUNCTION: We wrote to them a month ago; **therefore,** we should have received their reply.

You should use a semi-colon to separate independent clauses when you connect them with an adverbial conjunction. You can also use the adverbial conjunction to begin a second sentence. A comma always follows the adverbial conjunction, as shown above.

Many writers mistakenly use *however*, usually an adverbial conjunction, when they should write *but*, a coordinating conjunction. The words are close in meaning, however, so that you often need only to change the punctuation. For instance:

WRONG: We sent the shipment out, **however,** it did not arrive.

RIGHT: We sent the shipment out, **but** it did not arrive.

RIGHT: We sent the shipment out; **however,** it did not arrive.

The most common adverbial conjunctions are *however, therefore,* and *nevertheless.*

However, contrasts two ideas:

Robert was planning to recruit new salespersons; however, budget restrictions have limited hiring.

Therefore, shows that one idea causes another, and it can also state conclusions:

the United States has recently revised its import quotas; therefore, we can expect our shipments to increase.

Nevertheless, indicates that one idea is true in spite of another.

Mr. Kiester is very disorganized; nevertheless, he always seems to get results.

Other conjunctive adverbs include the following:

also	indeed	next
anyway	instead	otherwise
besides	likewise	still
furthermore	meanwhile	then
hence	moreover	this

PRACTICE A   Rewrite each of the following sentences, substituting an adverbial conjunction for each coordinating conjunction and revising the punctuation accordingly.

1. The company has replaced its president, E.Z. Spender, *and* it plans other changes in management.

   _____

   _____

2. Our customer account files are not up to date, *but* we have not lost sales revenue yet.

   _____

   _____

3. The OMNI 3683 Modem provides a direct interface with the mainframe, *and* the correspondent can easily research the date as a result.

   _____

   _____

4. The old system could make conversions in many currencies, *but* it could not adjust changes in exchange rates.

   _____

   _____

5. We were able to double new orders from Europe last year, *and* so we decided to increase our production facilities.

   _____

   _____

PRACTICE B   Combine each pair of sentences by using a semicolon and an adverbial conjunction.

1. Your questions can best be answered by M. Alphonse Gaston. I have forwarded your inquiry to him.

   _____

   _____

2. The casings are made of inexpensive plastic. The tape is of the finest quality.

   _____

   _____

3. We would like to know how long and how well Miss Kew worked in your office. Please tell us her job responsibilities there, also.

   _____

   _____

4. The new computers were installed last month. They have been tried by only half the people in the department.

_____

_____

5. Corporate Technology will discuss new research in Geneva all next week. We will write many reports to top management in the month following.

_____

_____

WORDS IN ACTION

A Choose the best answer.

1. Under our new licensing agreement with Mojo K.K., we can obtain their new megachip for a _____ of its retail cost.
   a. reduction   c. fraction
   b. distribution   d. segment

2. Effective _____ is one component of a good marketing strategy.
   a. distribution   c. variance
   b. fraction   d. autonomy

3. _____ to a recent article in *Business World*, Colossal Petroleum Corp. is planning a merger with Gouger, Inc.
   a. Preliminary   c. Supplementary
   b. Tentative   d. According

4. The company's past experiences in that area were not successful enough to _____ an additional investment.
   a. segment   c. convey
   b. warrant   d. incorporate

5. Our current manufacturing facility does not have the _____ to produce the circuit board in quantities sufficient to fill our projected sales orders.
   a. retail   c. sequence
   b. reduction   d. capability

6. The _____ report suggested that we continue research.
   a. preliminary   c. feasible
   b. potential   d. capable

7. Because of the current trade restrictions, an international licensing agreement with IRCO is not _____ at this time.
   a. phenomenal   c. feasible
   b. tentative   d. fiscal

8. Sr. Jorge Javier is the exclusive _____ of Visicomp software for Spain and Portugal.
   a. autonomy   c. distributor
   b. revenue   d. consumer

9. Pibbs Manufacturing Corporation plans to open a _____ outlet in Beaverton.
   a. revenue
   b. autonomy
   c. retail
   d. influence

10. Mr. Habib is conducting an important meeting and cannot be _____.
    a. expended
    b. influenced
    c. categorized
    d. interrupted

B   Write the word that matches each definition: autonomy, incorporate, interact, professional, retail.

1. engaged in an activity as a means of income
   _____

2. act on or with each other
   _____

3. become combined; merge, embody
   _____

4. self-government; independence, freedom
   _____

5. the sale of goods directly to the consumer
   _____

GUIDELINES

Commas

1. Always use commas to separate three or more items in a series; use a comma before the conjunction that precedes the last item:

   The shipment contained pressure gauges, float valves, and rotors.

2. Use a comma to separate a date from a number written in figures:

   In 1985, 508 tons of grain were shipped to Greenland.

3. Use a comma at the end of an introductory clause or phrase to prevent misleading word junctions:

   Not long before, she had learned the truth.
   If you like, Tom can repair the condenser.

   To the public relations head, reports seemed dull.

4. Use a comma to separate the coordinate clauses of a compound sentence (this means a comma before the conjunction when it is followed by an independent clause):

> We were going to the meeting, but we lost our way completely.
>
> Hal invited the department to a cookout, so he had to shop for food after work.

5. Use commas to set off appositives and nonrestrictive clauses:

> The accountant, Mr. Price, delivered a long presentation.
>
> Mr. Price, who delivered a long presentation, is the accountant.

6. Use a comma after long introductory clauses or phrases:

> Although the director arrived at the meeting half an hour late, none of the board members expressed disapproval.

7. Use commas to set off *Jr.*, *Sr.*, and titles that follow a name:

> George R. Blake, Sr., was famous for his wise investments.

8. Set off the name of a state, province, or country with commas when it is used with the name of a city:

> His years in Charlottesville, Virginia, were spent with a consulting firm.

9. Set off the year with commas when it is used with the month and day:

> The publication of the book on April 4, 1957, initiated an extraordinary chain of events.
>
> BUT: July 1924 felt like the hottest month in years.

10. Use commas to set off a direct quotation:

> "I will have your report ready by Tuesday," my assistant said.
>
> Then I thought, "But I need it on Monday!"

11. Use a comma or commas to separate two or more adjectives when the adjectives could be connected with *and* without changing the meaning:

> The hot, smoke-filled air in the seminar room forced the group to find another location for the meeting.
>
> BUT: The isolated little board room seemed inviting to them.

8.2 GRAPHS AND CHARTS

Objectives

1. Make graphs and charts.
2. Use semicolons correctly.

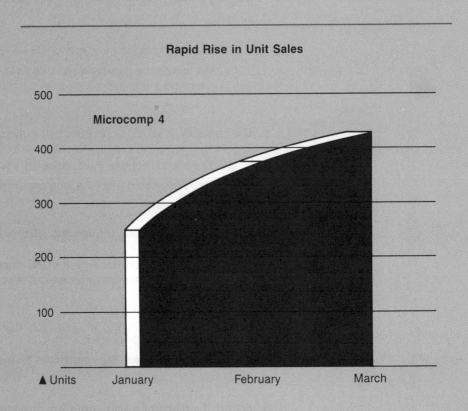

Rapid Rise in Unit Sales

Microcomp 4

500		
400		
300		
200		
100		

▲ Units   January   February   March

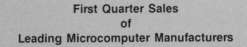

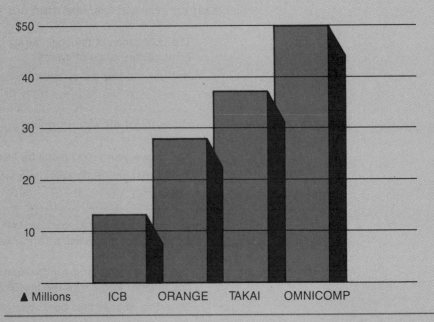

**First Quarter Sales
of
Leading Microcomputer Manufacturers**

$50

40

30

20

10

▲ Millions   ICB   ORANGE   TAKAI   OMNICOMP

Purpose   Do you remember the proverb "One picture is worth a thousand words"? In report writing the proverb is frequently true. We usually understand what we can see more easily than what we hear or read, particularly when dealing with numerical and comparative data. We are also more likely to remember what we see. Therefore, if you thoughtfully employ graphs and charts (often referred to as "visuals") in your reports, you can often clarify important points and save yourself a lot of writing.

Guidelines   There are a few basic rules to remember when you're planning to use visuals. The first is to keep them as simple as possible, since they are not particularly well suited for expressing complex relationships. You could, for example, use a graph to compare the sales of Product A with the sales of Product B over several years. But if you also included information about the relative pricing structures for the products, your graph would probably become too difficult to understand. Just as you should discuss only one topic in a paragraph, you should address only one subject in a graph.

Second, you should always provide a clear, concise caption to identify your visual. For graphs, place the caption below the visual; for charts, place the caption above the visual. If you are using several visuals, number them so that you can easily refer to them in your text.

Next, remember to discuss the visual in your text. Don't try to state your point by using the graph or chart alone. The visual reinforces a certain part of your text and makes a point memorable, but it does not work well by itself. Its purpose is to illustrate or clarify a point in your topic, so when your readers reach that point, tell them where to look.

Finally, try to consider the artistic aspects of composing and positioning your visual. The general appearance of the page is always important. Be careful in deciding upon the type of chart or graph to use, the size of the visual, the terminology which will best make the point, and where in the report the visual will produce the best effect.

Graphs   The most common types of graphs are the line graph, the bar graph, and the pie graph. Line graphs are particularly valuable for showing developments over a period of time. Bar graphs are best for showing comparative figures and relationships. Pie graphs are used only to show how a whole entity is divided.

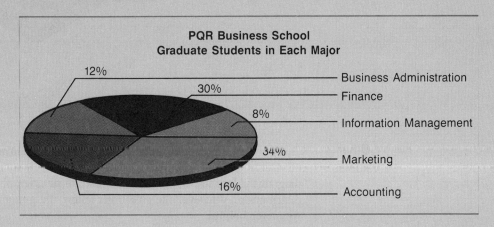

PQR Business School
Graduate Students in Each Major

12% — Business Administration
30% — Finance
8% — Information Management
34% — Marketing
16% — Accounting

Charts   Charts are best used to show structures and organizational relationships. An organizational chart can show the lines of authority and responsibility within a company. Such a chart might help employees better understand their roles in an organization that has many branches. Typically, such charts start at the top of the "chain of command," and then they proceed down and across, stating the title of each job, often using arrows to indicate supervisory responsibilities.

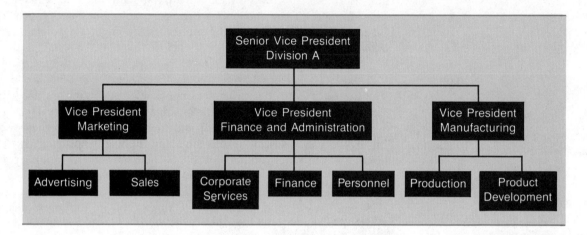

Flow Charts   A flow chart is similar to an organizational chart, but it is more concerned with progressions. It illustrates a schematic representation of a sequence of operations.

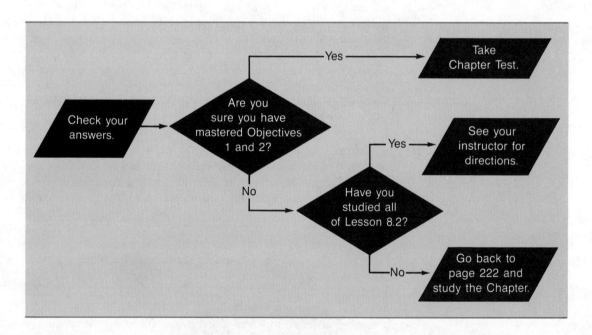

Other Visuals   Of course the type of information you are presenting will determine the types of visuals you will use. Technical writers make frequent use of illustrative diagrams. Maps are often used to illustrate demographic trends and geographical distribution. Whatever the situation, follow the guidelines and use visuals whenever helpful.

CHECKLIST

Graphs and Charts

1. Choose the type of visual that best represents the information you are transmitting. ☐

2. Keep your visuals as simple as possible. ☐

3. Provide clear and concise captions. Place your captions above charts and below graphs. ☐

4. Always refer to the visual in your text. Try to position the visual in a way that the reader reads about it before seeing it. ☐

5. Pay attention to clarity and the artistic aspects of your visual. If you plan to duplicate your report, only use visuals that reproduce clearly. ☐

ASSIGNMENT

Illustrate one of the situations below by designing an appropriate chart or graph.

1. **Line Graph** – Acme Manufacturing Co. produced 95 000 transistor switches ten years ago. For each two-year interval since then, Acme has doubled its production of transistor switches. Last year, however, production dropped by 50 percent.

2. **Bar Graph** – Illustrate the graduate business school enrollments for the following countries: Australia (50 000), Canada (48 000), Japan (85 000), United Kingdom (62 000), and the United States (220 000).

3. **Pie Graph** – Illustrate the results of a survey that asked 500 people who write frequently as part of their work, "What kind of writing do you do most often?" 45 percent named memos, 38 percent letters, and 10 percent short reports; the remaining 7 percent named various other kinds of writing.

4. **Organizational Chart** – Illustrate the corporate structure of a company that you are familiar with or one that you can imagine. Indicate job titles and lines of supervision.

5. **Flowchart** – Show the process of a product, beginning with its design and ending with its sale and delivery to a consumer.

Graph or
Chart

GUIDELINES
Semicolons

The semicolon indicates a stronger break than a comma, and is most frequently used in compound sentences where a comma would not be distinctive enough for clarity. Semicolons should be used sparingly. It is generally better to divide a compound sentence in two than to use a semicolon.

1. Use a semicolon between the elements of a compound sentence when these elements are not joined by a conjunction:

> The workers were participating in the development of a new industry; they could see that their work made a real contribution.

2. Use a semicolon when the clauses of a compound sentence are joined by a transitional word such as *however, therefore, moreover,* or *nevertheless:*

> The shipment arrived late; moreover, several items were damaged.

3. Use a semicolon to separate the main elements of a long or complicated sentence that includes commas:

> For their advertising display the engineers made models of clay, wood, and metal; painted murals; wrote descriptive copy; and collected pictures for a layout.

COMMUNICATION WORKSHOP
Readability Index

Throughout this book, we've been discussing ways to make your writing easier to read. Now we'll give you a way of measuring how readable it is.

Many studies have been made on the readability of written material, and various systems have been developed to measure this quality. Readability is generally considered to be influenced by length of word, sentence, and paragraph. Human interest references are also considered important, but they are difficult to measure.

Robert Gunning's Fog Index is one of the simplest of the formulas to use. Gunning directs a writing clinic and for decades has helped people improve their writing in many fields. His clients include some of the largest corporations in the world.

The Fog Index (so called because unclear writing interferes with comprehension as fog interferes with vision) is based on the assumption that too many long words and long sentences make a passage hard to read, and that short words and sentences make easier reading. However, Gunning does not recommend writing only three-word, monosyllabic sentences. He advises writers to use his index occasionally as a test to measure the complexity of their prose – not as a set of rules on which to model their writing.

The Fog Index is the probable years of schooling a native English reader needs to readily understand a piece of writing. Thus, a Fog Index of 5 indicates a reading level of someone who's had five years of schooling.

Formula

To find the Fog Index, follow these three steps.

1. Find the average sentence length:

   a. Take a 100-word sample – considering a word to be anything with space around it, including figures. Stop counting words with the sentence ending nearest the 100-word count. The result: the total word count.

   b. Count the number of sentences involved in the sample. Count independent clauses as sentences.

   c. Divide the total word count by the sentence count. The result is the first number in the formula: the average sentence length.

2. Find the percentage of "difficult" words:

   a. Count the number of "difficult" words – those of three or more syllables – in the total sample. These words may not be difficult in the usual sense, but they take longer to read than shorter words. Don't include proper nouns (capitalized words such as *Mr. Smith*), compound nouns (for example, *bookkeeper* and *afternoon*), or verb forms made into three syllables by *-ed* or *-ing* endings (for example, *credited* and *processing*).

   b. Divide the number of hard words by the total word count. The result is the second number in the formula: the percentage of "difficult" words.

3. Compute the Fog Index:

a. Find the sum of the average sentence length and the percentage of "difficult" words.

b. Multiply the sum by .4. The result is the Fog Index, or the probable number of years of schooling required to read the passage.

Example

> It has come to my attention that there is a problem in employee communication with wordiness, jargon, clichés, and multisyllabic words. I am of the opinion that we should attempt to eradicate this difficulty. We are not at the present time in a position to waste company time and money indulging in voluminous correspondence. Pursuant to this matter, be advised that I have, therefore, invited a readability expert to give a seminar this Friday, November 16, at 2:00 P.M., on methods of increasing readability in business writing. Please be advised that it is incumbent on every employee to attend this seminar.

1. The example consists of 101 words and 5 sentences. The average sentence is 101 divided by 5, or 20.2.

2. The number of words with three or more syllables is 22. Remember, *November* can't be counted because it's a proper noun, and *indulging* and *increasing* can't be counted because without the *-ing* ending they would have two syllables. The percentage of difficult words is, therefore, 22 divided by 101, or 21.7.

3. The sum of the average sentence length (20.2) and the percentage of difficult words (21.7) equals 41.9. Multiply this sum by .4 and you get 16.8. The Fog Index, therefore, is 16.8.

We recommend you check your writing regularly and try for a Fog Index of 10 or below. Studies show that material with a Fog Index of 11 or more is too difficult to read for most people.

DISCUSSION ACTIVITIES

1. Revise the above example by eliminating the jargon, clichés, and wordiness. Do a Fog Index on your revision.

2. Choose another passage from this text. If the Fog Index is over 10, make suggestions for rewriting it. (Why not send us a copy of your comments?)

3. What's the Fog Index of the report at the beginning of this chapter? (Choose three samples, and average the three scores.)

9

WORLD TRADE
COMMUNICATIONS

Trade Agreements

Import/Export
Communications

9.1 TRADE AGREEMENTS

1. Understand established channels of distribution.
2. Understand the basic types of agent and distributor agreements.
3. Understand the general format of license agreements.
4. Complete order forms correctly.
5. Write clear and concise telexes and telegrams.

148776 OMNIC
ATTN: ED FOWLER

RECEIVING REQUESTS FOR CUSTOMER TRAINING DAILY.
REQUEST SAMPLE OF INTRODUCTION TO SMALL COMPUTERS
COURSE IMMEDIATELY.

TARO TANAKA
OE DISTRIBUTORS

Answer international messages promptly.

1234567 OE
ATTN: TARO TANAKA

ALL TRAINING COURSES ARE LICENSED MATERIAL.
COMPLETION AND EXECUTION OF LICENSE AGREEMENT
REQUIRED BEFORE DELIVERY. WILL FORWARD ORDER FORM
AND LICENSE AGREEMENT.

FOWLER
OMNICOMP

Use the same method of response.

Sales and Distribution Channels	The customary business methods and established channels of distribution in individual countries influence a company's decision on how to sell its products in different countries.

Indirect Selling

Indirect selling is often done through commissioned agents who purchase products at their lowest possible price and receive a commission for their services from their foreign clients. Another way to sell indirectly is through export management companies, who act as the export department for several manufacturers of noncompetitive products. Export trading companies purchase goods for resale in foreign markets. Many export trading companies have offices all over the world, but they are often based in Europe and Japan.

Direct Selling

Direct selling requires you to deal directly with a foreign client, and you are responsible for shipping the products yourself. Direct sales are often handled by sales representatives who usually work under contract on a commission basis. Their contract defines their territory, method of compensation, and other terms. Sales representatives can sell products on either an exclusive or nonexclusive basis.

When products require periodic servicing, they are often sold via **foreign distributors**: merchants who purchase products at the greatest possible discount and resell them for a profit. Distributors usually keep a supply of spare parts and maintain facilities and personnel to service the product.

Most products are not sold directly to the end users, as foreign buyers are often not aware of international trade regulations.

License Agreements

Another way to enter a market is to give someone permission to manufacture or use your products for an agreed-upon fee. Such an agreement is called a **license**. A license gives official or legal permission to engage in an activity or obtain propriety right. When a company owns the proprietary rights to a product, patent, trademark, production process, or copyright, it can license to others these rights. Licensing is a common way for a firm to enter an unfamiliar market without risking a major investment. The company or person granting the license is called the **licensor**, and the person receiving it is called the **licensee**.

Licenses can be either exclusive or nonexclusive. An exclusive license gives its rights to one party only. In addition, the license can be transferable, which means that the licensee can, in turn, license the product to another party.

Licensing agreements usually contain a clause that specifies the market for which the license applies. This allows the licensor to control which markets are served by the licensee, and it prevents the licensee from directly competing with the licensor.

Licensing, however, can have its disadvantages. The licensor must be sure that the licensee maintains the quality of the product and respects the licensor's reputation. In addition, the licensor must carefully monitor the licensee to make sure that the terms of the agreement are being met.

Before entering into any type of agreement, however, make sure that you have carefully examined your market and determined its real potential. Always answer each of the following questions before deciding whether or not to enter a foreign market:

1. Are there any restrictions on the export or importation of your product?
2. Are your potential customers permitted to transfer payment from their country to yours?
3. What potential share of the market could you achieve?
4. Who are the potential buyers?
5. What price is competitive?
6. What selling techniques work best?
7. What credit terms are acceptable in the specific market?
8. Will your product have to be redesigned or repackaged?

Most agreements include the following basic items:

1. Name and address of both parties
2. Date when agreement goes into effect
3. Duration of the agreement
4. Provisions for terminating the agreement
5. Sales territory
6. Description of the product
7. Discount and/or commission schedule
8. Restrictions on sales of competitive products
9. Periodic reporting requirements
10. Breach of agreement guidelines, and legal implications

The following illustration of a license agreement gives the customers permission to use self-study course materials developed by a major computer company. These mateials, which consist of films, printed matter, and diskettes, instruct customers in the use and application of that company's products.

Case Study: Data General

Data General Self-Study Course License Agreement

Data General Corporation, Route 9, Westborough, Massachusetts ("LICENSOR" or "DGC") hereby grants to the company, government agency or other institution listed below as the Customer ("LICENSEE") a non-exclusive license to use the materials, including manuals, tape cassettes, drawings and related materials, comprising the self-study course(s) (the "Course") enumerated on the reverse side hereof on the following terms and conditions.

1. License—The license granted hereunder authorizes LICENSEE on a non-exclusive basis to use the Course to train its employees and the employees of its customers in the use and maintenance of the DGC equipment which is the subject of the Course. LICENSEE is not authorized to sub-license or copy the Course in whole or in part. This license is non-transferable.

2. Title—The original and any copies of the Course shall remain at all times the property of LICENSOR.

3. Fees—Fees for LICENSOR'S self-study Courses which may include video tapes, audio tapes, manuals, and other printed materials, will be stated in the DGC training price list in effect at the time LICENSOR accepts this order or as specified on an authorized DGC quotation in force at the time of acceptance by LICENSOR. Fees are exclusive of all excise, sales, use or like taxes and, therefore, are subject to an increase equal in amount to any tax LICENSOR may be required to collect or pay with regard to the license or delivery of any Course or Course materials.

4. Delivery—Delivery will be made F.O.B. point of origin. LICENSOR will not be liable for damages or delay in delivery or for failure to give notice of such delay when such delay is due to conditions beyond LICENSOR'S control.

5. Terms—Terms are net cash on or prior to delivery. LICENSEE may apply for open account credit; if such credit is approved by LICENSOR terms will be net 30 days from date of invoice.

6. Protection of Licensed Materials—LICENSEE agrees not to provide or otherwise make available the Course or any portion thereof to any person except for study purposes as described above in paragraph 1 without LICENSOR'S written consent. LICENSEE agrees to take appropriate action by instruction, agreement or otherwise with the LICENSEE'S employees and its customers' employees to satisfy LICENSEE'S obligations hereunder with respect to use, copying, modification and protection and security of the Course.

7. Terms and Termination—This license is effective from the date of receipt of the Course from LICENSOR. The license granted hereunder may be terminated by LICENSOR if LICENSEE fails to comply with any of the terms and conditions of this Agreement. Should LICENSOR so terminate this license, LICENSEE will return the Course and any copies thereof to LICENSOR within ten (10) days after notification from LICENSOR and will certify in writing that it has done so.

8. Warranty—LICENSOR warrants that the medium on which the Course is recorded will be free from defects in material and workmanship for a period of 3 months after shipment to LICENSEE. In the event that LICENSOR is notified of such defect within the warranty period, LICENSOR will replace the defective Course media upon its return to LICENSOR. LICENSEE agrees to obtain a return authorization number from LICENSOR prior to such return. EXCEPT FOR THIS EXPRESS WARRANTY, LICENSOR GRANTS NO WARRANTIES EITHER EXPRESS OR IMPLIED, WITH REGARD TO ANY COURSE OR COURSE MATERIALS, INCLUDING ALL IMPLIED WARRANTIES OF MERCHANTABILITY AND FITNESS FOR A PARTICULAR PURPOSE, AND SUCH EXPRESS WARRANTY OBLIGATIONS IS IN LIEU OF ALL LIABILITIES OR OBLIGATIONS OF LICENSOR FOR DAMAGES ARISING OUT OF OR IN CONNECTION WITH THE DELIVERY, USE OR PERFORMANCE OF THE COURSE OR COURSE MATERIALS.

9. Limitation of Liability—LICENSEE agrees that the express warranty obligation stated above is LICENSOR'S sole obligation and that LICENSOR has no obligation or liability for damages of any nature, including lost profits or for any claim or demand against LICENSEE by any other part. LICENSEE AGREES THAT LICENSOR SHALL NOT BE LIABLE FOR INDIRECT, SPECIAL OR CONSEQUENTIAL DAMAGES.

10. Customer Certification—Customer hereby certifies that it is the owner or lessee of the DGC equipment which is the subject of the Course.

11. General—The provisions of the license shall control over the terms of any present or future order or communication from LICENSEE. Acceptance by LICENSEE of any Course or Course materials from LICENSOR shall be conclusive evidence of LICENSEE'S agreement that the license for such course is governed solely by this Agreement. This Agreement supersedes all prior licenses, agreements or understandings between the parties relating to the subject matter and is intended by the parties as the complete and exclusive statement of the terms of this Agreement. This agreement shall be governed by the laws of the Commonwealth of Massachusetts.

Authorized Signatures:

Customer _____	Data General Corporation
Name _____	Name _____
Title _____	Title _____
Date _____	Date _____
Address _____	Signature _____
Signature _____	

Used by permission of Data General Corporation.

Discussion Questions

Using the terms of the licensing agreement, answer the following questions.

1. Can the customer allow another party to use the training course material? Why or why not?
2. Is this an exclusive license?
3. Can the customer make duplicate copies of the training course?
4. Is the licensor responsible for damages if the course is damaged in shipment?
5. Is the licensor responsible for any lost profits the licensee may incur as a result of using the course?
6. Who owns duplicate copies of the course, the licensor or the licensee?

WRITING ASSIGNMENT

Background   You (Taro Tanaka) are the director of sales of Oe Distributors. You have decided to order one copy each of the following self-study courses from Data General: Introduction to Small Computers, Fundamentals, Computer-Aided Instruction, RDOS User, Business Basic Language, and Nova 4 Maintenance. You also need ten student guides for the Introduction to Small Computers course. The bill is to be charged to the sales division at the attention of Kenji Miamoto.

Complete the order form on page 252. Oe Distributors is located at 14-1 Roku Waseda 4-chrome, Shinjuku-ku, Tokyo, and you want the courses to be shipped to that address. You are the contact person and have decided not to provide your phone number.

Specify that you need two video cassettes in the VHS format, and your magnetic format requires Mini Diskettes and 1600 BPI Magnetic Tape. Your operating system requirements are for RDOS. You need the course as soon as possible, and have enclosed a check for payment.

Make sure to follow the discount schedule when determining the prices, and follow the directions for completing the form.

Courses Offered:

COURSE TITLE	COURSEWARE FORMAT	MODEL NUMBER	LIST PRICE	ADD'L STUDENT GUIDE	
Introduction to Small Computers	Audio/text	1700-SS	$ 250	$ 40	PREPARATORY COURSES
Interactive Systems Concepts	Audio/text	1701-SS	295	45	
16-Bit Initial Symptom Recognition	Audio/text	1704-SS	350	50	
Data General Computer Hardware Fundamentals	Audio/text	1800-SS	295	45	
Elementary Programming Concepts: Computer-Aided Instruction	Tape or diskette/text	1702-CB	175	30	
CEO Word Processing	Audio/text	1786-SS	350	60	APPLICATIONS COURSES
COMPUCALC User	Text	1780-SS	75	N/A	
AOS, AOS/VS Operator	Audio/text	1710-SS	695	100	SOFTWARE COURSES
AOS, AOS/VS User	Audio/text	1712-SS	795	120	
RDOS User	Audio/text	1732-SS	725	110	
MP/OS Operating System and Utilities	Audio/text	1738-SS	550	85	
Business BASIC Language	Audio/text	1758-SS	595	90	
MP/PASCAL Programming	Audio/text	1770-SS	595	90	
Advanced MP/PASCAL	Audio/text	1771-SS	395	60	
NOVA 4 Maintenance	Video/text	1820-SS	2700	295	HARDWARE COURSES
NOVA 3 Maintenance	Video/text	1822-SS	2700	295	
6060 Disc Maintenance	Video/text	1851-SS	1295	295	
6100 Series Disc Subsystem Maintenance	Audio/text	1852-SS	950	150	
6026 Magnetic Tape Drive	Video tutorial	1853-SS	1200	295	

Self-Study Courses Provide Effective and Convenient Training	Self-study courses combine the benefits of intensive training with the convenience of self-paced instruction. You get in-depth, product-specific training at your site, your pace, and on your schedule. Educational Services currently offers self-study courses that cover a range	of hardware and software topics and are designed for students of all levels —from computer novices to high-level programmers. Self-study courses are offered in a variety of formats, including audio and video-assisted and computer-aided instruction.

HOW TO ORDER SELF-STUDY COURSES

1. Tear out the Self-Study Order Form/License Agreement on the opposite page.

2. Select the self-study courses that you wish to order. Using the Self-Study Course Discount Schedule below, calculate the cost-per-unit of the courses that you're ordering.

   Note that the Discount Schedule only applies to complete self-study courses. It does not apply to orders for additional copies of Student Guides.

3. Read the Self-Study Order Form/License Agreement carefully, and fill in all the requested information on both sides. Include your proper remittance with the completed – and signed – Order Form/License Agreement, and send it to the address listed on the form.

4. We cannot process your self-study order unless the Order Form is complete and the License Agreement is signed. To help us fill your order as quickly as possible, please be sure all the information is complete on both sides of the Order Form/License Agreement.

SELF-STUDY QUANTITY DISCOUNTS

Discounts are available for multiple copies of a particular self-study course or different courses, according to the Discount Schedule below:

Quantity Ordered	Discount
1	None
2 – 3	10%
4 – 5	20%
6 or more	Contact us for price quotation.

A WORD ON LICENSING

Data General courseware is licensed material. Full title and copyright, including but not limited to reproduction and broadcasting rights, remain with Data General Corporation. Completion and execution of Data General's standard self-study course License Agreement (located on the back of the Order Form) is required before delivery of the courseware can be made.

Data General Educational Services
Self-Study Order Form/License Agreement

Invoice to:	Ship to:
Company:	
Division:	
Attn:	
Address:	
City/State/Zip:	
Contact Name:	
Phone: Ext:	

Item #	Quantity	Model #	Description	Unit Price	Extended Price

Video Format (if appropriate)	Sub Total $	
3/4 inch videocassette	BETA 1 2 3 (circle #)	Tax Exempt # Sales Tax $
Other (specify)	VHS 1 2 3 (circle #)	*Total Order $

Magnetic Format (if appropriate)

☐ Mini Diskette (DESKTOP GENERATION systems)

☐ 800 BPI Magnetic Tape

☐ 1600 BPI Magnetic Tape

*All shipments made F.O.B. origin. Prepaid shipping cost will be added to your invoice based on your selected shipping mode. State and local taxes will be added to your invoice unless a Tax Exempt number is specified.

Operating System (if appropriate)

☐ AOS   ☐ AOS/VS   ☐ RDOS

Method of Payment – Must Be Enclosed

☐ Check enclosed

☐ Money Order enclosed

☐ Purchase Order enclosed

☐ License Agreement completed (Reverse Side)

Ship Via

☐ Air Freight

☐ Air Parcel Post

☐ U.P.S.

☐ Fastest Way

NOTE: This order and the materials delivered hereunder are subject exclusively to the terms and conditions of the License Agreement on the reverse side hereof which must be signed by an authorized representative of Customer.

For Internal Use Only:

Send to: **Data General Corporation**
            Attn: Educational Services, M.S. F019
            4400 Computer Drive
            Westboro, Massachusetts 01580

DGC Rep #:

ES Rep #:

Education Ctr:

Used by permission of Data General Corporation.

STYLE AND STRUCTURE

Telexes and Telegrams

Telex is a teletypewriter exchange service that allows you to transmit written messages quickly and directly. It is similar in operation to the telephone, except that machine-printed messages replace speech. In business, the telex transmission serves the same purpose as the memorandum – it communicates its message concisely and provides a written record of the message. It also conveys a feeling of urgency not found in other types of business communications. Telex is a machine-to-machine operation; however, both parties must have access to a telex machine in order to transmit and receive messages directly.

If one or both parties do not have access to a telex machine, they send a **telegram** when communicating between two domestic points, or a **cablegram** for international communications. When a cablegram is sent, the written message is delivered to the telegraph office or dictated over the telephone to a person at the office. Then the message is sent by a teletypewriter to the receiving station. There, the message is printed and then delivered by a messenger to the person to whom the message is addressed.

Telexes and cablegrams are often the most economical and efficient way to convey one-way information or to request information. They are generally less expensive than a long-distance telephone call, but since the number of words in the message determines the cost, you should always try to state the message as concisely as possible.

To minimize the cost of teletypewriter transmissions, you should omit unnecessary articles, prepositions, conjunctions, and punctuation. It is important, however, to retain the clarity of your message. Let's consider the following example.

Suppose that you are planning a business trip to London, and you want to send a telex to your local agent asking that you be met at the airport. Your initial message, if you were writing a memo, might read as follows:

> I will arrive tomorrow morning at Heathrow Airport on American flight
> 515 at ten o'clock. Would you please arrange to meet me there.

This message would then be condensed for telex transmission.

> ARRIVING TOMORROW 10AM AMERICAN FLIGHT 515 HEATHROW.
> PLEASE MEET.

These nine words convey the necessary message contained in the twenty-two words above, including the word "please," which creates a more polite tone. But consider the following message:

> ARRIVE TOMORROW. PLEASE MEET AT HEATHROW AT TEN.

The person who receives this message will be confused. The message does not specify whether to meet at ten o'clock in the morning or in the evening. Furthermore, by not indicating the airline or flight number, the message does not give the reader the information necessary to find the person at the airport. The reader will have to cable back and ask for further details. Thus the writer's attempt to economize on the initial message will actually require three transmissions.

Although a telegraph message should be brief, clarity is always more important than brevity. Complex messages are not well suited to the telex form, and detailed information that is not urgently needed should be sent in a follow-up letter.

In an attempt to save money, people often use abbreviations in their messages, writing YR for "your," or ASAP for "as soon as possible". However, you should try to avoid using abbreviations whenever possible. Abbreviations are often misinterpreted and occasionally undecipherable. A carefully chosen word can often replace a phrase, but a clear, concise message should be your main goal.

Use telexes for brief written communications that must arrive faster than standard mail. If possible, withhold any details that are not urgently needed and include them in a follow-up letter.

Remember that teletypewriters print in capital letters only. They cannot underline any words, and the keyboard does not contain a dollar sign ($), a number sign (#), an ampersand (&), quotation marks, or a semicolon.

PRACTICE A

Rewrite the following telex messages to make them clearer and more concise.

1. I HAVE RECENTLY LEARNED OF AN UPCOMING PRICE INCREASE IN YOUR PRODUCT. PLEASE LET ME KNOW IF THE CURRENT PRICES WILL REMAIN IN EFFECT THROUGH DECEMBER TWENTY.

_____

_____

_____

_____

2. YOUR SHIPMENT OF MACHINE SCREWS HAS BEEN DELAYED AT CUSTOMS. I WOULD LIKE YOU TO PLEASE CHECK YOUR COPY OF THE CUSTOMS INVOICE AND COMPARE IT WITH THE BILL OF LADING. LET ME KNOW IF YOU ARE ABLE TO FIND ANY IRREGULARITIES.

_____

_____

_____

_____

3. I HAVE JUST RECEIVED YOUR ORDER FOR TWENTY CASES OF WHANGO GOLF BALLS. IN YOUR ORDER, YOU NEGLECTED TO SPECIFY WHETHER YOU WANTED OUR STANDARD OR OUR SUPERFLIGHT BALL. PLEASE SEND A REPLY TO ME AS SOON AS YOU POSSIBLY CAN.

_____

_____

_____

_____

4. THE PLANE THAT I WAS GOING TO ARRIVE ON HAS BEEN UNAVOIDABLY DELAYED. CAN WE POSSIBLY CHANGE THE TIME OF OUR MEETING TO TOMORROW AT TWO O'CLOCK IN THE AFTERNOON?

_____

_____

_____

_____

5. IF IT IS AT ALL POSSIBLE, PLEASE CANCEL MY ORDER OF OCTOBER 31, NUMBER 21220. THE CLIENT WHO WAS GOING TO BUY THIS SYSTEM HAS DECIDED TO PURCHASE A LARGER MODEL. I WILL BE SENDING YOU A REVISED ORDER LATER THIS WEEK.

_____

_____

_____

_____

_____

PRACTICE B

Revise the following telex message.

1248567 MDR
ATTN: DOLORES MENDEZ
THERE IS A SERIOUS PROBLEM CONCERNING THE EXPORT OF THE ITEMS THAT WERE LISTED ON INVOICE NUMBER 60244X. TWO ITEMS WERE BACKORDERED. THIS HAS INVALIDATED THE CONFIRMED LETTER OF CREDIT NUMBER 249992 THAT WAS ISSUED BY THE USURIAN GUARANTY TRUST COMPANY. IN ORDER TO CLEAR UP THIS MATTER OF THE DISCREPANT DOCUMENTATION, PLEASE ISSUE A NEW LETTER OF CREDIT IN THE AMOUNT OF 725 DOLLARS. WHILE I AM WRITING, LET'S DISCUSS MY UPCOMING VACATION TIME NEXT MONTH. SINCE I HAVE THREE WEEKS VACATION, I THOUGHT THAT I WOULD TAKE SOME TIME NOW TO CONTINUE MY STAY IN EUROPE FOR MY VACATION. PARTICULARLY, I'D LIKE TO VISIT FRANCE AND SEE SOME OF THE PARIS SIGHTS. PLEASE LET ME KNOW IF THIS WILL CAUSE ANY PROBLEMS FOR YOU. THE WEATHER HERE HAS BEEN WONDERFUL. GIVE MY REGARDS TO EVERYONE IN THE OFFICE.
ALBERT VARMINT

_____
_____
_____
_____
_____
_____
_____
_____
_____
_____
_____
_____

WORDS IN ACTION

Choose the best answer.

1. Mr. Krebbs received a(n) _____ telex message from the home office this morning.
   a. modular
   b. oral
   c. exclusive
   d. urgent

2. Because of our strict credit policy, we must ask for _____ of the total price before we ship your order.
   a. distribution
   b. exhibition
   c. prepayment
   d. interest

3. CAMCO's training program begins in May and lasts for two weeks. The daily _____ last five hours.
   a. negotiations
   b. deposits
   c. modulations
   d. sessions

4. The shipment to Zambia was returned because of a _____ between the bill of lading and the invoice.
   a. deposit
   b. discrepancy
   c. modulation
   d. session

5. Since Ms. Oswego does not have _____ to a telex machine, we'll have to send her a cablegram.
   a. access
   b. discussion
   c. documentation
   d. interest

6. As a general rule, it's best not to _____ words in a telex message.
   a. abbreviate
   b. arrange
   c. expedite
   d. transmit

7. An _____ license gives certain rights to only one party.
   a. export
   b. exclusive
   c. interest
   d. import

8. Agents usually receive a _____ for their services.
   a. deposit
   b. distributor
   c. commission
   d. telegram

9. Mr. Tanizaki was responsible for _____ the international licensing agreement between Zippun Electronics and UNOCORP.
   a. accessing
   b. depositing
   c. interrupting
   d. negotiating

10. A _____ is similar to a telegram, but it is sent to a foreign destination.
    a. cablegram
    b. telegraph
    c. teletypewriter
    d. telex

Objectives

1. Understand the general terms and methods of international transactions.
2. Understand the various methods to receive payments.
3. Understand the general format of shipping documents.
4. Understand the general format of collection documents.

PROFESSIONAL HELP

Omnicomp International, a leader in manufacturing of computer products since 1978, maintains a marketing presence worldwide. These positions work in support of that international sales and marketing effort.

EXPORT DOCUMENTATION COORDINATOR

You will prepare shippers' letters of instruction, commercial invoices, certificates of origin, shippers' export declarations, ocean bills of lading, and banking documentation. This will involve correspondence with freight forwarders, bank consolates, and customs agents.

At least 2-3 years' experience in export documentation and computer-entry word processing, and excellent typing skills are required. Knowledge must include foreign trade terms, export payment and credit terms and pro forma invoices.

INTERNATIONAL CREDIT SPECIALIST

You will be responsible for credit and collection of international trade and international affiliate accounts including monthly reconciliation of affiliate accounts receivable, processing commission payments, and following up on deductions and returns. This will include coordinating problem solving with our international customer service department.

A BS in Finance or the equivalent experience, with at least 2-4 years international banking or collection experience, is required.

Please send résumés to Elena O'Malley, Omnicomp International, 17 Bunker Hill Road, Shrewsbury, MA 01545. An equal opportunity employer. M/F.

OMNICOMP INTERNATIONAL
17 BUNKER HILL ROAD, SHREWSBURY MA 01545

Language

Effective communication in international trade requires an awareness of language, culture, and the laws and regulations governing the import and export of goods. Through worldwide airmail, cable, telex transmissions via satellite, and international telephone service, the global exchange of language is faster and more efficient than ever before. And although less than 10 percent of the world's population speaks English as its native language, more than 75 percent of the world's correspondence is written in English.

Throughout this book, we have offered strategies to help you use English as a communication tool. We've suggested ways to use language to achieve specific goals, and we've stressed the importance of clarity. Remember the following guidelines, and use them to help maintain the clarity of your writing and to avoid misunderstandings.

1. Use precise, simple words whenever possible. As you revise, be sure that your words accurately convey your message. If you can use a simpler word, do so.
2. Use concise sentences. Remember, if you can eliminate a word without changing your meaning, eliminate it.
3. Use clear transitions. Indicate the relationships between ideas and the progress of your thoughts by including transitional words and phrases. Moreover, topic sentences and summarizing sentences help make complex information more understandable.
4. Limit the length of your paragraphs. Paragraphs should be clearly organized and reasonably short – in most cases, no longer than ten lines. Use your paragraphs to address a single thought, and make sure that all the sentences express ideas that are clearly related to that thought.
5. Use visuals whenever helpful. Graphs, charts, tables, and illustrations can supplement and clarify your writing.

Culture

We have also emphasized how important it is to understand and consider your reader. In import/export communications, this often requires you to understand your reader's culture as well. The culture of a country includes its society's values, attitudes, religious beliefs, arts, customs, and organization. Your sensitivity to and knowledge of a culture will have a direct effect upon your success in dealing with persons from another country. A strong cultural awareness is particularly important in conducting the public relations and marketing activities of a business.

So take the time to familiarize yourself with the way of life of any country that you may deal with, and learn to adapt your business procedures to it. The more you learn about a culture and its people, the more you will appreciate and respect them. Remember that real communication can take place only when both the sender and the receiver of the message understand and consider the needs of the other.

Shipper's Export Declaration

U.S. DEPARTMENT OF COMMERCE – SESA, BUREAU OF THE CENSUS – DIBA, BUREAU OF EAST-WEST TRADE

SHIPPER'S EXPORT DECLARATION
OF SHIPMENTS FROM THE UNITED STATES
Export Shipments Are Subject To Inspection By U.S. Customs Service and/or The Office of Export Control

READ CAREFULLY THE INSTRUCTIONS ON BACK TO AVOID DELAY AT SHIPPING POINT

Declarations Should be Typewritten or Prepared in Ink

Form Approved: O.M.B. No. 41-R0397

CONFIDENTIAL – For use solely for official purposes authorized by the Secretary of Commerce. Use for unauthorized purposes is not permitted (Title 15, Sec. 30.91 (a) C.F.R.; Sec. 7(c) Export Administration Act of 1969, as amended, P.L. 91-184).

Authentication (When required)

DO NOT USE THIS AREA	DISTRICT	PORT	COUNTRY (For Customs use only)

File No. (For Customs use only)

1. FROM (U.S. port of export)

2. METHOD OF TRANSPORTATION (Check one):
☐ VESSEL (Incl. ferry) ☐ AIR ☐ OTHER (Specify) _____

2a. EXPORTING CARRIER (If vessel, give name of ship, flag and pier number. If air, give name of airline.)

3. EXPORTER (Principal or seller – licensee)   ADDRESS (Number, street, place, State)

4. AGENT OF EXPORTER (Forwarding agent)   ADDRESS (Number, street, place, State)

5. ULTIMATE CONSIGNEE   ADDRESS (Place, country)

6. INTERMEDIATE CONSIGNEE   ADDRESS (Place, country)

7. FOREIGN PORT OF UNLOADING (For vessel and air shipments only)

8. PLACE AND COUNTRY OF ULTIMATE DESTINATION (Not place of transshipment)

MARKS AND NOS.	NUMBERS AND KIND OF PACKAGES, DESCRIPTION OF COMMODITIES, EXPORT LICENSE NUMBER OR GENERAL LICENSE SYMBOL (Describe commodities in sufficient detail to permit verification of the Schedule B commodity numbers assigned. Do not use general terms.)	SHIPPING (Gross) WEIGHT IN POUNDS (REQUIRED FOR VESSEL AND AIR SHIPMENTS ONLY)	"D" or "F" (Specify)	SCHEDULE B COMMODITY NO. (Include Commodity Control List italicized digit, when required)	NET QUANTITY SCHEDULE B UNITS (State unit)	VALUE AT U.S. PORT OF EXPORT (Selling price or cost if not sold, including inland freight, insurance and other charges to U.S. port of export) (Nearest whole dollar; omit cents figures)
(9)	(10)	(11)	(12)	(13)	(14)	(15)

VALIDATED LICENSE NO. _____   OR GENERAL LICENSE SYMBOL _____

16. BILL OF LADING OR AIR WAYBILL NUMBER

17. DATE OF EXPORTATION (Not required for shipments by vessel)

18. THE UNDERSIGNED HEREBY AUTHORIZES _____
TO ACT AS FORWARDING AGENT FOR EXPORT CONTROL AND CUSTOMS PURPOSES.   (Name and address – Number, street, place, State)

EXPORTER _____   BY _____ (DULY AUTHORIZED OFFICER OR EMPLOYEE)

▶ 19. I CERTIFY THAT ALL STATEMENTS MADE AND ALL INFORMATION CONTAINED IN THIS EXPORT DECLARATION ARE TRUE AND CORRECT. I AM AWARE OF THE PENALTIES PROVIDED FOR FALSE REPRESENTATION. (See paragraphs I (c) and (e) on reverse side.)

SIGNATURE _____   FOR _____
(Duly authorized officer or employee of exporter or named forwarding agent)   (Name of corporation or firm, and capacity of signer; e.g., secretary, export manager, etc.)

ADDRESS _____

DO NOT USE THIS AREA

▶ Declaration should be made by duly authorized officer or employee of exporter or of forwarding agent named by exporter.

ᵃIf shipping weight is not available for each Schedule B item listed in column (13) included in one or more packages, insert the approximate gross weight for each Schedule B item. The total of these estimated weights should equal the actual weight of the entire package or packages.

ᵇDesignate foreign merchandise (reexports) with an "F" and exports of domestic merchandise produced in the United States or changed in condition in the United States with a "D." (See instructions on reverse side.)

INTERNATIONAL TRANSACTIONS

Finally, you must understand the common practices and legal requirements governing international sales. Since laws reflect the culture that enacted them, there is a great diversity between the laws of different nations. Since most countries strictly monitor the flow of goods across their borders, importers and exporters must be familiar with both laws of their own country and those of the country they are dealing with.

Methods of Payment

One of the first things to consider when entering into an internationl transaction is the method of paying for the product. There are many ways to arrange payment, and choosing the best method depends on the relationship between the buyer and the seller.

Cash in Advance Most customers object to paying cash in advance for an obvious reason – customers don't like to pay for merchandise they haven't received. Nevertheless, unestablished customers without a healthy credit rating are often required to pay cash in advance. Many small orders often require prepayment as well.

Open Account Under this arrangement, the customer agrees to pay for the shipment at a later time. Open accounts should be used only when the seller has absolute confidence in the buyer's ability to pay.

Consignment Sales Here the customer receives merchandise on a deferred payment basis. The customer first sells the merchandise to a third party and then reimburses the seller within a specified time.

Drafts for Collection A draft or bill of exchange, is a written order, usually signed by the seller and addressed to the buyer, directing the buyer to pay a third person a specific sum of money at a specific date. This "person" can be a company, a bank, or an individual. The person who makes out the draft is called the *drawer*. The person who pays the amount on the bill is the *drawee,* and the person who receives the payment is the *payee.*

The seller, or drawer, usually presents the draft and shipping documents at a local bank. This bank then sends the draft and documents to a bank in the customer's city for collection. Documents are usually not released to the customer until the amount specified on the draft has been paid. After the customer pays, the collecting bank remits the amount to the seller's local bank.

Letters of Credit Under this method, the importer goes to a local bank to purchase the letter of credit. In most cases, the bank asks the importer to deposit, in local currency, all or part of the amount specified in the letter. The buyer describes to the banker the nature of the transaction, specifies the documents the seller needs to complete the transaction, and determines the date by which the transaction must be completed.

Then the importer's bank, or *issuing bank,* arranges for the payment to be deposited in a bank in the exporting country. This bank, referred to as the *notifying bank,* then issues the letter of credit to the seller. The letter tells the seller that the buyer has deposited the money to pay for the product, and it tells the seller what documents will have to be produced in order to collect payment.

Commercial Invoice

COMMERCIAL INVOICE

| SHIPPER/EXPORTER | DOCUMENT NO. |
| | EXPORT REFERENCES |

| CONSIGNEE | FORWARDING AGENT - REFERENCES |
| | POINT AND COUNTRY OF ORIGIN |

| NOTIFY PARTY | DOMESTIC ROUTING/EXPORT INSTRUCTIONS |

PIER OR AIRPORT

| EXPORTING CARRIER (Vessel/Airline) | PORT OF LOADING | ONWARD INLAND ROUTING |
| AIR/SEA PORT OF DISCHARGE | FOR TRANSSHIPMENT TO | |

PARTICULARS FURNISHED BY SHIPPER

MARKS AND NUMBERS	NO. OF PKGS.	DESCRIPTION OF PACKAGES AND GOODS	GROSS WEIGHT	MEASUREMENT

| DELIVERY TERMS | NET INVOICE VALUE $ | AMOUNT INSURED $ |

See addendum attached for detailed summary of billing and packing.

CERTIFICATIONS

Signed _____

Letters of credit can generally be divided into four categories:

1. **Irrevocable letter of credit issued by a foreign bank and confirmed by a domestic bank** Irrevocable letters of credit offer the exporter the greatest protection because the bank must honor any claim that complies with the terms of the letter, and no changes in these terms can be made without the seller's consent. This type of letter carries with it the obligation of both the foreign issuing bank and the domestic notifying bank.

2. **Irrevocable letter of credit issued by a domestic bank** This type of letter is, in effect, similar to the letter described above, except that the issuing bank and the notifying bank are the same. Thus the letter carries the obligation of only one bank. Here the importer deals directly with an agent of a bank located in the exporting country.

3. **Irrevocable letter of credit issued by a foreign bank, but unconfirmed by a domestic bank** This means that the notifying bank merely notifies the seller that the issuing bank has established the account to finance the transaction. The notifying bank assumes no obligation to honor the letter if the foreign bank withholds payment. Thus the exporter is not fully protected.

4. **Revocable letter of credit** Revocable letters of credit offer the exporter no real assurance of payment. The terms of such a letter can be modified at any time, and the letter itself can even be cancelled without notice. This letter is basically a nonbinding agreement between the importer and the exporter, and for this reason it is used less frequently as other letters of credit.

Shipping Procedures

Freight Forwarders

In order to show that the necessary regulations and procedures have been followed, international shipments require a number of documents. Most of these forms, as well as the actual shipping procedure, are usually handled by freight forwarding agents. Exporters hire freight forwarders to facilitate the efficient transport of the their goods. Freight forwarders secure the best possible rates from airlines or ocean carriers, and they produce the documentation necessary to prove that each shipment meets the legal requirements of the exporting and the importing countries. The seller pays the forwarding agent a commission for performing this service and then, depending upon the terms of the sale, passes this cost along to the buyer.

Along with the freight forwarder's commission, it is common to charge a percentage of the total sale to pay for the shipment itself. In other cases, the buyer pays for the actual transportation of the product. In international trade it is common to ship merchandise in one of the following ways:

1. **C.I.F.** (cost, insurance, freight) When the seller quotes a price under these terms, it includes the price of the merchandise itself, the insurance itself, and all transportation charges, duties and fees.

2. **F.O.B.** (free on board) This means that the seller is only responsible for delivering the goods onto a specified carrier, either at an inland point of origin or a port of exportation. From there, the buyer is responsible.

3. **EX** (from **point of origin**) This method excludes all costs from the specified point of origin. The buyer pays for all transport charges and fees.

Bill of Lading

SHORT FORM BILL OF LADING	NAME OF CARRIER
(Non-Negotiable Unless Consigned To Order)	

SHIPPER/EXPORTER (2) (COMPLETE NAME AND ADDRESS)

DOCUMENT NO. (5)

EXPORT REFERENCES (6)

CONSIGNEE (3) (COMPLETE NAME AND ADDRESS)

FORWARDING AGENT-REFERENCES (7) (COMPLETE NAME AND ADDRESS)

POINT AND COUNTRY OF ORIGIN (8)

NOTIFY PARTY (4) (COMPLETE NAME AND ADDRESS)

DOMESTIC ROUTING/EXPORT INSTRUCTIONS (9)

PIER/TERMINAL (10)

VESSEL (11) FLAG	PORT OF LOADING (12)	ONWARD INLAND ROUTING (15)
PORT OF DISCHARGE FROM VESSEL (13)	FOR TRANSSHIPMENT TO (14)	

PARTICULARS FURNISHED BY SHIPPER

MARKS AND NUMBERS	NO. OF PKGS.	DESCRIPTION OF PACKAGES AND GOODS	GROSS WEIGHT	MEASUREMENT
(16)	(17)	(18)	(19)	(20)

FREIGHT AND CHARGES PAYABLE AT			PREPAID ☐	COLLECT ☐
	PREPAID	COLLECT		

RECEIVED the goods or the containers, vans, trailers, pallet units or other packages said to contain goods herein mentioned, in apparent good order and condition, except as otherwise indicated, to be transported, delivered or transhipped as provided herein. All of the provisions written, printed or stamped on either side hereof are part of this bill of lading contract.

IN WITNESS WHEREOF, the Master or agent of said vessel has signed _____ bills of lading, all of the same tenor and date, one of which being accomplished, the others to stand void.

TOTAL

BY _____

FOR THE MASTER

DATED

B/L NO.

Shipping Documents

The shipper or forwarder must prepare a number of shipping documents necessary to move the shipment through customs, allowing it to be loaded aboard a carrier, and to deliver it to a foreign destination. The specific documentation required depends upon the nature, origin, and destination of the shipment.

One specific common shipping document is the export license, which authorizes the shipment of goods abroad. Export licenses are issued for each specific transaction or for a group of transactions. The limits or restrictions on the goods that can be exported are also specified in the license. Exporters in the United States must submit an application for an export license to the Office of Export Administration.

Export Declaration

Another common document is the shipper's export declaration. Most exporters must complete this document for their shipments. It is used for compiling export statistics and for enforcing export control regulations.

In order to collect payment, the shipper usually must complete the following documents to prove that the terms of the sale were completed: a commercial invoice, a consular invoice (when required), a bill of lading, an insurance policy or a certificate that confirms that the shipment has been fully insured, and a certificate of origin.

Commercial Invoice

In many cases, the only document the seller must provide is the invoice. An invoice, as we explained in Chapter 5, identifies the shipment, the seller, the buyer, and the terms of the sale.

The two most common types of invoice used in international trade are the pro forma invoice and the commercial invoice. The main difference between the two is that the pro forma invoice does not accompany the shipment and the commercial invoice does. A *pro forma invoice* is, in fact, a bid that formally informs the buyer what will be shipped, by what means, and for what cost. The *commercial invoice* is delivered to the forwarding agent with the shipment itself. It serves as a means of identification and as a basis for further documentation. The two documents are usually similar in appearance, and in some cases they are identical.

Consular Invoice

The *consular invoice* is the exporter's evidence of the value of the shipment. The consular invoice is only required in certain countries or for shipment of restricted goods. The document is similar to the standard commercial invoice, but it is usually written in the language of the importing country on special forms that can be obtained only from a consulate. Exporters must also pay the consulate either a fixed amount or a percentage of the shipment's cost to certify and notarize the invoice. In some countries, errors or inaccuracies on the consular invoice are punishable by fines, so it is important that exporters complete the forms carefully. As a general rule, it is best if the importer assumes responsibility for the cost of consular certification and any fees associated with it.

Consuls always retain certain copies for their own files and for customs officers in the place of destination. The copies that they return to the exporter, together with other essential documents, are usually sent to the collecting bank, which

Certificate of
Insurance

INSURANCE CERTIFICATE

SHIPPER/EXPORTER	DOCUMENT NO.
	EXPORT REFERENCES
CONSIGNEE	FORWARDING AGENT - REFERENCES
	POINT AND COUNTRY OF ORIGIN
NOTIFY PARTY	DOMESTIC ROUTING/ EXPORT INSTRUCTIONS
PIER OR AIRPORT	

EXPORTING CARRIER (Vessel/Airline)	PORT OF LOADING	ONWARD INLAND ROUTING
AIR/SEA PORT OF DISCHARGE	FOR TRANSSHIPMENT TO	

PARTICULARS FURNISHED BY SHIPPER

MARKS AND NUMBERS	NO. OF PKGS.	DESCRIPTION OF PACKAGES AND GOODS	GROSS WEIGHT	MEASUREMENT

DATE OF POLICY	SUM INSURED $	AMOUNT IN WORDS	DOLLARS

SPECIAL TERMS AND CONDITIONS: SHIPMENTS ON DECK or AIR CARGO when Insured Under this Policy are subject to terms and conditions specified on the reverse side hereof. SHIPMENTS SUBJECT TO AN "UNDER DECK" BILL OF LADING are Insured.-

THIS INSURANCE IS ALSO SUBJECT TO THE FOLLOWING AMERICAN INSTITUTE CLAUSES CURRENT ON THE DATE OF ISSUANCE OF THIS POLICY:-
MARINE EXTENSION CLAUSES   **S. R. & C. C. ENDORSEMENT**   **WAR RISK INSURANCE**

WHEN GOODS ARE SO DESTINED THIS INSURANCE IS SUBJECT TO:-
SOUTH AMERICAN 60 DAY CLAUSE

This Policy not transferable unless countersigned by an authorized representative of this Company or the Assured. Countersigned:

IN WITNESS WHEREOF, this Company has executed and attested these presents.

Secretary   *President*

266

delivers these documents to the importer after payment has been made or the draft has been accepted. The documents are necessary for presentation to customs when the importer declares the shipment. They should arrive at the same time as, or preferably before, the shipment.

Bill of Lading

A *bill of lading* is both a receipt for goods sent by ship or railroad and a contract between the shipper and the carrier. It defines the terms and conditions under which the goods are transported from one point to another. It also describes the goods, their value, and the shipping charges. When the carrier is an airline, the bill of lading is usually referred to as an air waybill.

The bill of lading shows that the shipment is *consigned* to the carrier, making the carrier responsible for the goods. If you are sending the shipment, you are called the consignor; if you are receiving the shipment, you are called the consignee. The bill of lading lists the consignor, the consignee, and the transportation company to which the shipment is consigned.

There are two types of bills of lading: *straight bills* and *order bills*. A straight bill of lading shows that the shipment is consigned directly to the consignee and cannot be transferred to another party. Thus straight bills of lading are considered "not negotiable." You can transfer order bills of lading to another person, which means they are negotiable. As the owner of a shipment, you can endorse the order bill to another party while the shipment is in transit, and the party assumes the rights of the original consignee.

Certificate of Insurance

A *certificate of insurance* defines a policy between an insurance company (the insurer) and the forwarder, consignor, consignee, or owner of the shipment (the assured). It states that for a specified payment, or premium, the insurer agrees to pay the assured for any loss or damage to the shipment while it is being transported. The certificate describes the nature and quantity of the shipment, its value, any identifying numbers, the vessel or vehicle carrying the shipment, and the terms of the policy. The document is either kept by the assured and used for banking purposes or issued to the freight forwarder needed to assemble a complete set of shipping documents.

Certificate of Origin

In addition to the previous documents, many countries require a *certificate of origin*. This document simply certifies that the products being exported were actually manufactured in the exporting country. Certificates of origin are generally required between countries that maintain special trade agreements and whose products are charged with reduced tariff rates and duties. In some cases the certificate of origin is incorporated into the consular invoice form, and in others the certificate replaces the consular invoice.

Standard Document Form

One of the problems of international trade is the excessive amount of documentation required. A typical transaction often requires more than forty separate documents to be filled out by as many as twenty-five people. Most of these people simply transfer information from one document to another. Such paperwork delays shipment, increases costs, and reduces profits.

During the past several years, many governments have been developing a standard format that will simplify international trade paperwork. This format allows the shipper to enter all necessary information only once; then others duplicate it on similar forms to serve many purposes. The *U.S. Standard Master*, is

Certificate of
Origin for
Japan

CERTIFICATE OF ORIGIN FOR JAPAN

No..............

Name of Applicant..

Address..

Marks and Numbers	Number of Packages	Place of Origin	QUANTITY AND DESCRIPTION OF COMMODITY	Value

I hereby certify that the commodity enumerated above has been produced (or manufactured) in the place of origin above mentioned.

Date..19..... Signature..

Title..

(Remarks)   Certificate will cease to be valid after four months from the date of its issuance.

The ...., a recognized Chamber of Commerce under the laws of the State of

...., has examined the manufacturer's invoice or shipper's affidavit concerning the origin of the merchandise and,

according to the best of its knowledge and belief, finds that the products named originated in..

Secretary..

often used as a bill of lading, a certificate of insurance, an invoice, a certificate of origin, a dock receipt, and a shipping-instructions form.

Carnets The *carnet* is a customs document that eliminates extensive customs procedures and payment for duty and tax for temporary imports. As a result of various customs conventions, you can use carnets in the following countries:

Australia	Germany	Ivory Coast	Romania
Austria	Greece	Japan	South Africa
Belgium	Hong Kong	Korea (South)	Spain
Bulgaria	Hungary	Luxembourg	Sweden
Canada	Iceland	The Netherlands	Switzerland
Cyprus	Iran	New Zealand	Turkey
Czechoslovakia	Ireland	Norway	United Kingdom
Denmark	Israel	Poland	United States
Finland	Italy	Portugal	Yugoslavia
France			

Summary We have discussed just a few of the many documents required to complete an international transaction. Although they might seem intimidating and confusing, they are, for the most part, handled by freight forwarders and are not the concern of the average import/export businessperson. A familiarity with these forms is helpful, however. In order to help you remember all the documents, you can categorize each document into one of three groups:

Transport-Related Documents These refer to all forms used in the actual shipment of goods. They include the following: all bills of lading or waybills, insurance certificates, shipping and delivery instructions, dock receipts, terminal and handling documents, and dangerous or hazardous materials documents.

Transaction-Related Documents These are documents used in the sales procedure between the exporter and the importer. They include all invoices, letters of credit, and bills of exchange.

Government-Related Documents This category includes all documents that are required by the governments and customs of the importing and exporting countries. They include consular invoices, certificates of origin, import and export licenses, export declaration forms, and any other customs-entry forms and inspection certificates.

Of course, the actual documents needed for a specific transaction depend upon the two countries involved, and it is important that the exporter and the importer become familiar with the rules and regulations of the country they are dealing with. For although the freight forwarder handles most of the details of the international shipment, the buyer and the seller are ultimately responsible for any problems in the transaction.

Special Report: Japan

TRADING PROCEDURES

Import Channels

Most exporters to Japan conclude a format agreement with an importer. In most cases this importer is a specialized trading company, but individual agent agreements are also common.

Japan's very specialized distribution system makes it very difficult for most companies to distribute their products. A simpler pattern of distribution, however, is now in place for handling many categories of consumer goods.

Japan's general trading companies are represented in about all the world's major cities. As a small manufacturer in Japan, you can rely on these trading companies to help you sell your products abroad.

In Japan many foreign companies are allowed to import, warehouse, market, and service their own products, as long as the products are on the government's list of approved products. However, most foreign companies do not start a direct sales operation without the existence of independent Japanese representatives.

Advertising

Originally, Japanese advertising agencies financed certain media – initially newspapers, later radio and television – by purchasing space or time in advance and then selling it to companies interested in advertising their products. For this reason many companies in Japan continue to rely on advertising agencies, but now the agencies primarily produce advertising copy.

If exporters want to distribute a product successfully in Japan, they should plan an intensive advertising campaign to establish the product's image. They should not assume that a successful campaign in their own market will work in Japan. All manufacturers, of course, should follow similar guidelines for selling their products in other countries.

Import Insurance

The Japanese government has import insurance for importers who fail to receive their goods after they've made payment. The policy provides coverage when the freight is lost or damaged during shipment, when the shipment is not delivered because of the exporter's bankruptcy, fraud, or credit uneasiness, or when there is a military takeover in the exporting country.

SUMMARY OF REQUIREMENTS OF DOCUMENTS

Exporters and importers should make sure their shipper list all weights and measures in the metric system on all documents accompanying shipments to Japan.

Commercial Invoice Exporters do not have to use a special form of the commercial invoice. They need, however, at least two copies on their shipper's letterhead.

For shipments of printed materials, sales samples, or other items of no commercial value, the exporter should write on the commercial invoice "No Commercial Value. Not for Resale." If this is not done, Japanese customs may assess duties that will be charged to the consignee. Exporters do not need a commercial invoice for shipments by mail.

Certificate of Origin Importers need a certificate of origin for foreign merchandise granted duty concessions by Japan under the General Agreement of Tariffs and Trade (GATT) and the Generalized System of Preference. Certain items are exempt from this requirement. Exporters should submit the certificate of origin to their local chambers of commerce (which usually require an additional copy) or to a Japanese consular or diplomatic official at the place of production, purchase, or shipment. The signed document certifies that the products were actually manufactured in the exporting country.

Consular Invoices are not required, but the consulate will legalize the invoice upon request by the exporter if this is required by the sales contract, a letter of credit, or a request by the importer.

Import Declaration or Approval Importers need to prepare and file a declaration of import from an authorized foreign exchange bank in Japan for items under quota and certain other specified items. The import declaration must show the shipping number, description, quantity, and value of the goods; the place of origin, purchase, and shipment of the goods; and the name of the registered mark and nationality of the vessel or aircraft by which the goods are carried. Once the import declaration has been accepted by customs, it cannot be altered without special approval of customs.

Packing List Exporters should include a packing list, but it's not required.

Bill of Lading Exporters are usually required to send three signed original bills of lading through their banking channels and to send at least two unsigned copies are sent to the consignee. The bill of lading should show the name of the ship; the shipper; consignee(s); the marking and number of packages; and a description of the goods, including the gross metric weights and measures.

Import License Importers need an import license only for commercial shipments of import quota items. Validity is six months. All other imports require an import declaration.

SAMPLES AND ADVERTISING MATTER

Samples and advertising matter – brochures, photographs, films, and samples of no commercial value and so forth – are exempt from customs duty. Samples having commercial value are permitted duty-free entry provided they are to be exported from Japan within one year from the date of the permission for duty-free import.

Importers do not need an import license for goods bearing the markings "Trade Sample, Not for Sale" valued at less than US$2000. With the approval from the Director of Customs, foreign goods temporarily may be taken from a bonded area for use as samples. As a signatory to the International Convention to Facilitate the Importation of Commercial Samples and Advertising Material, Japan admits valuable samples temporarily duty-free under deposit or bond for the amount of duty.

WRITING ASSIGNMENT

Background

The Leon Neeper Company manufactures stainless steel products used in the production of ovens and ranges. Neeper's European agent is currently negotiating an important contract with Schnellfeuer GmbH, a German stove manufacturer. The contract would allow Neeper to produce all the rangetops for Schnellfeuer's electric stoves for the next two years.

R. Verman, Neeper's business manager, has just learned that next month there will be an 11-percent increase in the price of steel from the wholesalers. This increase will directly affect the negotiations with Schnellfeuer. An 11-percent increase in the raw materials will require a 15-percent increase in the price of the finished product.

You (R. Verman) must contact your agent, Hans Braun, immediately, and apprise him of the new situation. Since the price of the rangetops has already been agreed upon, Mr. Braun will have to realize a 15-percent savings by convincing Schnellfeuer to assume a greater portion of the shipping costs. Originally, Neeper's bid included cost, insurance, and freight (C.I.F). This means that the seller provides for the transportation of the product, including any export taxes and fees, and is responsible for insuring the shipment against any loss or damage until the product is delivered.

Now you would like Mr. Braun to renegotiate the shipping arrangements. Ideally, Neeper would deliver the ranges F.O.B. (free on board) New York, from where Schnellfeuer would be responsible for shipment and insurance. If this cannot be agreed upon, Neeper will deliver the rangetops C.F. (cost and freight), and Schnellfeuer must pay for all insurance.

Prepare a telex to Mr. Braun (telex number 9266214) telling him about the situation and informing him of his options in the negotiation. First write a draft of the message, and then rewrite it in the appropriate style, being as concise as possible.

Goal: _____

Audience: _____

FIRST DRAFT

_____

_____

_____

_____

_____

_____

_____

_____

_____

_____

_____

MESSAGE-SENDING BLANK

Send this message as a

____ Telex message (Telex #_____)

____ Domestic telegram for
        _____ telephone delivery
        _____ messenger delivery

____ Cablegram for overseas delivery

Send to

Name _____ Title _____

Company _____

Address _____

_____

_____

Message:

_____

_____

_____

_____

_____

_____

_____

_____

_____

_____

_____

_____

_____

_____

_____

_____

Choose the best answer.

1. A _____ states that the shipment being exported was actually manufactured in the exporting country.
   a. bill of exchange
   b. certificate of origin
   c. letter of credit
   d. pro forma invoice

2. The terms of a revocable letter of credit can be _____ at any time.
   a. cancelled
   b. consigned
   c. enacted
   d. issued

3. A bill of lading is a contract between the shipper and the _____.
   a. vessel
   b. vehicle
   c. consulate
   d. carrier

4. A(n) _____ letter of credit gives the exporter the greatest protection because the bank is obligated to honor it and its terms cannot be altered.
   a. assured
   b. commercial
   c. endorsed
   d. irrevocable

5. When a shipment is _____ to a carrier, the carrier is responsible for it.
   a. consigned
   b. endorsed
   c. issued
   d. enacted

6. A _____ is a common way for an importer to finance an international transaction.
   a. bill of lading
   b. certificate of origin
   c. consular invoice
   d. letter of credit

7. The _____ must pay a premium to the insurance company, which assumes the responsibility for any loss or damage to the shipment.
   a. assured
   b. carrier
   c. consulate
   d. transport

8. Each country _____ laws to regulate the flow of goods across its borders.
   a. consigns
   b. enacts
   c. endorses
   d. issues

9. The carrier _____ the shipment from its port of origin to its destination.
   a. cancels
   b. consigns
   c. endorses
   d. transports

10. The attitudes and beliefs of a society are part of its _____.
    a. culture
    b. customs
    c. diversity
    d. requirements

COMMUNICATION WORKSHOP
Customer Service Procedures

When a company places a guarantee on its products at the time of sale, a liability exists for the length of the guarantee. In addition to the warranty or guarantee on the product itself, companies often assume full responsibility for replacing the product if it was shipped C.I.F. and was lost or damaged in transit.

The following memorandum illustrates Omnicomp's customer service procedures involving goods shipped C.I.F.

OMNICOMP INTERNATIONAL
17 BUNKER HILL ROAD, SHREWSBURY MA O1545

Memorandum

TO: Customer Service Department

FROM: Larry Fine

SUBJECT: LIABILITY FOR LOST SHIPMENTS
               OR PRODUCTS DAMAGED IN TRANSIT

Omnicomp will assume full responsibility for replacing goods shipped C.I.F. that are lost or damaged in transit.

1. When we receive a communication from a C.I.F. customer reporting missing materials, we will take the following actions.
   a. The accounts correspondent must check original shipping documents to determine whether (1) goods were short-shipped or (2) shipment was delayed or lost in transit.

   b. If goods were clearly short-shipped, the accounts correspondent must replace the shipment immediately, following our standard instructions for short shipments, and then notify the customer of the action that was taken.

c. If it appears that the shipment was sent complete, the operations supervisor must judge whether the missing shipment (1) may still be in transit or (2) is unlikely to reach its destination.

In the former case, the accounts correspondent should send a telex or cable to the customer detailing the number of packages originally shipped, the shipping method used, and the date of shipment. Also, the customer is asked the number of packages received. The accounts correspondent should advise the customer to notify us within a reasonable time if the missing packages still are not received.

If it appears (because of the length of time since the shipping date) that the missing materials will not arrive, then the accounts correspondent will reship the missing items. When the accounts correspondence advises the customer of this action, he or she must request the return of the original shipment if it should arrive at a later date.

d. When replacing lost-in-transit materials, the operations supervisor must determine whether or not to file a full or partial claim with the insurance carrier.

If the delay in receipt is the fault of Omnicomp's Shipping Department (short in packing), no claim will be filed with the insurance carrier for the replacement shipment.

If the delay is due to materials being lost or damaged in transit, the insurance company will pay for any loss or damage up to the amount specified in the certificate of insurance.

e. Whatever action is finally selected, be sure to notify the customer immediately, either by telex, cable, telephone, or letter, depending upon the urgency of the situation.

2. We will either replace goods damaged in transit at no charge (including transportation costs) or issue a credit to the customer's account.

a. The accounts correspondent should answer communications from customers promptly and in like manner; that is, a telex should be answered by a telex, a phone call by a phone call, a letter by a letter. Since not receiving materials can cripple a company's efforts to conduct business, the accounts correspondent should resolve all reports of missing materials quickly and advise the customer what action is being taken.

b. Whenever reported problems cause an invoice to remain open and become overdue, the accounts correspondent must report the problem to the collection department. The accounts correspondent should send a statement to the collection departmen for review, editing, and eventual adjustment when the situation has been cleared up, check the account before the next billing cycle to make sure the adjustment was made correctly. If the adjustment is completed within a billing cycle, no such communication is necessary.

Please review the above procedures. We need to make sure that each transaction is fair to our customers and to Omnicomp.

DISCUSSION ACTIVITIES

1. You are an accounts correspondent in Omnicomp's Customer Service Department. Be prepared to answer the following questions.

   a. What do you do when you get a letter from a C.I.F. customer reporting missing goods?

   b. What information do you look for when you check the original shipping documents after you get a report on missing goods?

   c. What steps do you take if the missing goods were clearly short-shipped?

   d. What are the responsibilities of the operation supervisor?

   e. If the shipping department sent a shipment complete, and you judge it to be lost, what do you do? What do you tell the customer?

   f. Under what circumstances do you reship goods? What are the customer's responsibilities?

   g. When a shipment is lost, do you always file a claim with the insurance carrier?

   h. What does "short-shipped" mean?

   i. How do you contact the customer?

   j. If the customer doesn't want a replacement for the damaged goods, what other option do you have?

   k. What is the customer's responsibility when you replace damaged goods?

2. You're an irate Omnicomp customer who has been charged incorrectly for goods that never arrived. You've notified Omnicomp, you've received a letter explaining what action Omnicomp will take (based on the customer service procedures). Will you be satisfied? Explain why or why not.

10
PRESENTATIONS

Preparation

Organization and
Delivery

OE DISTRIBUTORS

14-1 Roku Waseda 4-chome, Shinjuku-ku, Tokyo 160 Japan

January 7, 19..

Mr. Andrew Mason, Marketing Services Manager
Omnicomp International
17 Bunker Hill Road
Shrewsbury, MA 01545

Dear Mr. Mason:

Now that Oe has become an Omnicomp distributor, we are anxious to train our sales staff in presenting your products effectively. In particular, we would like to request the services of an Omnicomp training consultant for an intensive course in the various uses of your Spellgramm program.

In our area, we feel that Spellgramm is ideally suited for clerical staff (bilingual secretaries), and we have defined the corporate sector as our primary market. We consider educational institutions to be our secondary market. Since each of these markets is serviced by different sales representatives, we would like to have two different training presentations: one for the business sector and the other for the educational market.

I look forward to hearing from you.

Respectfully yours,

Taro Tanaka
Director of Sales

OMNICOMP INTERNATIONAL
17 BUNKER HILL ROAD, SHREWSBURY MA 01545

February 2, 19..

Mr. Taro Tanaka, Director of Sales
Oe Distributors
14-1 Roku Waseda 4-chome
Shinjuku-ku
Tokyo 160 Japan

Dear Mr. Tanaka:

SUBJECT: SPELLGRAMM TRAINING PRESENTATIONS

Thank you for your letter of January 7 requesting staff training. We are proud of the Spellgramm software and believe that staff training is an important part of its success.

Mr. Mason asked me to respond directly. I am pleased to confirm that we can provide the training sessions you requested. I plan to give two different presentations: one aimed at the business sector and the other aimed at the educational market. The goal of both sessions will be the same: to enable your representatives to explain Spellgramm's features and benefits and to demonstrate its use.

To help me prepare for these presentations, would you please answer the following questions:
  a. Are your sales representatives familiar with word processing terminology?
  b. Are your representatives experienced with other Omnicomp software products? If so, which ones, and to what extent?
  c. How many representatives will attend each session?

Again, thank you for your interest. I look forward to productive training sessions with both you and your sales staff.

Sincerely yours,

Randall Drake

Randall Drake
Training Consultant

cc: A. Mason

Importance   Casual conversation is a part of our everyday lives, but when we are asked to prepare and deliver some sort of formal communication, panic is usually the first reaction. But there is a need for the information that you have to prepare and deliver, and to satisfy that need, your communication has to be effective.

There are many reasons to give a formal presentation: to create an awareness of need, to point out problems, to describe progress, to ask for help, and to influence the decision-making process. But in each case, it is in the speaker's best interest to be sure that the message gets through clearly. Management will not act positively on something it doesn't understand. The effectiveness of the communication process will be determined to a large extent by the degree of effort you, as the speaker, put into developing your presentation and ensuring that accurate reception and understanding will take place.

If all goes well, there is understanding between the speaker and the listeners. But how complete is the understanding? Do the receivers understand what was sent, or do they understand what they received, because what was sent and received can be vastly different.

To develop our skills as speakers, we must know the proper steps to take. Poor communication wastes everyone's time and energy, and there is no reason for it to occur. It is the speaker's responsibility to ensure that the message is clearly transmitted and correctly received. The barriers to effective communication can exist only in an atmosphere of apathy, and with common sense, they can usually be overcome. Communicating, at its best, benefits both the speaker and the listener. But hearing is not necessarily the same as understanding, and speaking is not necessarily the same as communicating.

Good presentations cause something to happen. The presenter knows beforehand exactly what reaction he or she wishes to cause, and every word, thought, and concept in the presentation should directly support that goal.

Goals   A successful presentation begins with careful preparation, and the first step in a careful preparation is to define your goals. What results do you want your message to bring? It's probably safe to assume that you are going to make your presentation for a very good reason. Don't forget that reason as you begin your planning. Too many presenters jump ahead to the "What am I going to put into it?" step as their first planning effort, and that is not the best place to begin.

First, identify the specific objective you have for giving the presentation. If you are vague or unsure of the objective, or if you fail to develop your presentation around it, your audience may ask themselves, "What is the purpose of this, anyhow?" By identifying a purpose, you will eliminate the nagging problems before they arise and you will also reduce your preparation time considerably. Most important, you will have taken the first step toward developing an effective presentation.

As in business writing, the best procedure to follow is to identify your objective in one sentence and write it down. Then refer to the sentence during the preparation of your presentation. Each item included in your presentation should be weighed against the defined objective; keep the supportive material, eliminate the rest. When you give your presentation, you don't want to wander off on tangents; you want to be certain that the purpose of your presentation is made clear to your audience.

You can easily test the validity of this important step. The next time you are in the audience at a presentation, analyze that presentation. See if the presenter's objective is clearly identifiable. Judge whether or not the main points offer direct support to the objective. If the objective is not clear, and the main points offer little support, you may find that the presentation wanders away from what the speaker is trying to say. At the same time, you will probably find that your attention is wandering too. You might even get a little irritated!

Of course, you could do the presenter a favor by tearing out this section of this book and mailing it to him or her, anonymously, of course. After all, the presentation did irritate you, didn't it?

Identifying your objective should be the easiest task in preparing your presentation, but don't underestimate its importance. Without a clearly defined purpose for giving your presentation and a presentation developed around that objective, chances are you will only waste time – yours and your audience's. Even worse, someone may tear out this section of the book and mail it to you, anonymously, of course.

Audience

It's usually true that the most effective presentations are those prepared with a particular audience in mind. By tailoring the presentation to the specific likes, dislikes, knowledge, and attitudes of an audience, the odds for success increase considerably. And while it is impossible to acquire complete knowledge of an audience's personality, certain key considerations should be employed. This is what is called audience analysis.

Analyzing your prospective audience is a lot like conducting market research on a prospective consumer group. In each case you want to discover what might please and displease the consumer. In both cases you would use the results of the analysis to accentuate the positive and eliminate the negative elements.

An excellent presentation can fail if some aspect is not palatable to your audience. Take the case of the fellow who worked diligently on his presentation but didn't consider who was to be in his audience. All through the presentation the company president, who was the key member of the audience, kept looking away from the presenter, rubbing his eyes, and looking very uncomfortable. At the conclusion, the president made a remark about having to be elsewhere, and hastily departed. Other members of the audience, obviously affected by the attitude, were also noncommittal about the presentation. The presenter, understandably concerned, later asked the president's assistant if something about the presentation had annoyed the president. The assistant informed him that the president was particularly sensitive to glare, and the presenter had used clear-background slides for his briefing, creating a harsh glare in the darkened room that caused considerable discomfort to the president. Talking to the aide was good audience analysis. Unfortunately it should have been done before the presentation.

As a presenter, you must be aware of the many differences that will exist among potential audience groups. The last thing you want to do is unwittingly offend any member of your audience. A planned audience analysis will provide the insight needed in each of the subsequent steps in preparation and, in many cases, put you more at ease when it's time to speak.

Since the audience analysis is an important part of your preparation, it's a good idea to write it down. As you progress through the preparation steps, your presentation will develop an identity of its own and you can begin "tailoring" it to your own specifications. To get started on the right track, however, the following list of analysis questions is a good guide:

Audience Analysis Checklist

1. Who is my audience?
2. How much do my listeners know about the subject?
3. Are they at the decision-making level in the company?
4. What language will they best understand: technical, business, financial, everyday English, or what?
5. Are there leaders in the group who could influence the others?
6. Should I address myself to the whole group or to only certain individuals?

7. What are their reasons for attending my presentation?
8. What information or technique is likely to gain their attention?
9. What information or technique is likely to get negative reactions?
10. Is the audience likely to be friendly or unfriendly, sympathetic or hostile?
11. Will they be in a hurry for the presentation to end?
12. Is there likely to be opposition, or even debate?

When you answer these questions, try to be as objective and realistic as possible, and you will gain a "feel" for your audience. Remember, the purpose of performing your analysis is to predetermine what conditions, opinions, attitudes, prejudices, and emotions will exist during your presentation, and then to tailor your approach to counter the negative and develop the positive.

Materials

In most instances, you will have sufficient knowledge of the subject matter of your presentation. This qualifies you to determine which material to use in preparing your presentation. Here are some good ideas to help you get started in the right direction.

Begin by gathering any information that might be useful. Put your personal knowledge of the subject into descriptive phrases, write it down, and include it with your other material: books, documents, reports, papers, and publications. Also think of visual materials to accompany your speech, such as charts and graphs. You'll probably find much more material than you will be able to use.

Once you've completed the process of collecting potentially useful material, the process of elimination begins. Time limitations and limited attention spans demand that you distill your material down to the most important essentials, with a reasonable amount of supporting data. Some of this supporting data will find its way into the actual presentation; the balance can be included in follow-up or hand-out material following the presentation.

Your earlier preparations will help you begin the distillation. Each piece of selected material should be weighed against the purpose, or goal, of the presentation and considered with the audience analysis in mind. If the material does not support your goal or doesn't suit the potential audience, it should be excluded.

Always ask yourself the question "Why am I using this?" Try to look at the materials as your audience might. Amplify the "Why" by asking "What contribution will this make to my objective?" Any material that can't stand up to this critique should be eliminated. Of course, this cut isn't always as painless as it might seem. There is a natural inclination to include associated material that you find interesting or informative. Unfortunately, this material doesn't always hold the same interest for your audience. It might even undermine the importance of the more essential items you want to convey. Always bear in mind that your presentation is a service to your audience, and if your interests must become secondary to theirs, that's a small sacrifice to make to achieve your goal. So be merciless in eliminating everything that doesn't make a direct contribution to your presentation's objective.

Organization

Once you've done this, you have to concern yourself with putting your material in some kind of order. Don't worry about the introduction and the closing yet. Most of what you have will probably be included in the main body of the presentation. Once the body is done, the introduction and the closing have a way of taking care of themselves.

Looking at your material, you should select three or four main ideas about your subject and list them in a logical sequence. These ideas will become the initial outline of your presentation. For each main idea, select two or three supporting ideas and list them under the particular ideas they support. This will complete the outline and establish the basis for the actual writing to come later.

Remember that the outline, at any stage of development, is very flexible. You can rearrange at any time to fit the nature of the presentation or the audience. You have several options in deciding the arrangement of the final presentation.

At this point your tentative outline is pretty well completed. Before you go any further, take another look at it, item by item, and be sure that each statement, each main idea, and each subordinate idea will be unequivocally clear to your listeners. Also be sure that each leads to your goal. If it is clear, concise, and convincing, it's ready. If something is vague and unclear, add any information needed to clear it up. When you've finished, you'll be ready to write.

PRACTICE A

Identify the audience and goal for the following presentations.

Example

1. Mr. Drake is a training consultant for Omnicomp International. He is giving training presentations to sales representatives who will be selling Omnicomp software targeted toward two major markets: the private sector and the educational market. All the representatives have previous experience selling Omnicomp software, and they understand word processing terminology. By the end of the presentation they will be able to explain the features and benefits of *Spellgramm* and demonstrate its use.

Goal: *to enable representatives to explain the features and benefits of Spellgramm and to demonstrate its use*

Audience: *experienced sales representatives*

2. Ms. Benaquist is a research analyst who has just completed a marketing survey for a cosmetic company preparing to launch a new perfume. In her presentation to the board of directors, Ms. Benaquist will identify and locate the primary and secondary markets. The presentation will be short, with few details serving to inform the board of her general findings. A more thorough presentation discussing details of advertising and distribution will be scheduled later in the week.

Goal: _____

_____

Audience: _____

3. Mr. Gregory Metcalf is on the public relations staff of a large multinational company that has begun construction of a new computer manufacturing plant. Tonight he will speak to the general public on the beneficial aspects of the new plant. His purpose will be to gain community support.

Goal: _____

_____

Audience: _____

4. Carol Richardson is a representative for Apelco Hospital Supply Company. She will present the latest radiological equipment to a large group of hospital administrators. She hopes to create interest in the very expensive equipment and to generate future sales.

Goal: _____

_____

Audience: _____

5. Tobe Heavy Industries Limited has just purchased four new electronic typewriters. Previously the company used extremely outdated models. Mr. Linn from Key Typewriter Sales will demonstrate the use and maintenance of the new typewriters to the administrative staff. The staff is reluctant to use the sophisticated typewriters because it is accustomed to the older models.

Goal: _____

_____

_____

Audience: _____

PRACTICE B
Eliminate the one piece of information in each example that does not fit the goal of the presentations in *PRACTICE A*.

1. a. *Spellgramm* has a 70 000-word inventory.
   b. *Spellgramm* automatically hyphenates, capitalizes, and abbreviates.
   c. *Spellgramm* took five years to be developed.

2. a. The primary market is female, ages 18–35.
   b. Perfume is a luxury product.
   c. There is a large market in urban areas as opposed to rural areas.

3. a. The computer manufacturing plant will create new jobs.
   b. Other industries will come to the area, creating more jobs.
   c. G. Metcalf pioneered efforts in computer manufacturing.

4. a. Only hospitals with financial backing can deal with rising costs.
   b. A high percentage of hospitals are updating their radiological equipment.
   c. Major medical schools are now teaching with this equipment.

5. a. The typewriter was discovered in 19..
   b. The typewriter must be kept clean.
   c. Dust particles can clog the new typewriter.

CHECKLIST

Preparation

1. Define your goal by asking yourself the purpose of your presentation. ☐

2. Analyze your audience and tailor your speech to fit their needs and interests. ☐

3. Weigh all points in your speech; if any don't support your objectives, eliminate them. ☐

4. Select relevant supportive data and visual aids. ☐

5. Select three or four main ideas to present, and order them logically. ☐

DISCUSSION ACTIVITIES

1. Along with speaking to the general public about the beneficial aspects of the manufacturing plant, Mr. Metcalf will be speaking to public officials about the safety aspects of the plant. This group is much more knowledgable about health hazards than is the general public. In what ways will Mr. Metcalf's presentations be different? Will the goals be different? How will audience analysis affect the presentations?

2. Randall Drake from Omnicomp International wrote a letter to Taro Tanaka in order to gain information about his audience. What are other ways to gather information about the audience? Is it always possible to get information about your audience before a presentation? If not, what can be done to plan your presentation effectively?

3. Have you ever been to a presentation in which the speaker did not consider the audience? What were the consequences?

4. You (Ellen Svitek) are a sales representative for an educational publishing company. Your product is *Storytime,* a set of audio cassettes designed to help students develop language and reading skills through listening.

   Storytime allows students to work independently, listening at their own pace to interesting stories and then answering challenging questions. After the students have answered the questions, a character in the story gives the correct response.

   Each *Storytime* package contains twelve cassettes, a teacher's manual, and duplicating worksheets. Each cassette consists of two fifteen-minute lessons on each side, and every lesson presents important language and reading skills.

   You have been asked to give two presentations on *Storytime:* one to interested parents and the other to school administrators. Explain how the goals, relevant supportive data, visual aids, and main ideas differ for both presentations.

Objectives

1. Give presentations.
2. Evaluate presentations.

Relate the introduction to the audience's interest and knowledge.

Mention features and benefits.

Summarize the major features and benefits.

Presentation: SPELLGRAMM TRAINING SESSION
FOR THE BUSINESS MARKET

OUTLINE

I. (Introduction) Correct spelling, punctuation, and grammar are vital to the success of your business. The quality of your correspondence reflects the quality of your products.

II. Spellgramm corrects spelling, capitalization, and hyphenation errors.

III. Spellgramm corrects many of the most common mistakes in grammar and sentence construction. Users will have the only grammar correction package on the market.

IV. Spellgramm benefits users in other ways. It improves the image of their businesses, and it increases productivity of their secretarial staff.

V. (Conclusion) Omnicomp's Spellgramm will make your customers' business more successful by helping their employees write error-free correspondence. Spellgramm is the only piece of software that corrects grammatical errors.

Introduction   Your presentation should have three main parts: the introduction, the body, and the conclusion. The introduction is the first thing the audience hears, so take the opportunity to grab its attention and make it want to hear what you have to say. The introduction should relate to the audience's interest and knowledge. An effective introduction might contain a vivid example, an important and authoritative quote, impressive or frightening statistics, or an anecdote. Be careful with humor, however.

Since the introduction comes first, write it last. The introduction reflects the total tone and content of your speech, and that can best be assessed when the speech is completed.

For the body, you've already developed an outline of your major ideas and supporting information. The only thing to keep in mind is that they should be presented logically and with confidence. Don't leave yourself open to embarrassing or potentially unanswerable questions. Make your words work for you. If you ask questions in your speech, either answer them yourself or indicate that they are not answerable. Choose words that are strong and positive in support of your main ideas, don't allow yourself to fall into the "maybe, possibly, might" syndrome. Facts are much more impressive. Giving the percentage of students whose English grades went up after using Spellgramm for a semester is more persuasive than saying students' grades may improve after using Spellgramm.

Conclusion   Good presentations should have an ending as distinct as the beginning. Remember that your conclusion, or summation, is your way of wrapping it all up neatly and saying good-bye. If you haven't stated your case well in the body, it's too late to try to cram material in at the close.

When you get ready to conclude, prepare your audience by using a tone of finality in your voice and by the use of such expressions as "In summation..." or "We can conclude that..." This will allow your listeners to collect themselves and to give you their undivided attention.

As with the introduction, the conclusion should be strong and persuasive. It will be the last thing the audience hears (with the exception, possibly, of some questions), so use it to clearly restate your main ideas and to thank your audience for listening.

Delivery   Every step you've taken this far in the preliminary preparation of your presentation has pointed you in one direction: choosing the words and writing your presentation. We hope you have been careful in selecting and arranging the materials you will use. But remember one very important thing: your presentation will consist primarily of the spoken word. It will be heard, not read. So write for the ear, not for the eye. Keep your words and sentences simple and informational. By doing this, you will reduce the risk of losing your audience.

Remember that you will have to speak the words and the audience will presumably hear them. So keep your presentation simple. Unlike the reader of a written report, your listener will not be able to go back and reread your message and study your argument.

Think of your presentation as a one-sided conversation, and choose your words accordingly.

1. Use your speaking, not your written, vocabulary. Short sentences, complete with contractions, are characteristic of spoken English, and so are simply constructed ones. They are also the most readily understood.

2. If you can't handle humor, don't use it.

3. Don't use long sentences if you have a breath-control problem. To keep your sentences short, avoid using too many conjunctions. Don't link too many thoughts together in the same sentence with *and*'s, *but*'s, *also*'s, and *or*'s. Make your points as clearly and simply as possible.

4. Avoid the use of technical jargon, terms, or acronyms that will not be understood by everyone in the audience. If such terms must be used, be certain to offer an explanation so you don't lose half of your listeners. Use terms of common reference as often as possible. And avoid words that are difficult to pronounce.

5. At some presentations it is appropriate to solicit questions from the audience. Stated clearly and briefly: "I would be glad to answer any questions you may have." If there are no questions, don't beg for them, merely exit gracefully. You've done your job.

Too many presenters never rehearse and, unfortunately for the members of the audience, it shows. It's simply not enough to have a good presentation down on paper because effective communication doesn't take place until the information is properly transmitted and correctly received. There's only one way to be sure that the written presentation can be transmitted and understood by the audience, and that is to simulate the actual presentation.

There are three good methods of practicing a presentation before actually giving it. While each method is effective on its own, a combination of two or all three is highly recommended.

1. First, take your presentation (include your visual aids, if any) and find a room where you won't be interrupted. Now try to imagine that your prospective audience is in the room with you and make your presentation as if it were the real thing. Pretend there are real people out there and remember to look at them as you deliver the presentation. This method will provide you with the feel of the material and the flow of the presentation. It will also give you the necessary practice for effective use of your visual aids. If you go through this simulated presentation several times, you'll notice an increasing familiarity with the material and an increasing ease of delivery.

2. Another method is to record your complete presentation on tape to hear how you sound and to hear whether your ideas are coming through as you planned. It is perhaps the best way to be objective, from the audience's viewpoint, and will help you to discover flaws that might otherwise have escaped your attention.

3. The third method is to deliver your presentation to an actual audience. Have some knowledgeable co-workers and, if possible, some representative members of your target audience listen to your practice presentation. Be certain that your audience gears itself to react in a manner typical of the individuals with the knowledge, interest, and attitudes of your target audience. This kind of rehearsal is an effective way to try out your techniques, to make sure your ideas are getting across, and to field questions from the audience, some of which you may not have anticipated.

Once you have completed the rehearsal, the flaws you've identified can be quickly corrected. Also, it's good to keep in mind whatever comments you have received from your practice audience. Critique the presentation for grammatical and technical content, and rewrite where necessary. If the rewriting is considerable, it's advisable to rehearse with the new content.

Location

To be fully effective, a presentation must be well staged. Proper staging of a presentation depends on controlling the environment to the maximum possible extent. There are three aspects of environment that can usually be controlled: space, lighting, and mechanics.

While the actual amount of space allocated for your presentation may be out of your hands, you should have control over the arrangement of this space. The consideration given to space arrangement can be divided into two factors.

The screen should be high enough so that the audience has an unobstructed view. From the person nearest to the front to the one in the rear, there should be no obstacle to vision. In most situations the bottom edge of a screen should be at least 4 to 4½ feet from the floor. With the screen at this height, most people will have an unobstructed view, and the screen will not be too high for viewing comfort.

Extremely wide horizontal angles of vision should be avoided. In an oblong room the screen should be parallel to the shortest wall. If the screen is set parallel to the longer wall, the angle of vision at either side becomes too great for easy viewing.

The screen should be at a right angle to the center line of projection to eliminate "keystoning," a distortion of the image in which parts of the picture are enlarged out of proportion or thrown out of focus. To eliminate keystoning, either raise the projector until the correct angle is acquired or tilt the screen until all portions of the image are accurately projected.

Proper lighting is important to relaxed viewing. Without question, the less the room light, the more brilliant the image on the screen and the greater the contrast. Brilliance and glare can be annoying and can cause eyestrain. A proper level of room light reduces the contrast and permits the audience to see well enough to take notes during the presentation.

Remember to familiarize yourself with the mechanical operation of your projection system. As far as your audience is concerned, the mechanical functioning should be "in the background" and should not draw attention away from your presentation. Find out ahead of time if there are special considerations, such as rear-projection, which if not projected through a mirror, will project your slides with the images reversed. It's your responsibility to assure that things go smoothly, and the time you spend to achieve this is time very well spent.

Presentation Techniques

No matter how well prepared a presentation may be, ultimate success depends largely on how effectively you deliver your message. It is through the skillful use of your voice and body that you will sustain audience interest and communicate your ideas.

With practice, a good technique can be developed that will be effective for any type of briefing or presentation. These delivery techniques are important, but they should not be cultivated for their own sake. Good presentation techniques are used to communicate, not to showcase the speaker.

First, maintain the center of attention. If you are the presenter, you are in control. If the audience knows more about the subject than you do, they wouldn't be there. Once you realize that you are in command of the situation, it follows that your appearance, behavior, and technique will set the mood for what follows.

You must, at the very outset, show an air of confidence. If you have prepared for this moment, you know your material and there is nothing to be nervous about. Don't hurry and don't lag. Relax and enjoy it.

Voice Control

One of the most significant behavior patterns used to display confidence and poise is effective voice control—a big factor in holding the attention of an audience. A monotonous, unvarying voice tone does not invite an audience to listen. To command attention, your voice must be pleasant, have variety, and be easily heard. You should vary the rate, pitch, and volume while speaking. Let's examine these three factors.

The average speaker talks at a rate of 140 words per minute. Good speakers will maintain this average but will also be flexible. They can either slow down or speed up as required. To emphasize a point, you may want to slow down to well below 100 words per minute. To provide a change of pace for a rapid transition or a quick example, you might want to sail along at 175 words per minute. Variety is the key to both avoiding monotony and emphasizing certain parts of your material. Don't depend on a fast rate of delivery to cover more material. Variation of rate is a tool for voice control, not quantity control.

Neither a low rumble nor a shrill scream can be tolerated for continued listening. A good speaking voice has both an acceptable range and a flexible pitch. Normal speaking pitch varies with the individual, however. For every voice there is one key at which it functions most effectively and pleasantly. The best approach is to pitch your voice high enough to allow you to lower it for contrast, and low enough to allow you to raise it for the same purpose. Use a variety of tones and rhythms to contribute expressiveness to the presentation. While stating your conclusion, you should use voice pitch to impart a tone of finality, clearly indicating that your presentation is over.

A high or low volume, when used exclusively, is a poor speaking technique. The volume of your voice must be adjusted to the conditions under which you are speaking as well as to the nature of your material. You should be heard without strain, but not at the expense of your audience's ears. As with rate and pitch, volume should be varied for emphasis and an interesting change of pace. Also, the presence of a microphone should not confuse you. Properly adjusted, the microphone should handle your normal speaking volume without the necessity to either whisper or shout into it.

For communicating with your listener, there is no substitute for clear speech. The audience can't understand muffled and indistinct words, and the reaction you might get could well be indecision, disinterest, or even chaos. To be quickly understood, you must speak each word clearly. Articulation, along with correct pronunciation, will hold the attention as well as the respect of your audience.

Body Movement

In addition to voice control, you should have a relaxed and rather free body action. This includes gestures, facial expressions, posture, and movement. To be really effective, you must use your muscles freely, naturally and with sincerity. All body action should stem from an honest and strong inner impulse to communicate. Insincerity in body movement is usually identifiable, and it detracts from the credibility of the presentation. Try to be natural.

Your posture can work for or against you. Good posture gives your listener an impression of force, purpose, and directness. Don't have your feet too widely apart, but don't have them so close together that movement becomes awkward.

Move only when there is a reason to move. The movement should contribute to your presentation – a change of stance on transition statements or "moving in" on your audience to emphasize a point.

If a lectern, or speaker's stand, is provided, it is really there for one purpose – to hold the speaker's notes or papers. Don't hide behind it or lean on it for support. You should be the symbol of strength, knowledge, and control in the room, not of the lectern.

A lot of people are concerned about what to do with their hands. The best answer to this problem is to leave them alone. Hands know how to take care of themselves, given the chance. Just as they have all of your life, they will become part of whatever spontaneous gestures you use, without conscious effort on your part.

Eye Contact

Good presenters always maintain eye contact with the audience. The ideal method is to establish a series of short eye contacts with as many audience members as possible during the presentation. In a very large audience, this practice is normally limited to the first several rows of people. Good eye contact accomplishes two things – it makes the audience more responsive because they're being spoken to, not spoken at, and it gives the presenter the opportunity to evaluate, almost instantaneously, how well your material is going over. Eye contact takes place intermittently and for a short duration while you cover material that you are familiar with. The audience fully expects that you will, from time to time, refer to your script, notes, or outline.

Use visual aids effectively. Make sure each chart is quickly understood, and use it in its entirety. Do not leave any visual on display after it has served its purpose, or it may distract the audience.

You must also consider what the audience will see as they watch you. It's been said that every presenter actually gives two presentations. The first is with dialogue, which is heard, while the second is with body actions, which are seen. When these two are interwoven to reinforce each other, the audience will listen and believe the composite story. When the two are inconsistent – the words saying one thing and the body action another – the words are discounted in favor of body language. The eyes of your audience are much more perceptive than its ears. This only serves to reinforce the fact that a well-prepared presentation is only half the battle. How you present it and how you look while presenting it are as important as how well you prepared it.

The practical experience you gain from each presentation you give will be invaluable in improving your future endeavors. Public speakers aren't born; they're cultivated. Knowing the proper techniques and practicing them can make you a better presenter and communicator.

SPEAKING ASSIGNMENTS

1. Here are some examples of the types of introductions described above that are appropriate for the *Spellgramm* presentation to the business or educational audience. Identify the type of introduction and audience, and give the same kind of introduction for the other audience.
   a. A survey of 2000 business executives from all levels of management showed that the ability to communicate is the main factor leading to promotion – above ambition, drive, education, experience, self-confidence, and good appearance.

b. Peter Drucker, a highly respected business management consultant and educator, said he considered the one basic skill most necessary for success in business to be "the ability to organize and express ideas in writing and in speaking.

c. I want to tell you about a man I know who became vice president of a large company even though he had only a high school education. He also had *Spellgramm*. . ."

d. Have you ever received something like this on a paper? (Show transparency of (1) "Having hung by the heels in the 30-degree temperature all night, I found the venison made a delicious breakfast" and (2) "Nearly every business has been directly concerned with a profit.")

e. Correct spelling, punctuation, and grammar are vital to your students' success, both before and after graduation.

2. The major subpoints of Drake's speech are outlined below. Choose the most relevant ones and describe those subpoints that belong to the appropriate main ideas of Drake's speech.

   a. It verifies the spelling of more than 70,000 words.

   b. It locates misplaced modifiers.

   c. It requires a memory of only 128K.

   d. It automatically capitalizes proper nouns and the initial words of sentences.

   e. It finds incorrect tense sequences.

   f. It's available in either British or American English.

   g. It locates incorrect pronoun referents.

   h. In addition to its standard word base, *Spellgramm* allows you to enter industry-specific terminology and the proper names of clients.

      (1) *Spellgramm* corrects spelling, capitalization, and hyphenation errors.

      (2) *Spellgramm* corrects many of the most common mistakes in grammar and sentence construction. Users will have the only grammar correction package on the market.

      (3) *Spellgramm* improves the image of their business and increases the productivity of the secretarial staff.

3. Revise the following conclusion to Randall Drake's speech according to the guidelines discussed in this lesson.

   > Well, it certainly has been a pleasure coming here and talking to all you folks. I hope you remember to tell your clients that *Spellgramm* offers practicality, flexibility, and speed. If you have any questions or problems, my address and phone number are on the brochure.
   > Thanks for having me. By the way, did I mention that *Spellgramm* does abbreviations?

4. Discuss the advantages and disadvantages of each method of practice described in "Guidelines for Speaking."

5. Take the outline you suggested in Exercise 2 and deliver an informal speech from it, using one of the practice methods just described. If you need more information on *Omnicomp Spellgramm,* see Chapter 5.

6. Evaluate a speaker's presentation in Exercise 5. Use the checklist on the delivery of presentations.

CHECKLIST

Delivery of Presentations

1. Make sure the seating is adequate. □

2. Make sure the viewing angles are adequate for all members of the audience. □

3. Find out if the windows need to be covered. □

4. Check the public address system in advance. □

5. Check for possible outside noise distractions during the briefing. □

6. Make sure all the pieces of the presentation go together. □

7. Do not attempt to cover too much material. □

8. Position yourself to be both seen and heard. □

9. Maintain the center of attention. □

10. Use a natural speaking voice. □

11. Do not overuse your notes. □

12. Do not use unfamiliar words. □

13. Communicate your purpose. □

14. Use each visual in its entirety. □

15. Make sure each visual is quickly understood. □

16. Do not leave any visual on display after it's served its purpose. □

17. Leave a good personal impression. □

18. Show enthusiasm. □

19. Thank all support personnel for their contributions. □

COMMUNICATION WORKSHOP
Listening Guidelines

Importance of Listening

Communication is a two-way process, involving the sending and receiving of messages. Throughout Chapter 10 we've recommended ways for a speaker to send a message effectively; here we will suggest ways you can ensure receiving it. And although our recommendations here will focus on listening to presentations, most guidelines can be applied in other listening situations, enabling you to increase your knowledge, broaden your experience, follow directions better, eliminate misunderstanding from conversation, and develop rapport with others.

Although listening is the most frequently used of the communication skills, until recently it has been the most neglected in terms of training. On the average, business people spend one third to one half of their workday in situations where they must listen.

To help employees communicate better and thereby increase productivity, major corporations have listening training seminars for executives, supervisory personnel, and other employees. These programs are needed because studies show that most people listen at a 25-percent level of efficiency. Information traveling through an organization gets distorted by as much as 80 percent, causing costly mistakes and the need for more paperwork.

Barriers to Listening

Listening, unlike hearing, requires use of the mind as well as the ears, and sometimes the eyes as well. For a number of reasons, we don't always put all these faculties to good use.

Distractions – Temperature, seating comfort, lighting, noise, odors, and persistent unrelated thoughts distract our attention.

Strong emotions – Prejudice toward the speaker, the subject, or the mode or expression often distorts our perception of the message.

Brain speed – Because you can think many times faster than a speaker can talk, your mind may wander to fill in the time if you don't occupy it with relevant thoughts.

Listening Guidelines

1. Determine your purpose for listening. Is it to get information, make a critical judgment, or for some other purpose? Generate self-interest: think of some benefits you can derive by listening. Then plan how you'll fulfill your purpose. If you're listening to learn a process, for instance, you'll want to note the essential steps. If critical evaluation is your goal, you'll want to get the main ideas and then weigh, question, and analyze them.
2. Review what you already know about the topic and the speaker. If an agenda or other relevant materials are available, look them over.
3. While waiting for the speaker to begin, prepare to listen. Eliminate or tune out distractions. Encourage the speaker by looking attentive.
4. Hear the speaker out. Don't be swayed by appearance, personality, or style of delivery: focus on the message. Keep an open mind and be sure you hear and understand the whole message before passing judgment.
5. Listen actively. Note the speaker's feelings and attitudes as well as words. Look for nonverbal communication – for example, gestures, expressions,

pauses, and inflections. Relate what you hear to what you know. Visualize information and restate it in your own words. Anticipate questions the speaker will probably answer.

6. If you're listening to evaluate something (for example, a product), question the validity, reliability, and timeliness of the product. Search for omissions. Ask whether the proposed solution is practical and whether there are alternatives.

7. Support listening with other communication skills, such as:

Reading – Supplement listening by reading materials on the topic to be discussed, studying the visuals presented during the talk, and jotting down unfamiliar words and concepts to research after the talk.

Speaking – To help yourself understand and retain content, mentally rephrase what you hear. Ask questions to clarify your understanding, and later try to explain the gist of the message to a co-worker.

Writing – Perhaps the most helpful aid to listening is note taking. It makes you pay attention to the speaker because it involves you physically so your mind is less apt to wander, and it increases the chances that you'll review what you've heard.

Three popular ways of organizing notes are (1) the outline method described earlier; (2) the précis, a summary in paragraph form; and (3) the fact-versus-idea division, in which notes are organized in two columns, one for facts and one for ideas.

Whatever method you use, remember that note taking should be an aid to listening, not a substitute for it. Don't spend more time taking notes than listening. Concentrate on the message, not on your method of recording it.

Don't try to get down every word. Listen for expressions heralding main points, such as "The most significant reason..." and "On the other hand,..." and for expressions signifying supporting details, such as "for instance...." Also note questions posed by the speaker, pauses, gestures, and changes of emphasis. Identify important parts of the speech with brackets or underscores. And be sure to review your notes as soon as possible after the speaker concludes, in order to clarify and organize them as needed.

DISCUSSION ACTIVITIES

1. Evaluate your own listening habits and suggest areas and methods of improvement.

2. You've been asked to introduce a speaker at a conference. Interview someone for five minutes to get relevant data (real or fictional), listening intently. Then present the speaker to the audience.

3. Have as many people as possible listen to a speech or follow a discussion by several people. Ask everyone to take notes. Then have several listeners present findings to the group in the form of an oral presentation. Ask the audience to use the presentation checklist in this chapter to check each presenter's effectiveness as a speaker. Then have the group follow the guidelines for listening while each presenter reports his or her findings. Have the audience decide which of the presenters was the best listener and/or presenter.

PRACTICE FOR GUIDELINES

PUNCTUATION   Punctuate the following letter. Be careful to avoid making fragments. (page 19)

Dear Ms. O'Malley:

In answer to your request for a recommendation for Ed Fowler I can't praise him enough he worked part-time as a salesperson at the Campus Stereo and Camera from 19.. to 19.. while he was in college Ed was adept at learning to operate equipment he was also a patient friendly teacher with clients who needed instruction and an enthusiastic salesperson I was very sorry to see him leave when he graduated to take a job in Rhode Island

Please call me if you need further information

Sincerely

John A. Zarnowski
Manager
Computer Stereo and Camera

COMPLETE FORMS   Revise the sentences. Use complete forms of the verbs. (page 26)

Example   1. Our company has always and will always be the first in word processors.
Our company has always been and will always be the first in

word processors.

2. The applicants are disappointed because they had hoped to have been hired by now.

3. The department meetings have never and will never be shorter than two hours.

4. I am surprised to be selected for the job.

5. The sales representatives aren't happy because they had wanted to have received the Babco order.

_____

_____

PROGRESSIVE TENSES   Give the correct form of the verb in the following sentences. (page 27)

1. Mr. Jones _____ (have) lunch at the moment; can he call you later?

2. I _____ (type) for three hours when you came in.

3. Ms. Sloan _____ (work) here for the past ten years.

4. A week from tomorrow we _____ (fly) to Sydney.

5. By the time the train arrives, we _____ (wait) for forty-five minutes.

MODAL AUXILIARIES   Revise the sentences. Check the modal auxiliaries and make sure they are consistent with the rest of the sentence. Make the necessary changes. (page 61)

Example   1. Mr. Jones will arrive tomorrow morning, and we meet for lunch at 1:00.
Mr. Jones will arrive tomorrow morning, and we will meet for lunch at 1:00.

_____

2. The director of operations thought she can present the proposal last week.

_____

_____

3. Mr. Webber thought he may purchase a more efficient copier.

_____

_____

4. The employees felt they shall have better insurance benefits.

_____

_____

5. The memo confirmed that the finance department will meet at 3:00 last Tuesday.

_____

_____

Make subject and verb agree in the following sentences. (page 62–63)

Example

1. Our customer service department handle complaints.
   Our customer service department handles complaints.
   _____

2. The budget committee work closely with the planning committee.
   _____
   _____

3. Replacement parts and services is available.
   _____

4. Either Model 1AO or 1AP fit the mainframe.
   _____

5. Neither the receptionists nor the administrative assistant place the orders.
   _____
   _____

6. The service, always fast and reliable, make our product the best.
   _____
   _____

7. Each of the staff members have a different responsibility.
   _____

8. One of the customers are dissatisfied with the product.
   _____

9. A number of clients has placed that order.
   _____

10. The division head are planning to meet with the buyers today.
    _____
    _____

THE COLON

Rewrite the sentences by using colons correctly or not at all. (pages 76–77)

Example

1. The trainees need to learn: marketing, accounting, and office procedures.
   The trainees need to learn the following: marketing, accounting, and office
   procedures.

2. The vice president reported: "With the current state of inflation, the company must produce 5 percent more sales in this quarter."

_____

_____

_____

3. Interoffice communications such as: the memo or transmittal should be concise.

_____

_____

4. The rule is: no customers are permitted in the office.

_____

_____

5. At our next meeting we will discuss: major competitive products and sales goals for the next quarter.

_____

_____

_____

SUBORDINATION   Combine the following sentences by using subordinating conjunctions. (page 87)

Example   1. There is no market for your product. I cannot give you an order.
Because there is no market for your product, I cannot give you an order.

2. Some companies offer in-service training. Other companies don't.

_____

_____

3. I worked as an assistant. I had enough experience.

_____

_____

4. She has sold the most. She will get a promotion.

_____

_____

5. You have excellent qualifications. We are not hiring.

_____

_____

Underline the clauses in the following sentences and write an *R* to identify a restrictive clause or an *N* to identify a nonrestrictive clause beside each sentence. (page 88)

Example

1. The contractor who makes the highest bid gets the job. _____R_____

2. The memo, which is a common form of interoffice communication, allows one to transmit information accurately. _____

3. The computer system that you recommended isn't adequate for our needs. _____

4. Bill Jones, who had been with the company for twenty-five years, finally retired. _____

5. Her performance, which impressed her supervisor, led to a raise. _____

PRONOUN CASE

Check the following sentences for pronoun errors. Make necessary changes. (page 102)

Example

1. Between you and I, we must increase sales.
   Between you and me, we must increase sales. _____

2. She is more experienced with promoting the new line of software than I.
   _____
   _____

3. They consider us to be extremely incapable of producing a marketing strategy.
   _____
   _____

4. The entire advertising department – Leslie, Reuben, and me – agreed to work overtime.
   _____
   _____

5. There were only Ms. Robbins and me left to handle the remaining letters of complaint.
   _____
   _____

6. This department could use some enthusiastic people like they.
   _____
   _____

7. You have forgotten two people, Bill and I.

_____

8. He will consult whoever is available.

_____

THE APOSTROPHE   Add apostrophes where needed to the following sentences. (pages 112–113)

Example   1. Ms. Browns response didn't address the problem.
   Ms. Brown's response didn't address the problem.
   _____

2. Theyll never finish by the three-oclock deadline.

_____

3. The personnel supervisor is revising the employees insurance package.

_____

4. Ive never seen such an incompetent sales department!

_____

5. We have asked two other persons for their opinions on this matter.

_____

CAPITALIZATION   Use capital letters where necessary in the following letter. (pages 124-126)

35 linden lane
dallas, texas 75238

february 15, 19..

speedy moving company
19 canal street
new york, new york 10011

dear mr. manager:

on february 3, one of your movers severely damaged my
valuable antique chair when he dropped it from the truck. on
february 4, i called your office and explained the situation to
mr. moriarti in the customer service department. he told me
that the value of the chair would be deducted from my bill.

yesterday the bill arrived, and only $100 was deducted for damages in transit. the insured value of my chair, however, is $600. because of the damage, i was also unable to enter the piece in an annual antique show.

i trust you can understand my disappointment, not only in losing a piece of valuable furniture, but in missing the antique show. because of my loss, i have enclosed payment less another $500 for damages.

sincerely yours,

karen bond

PRONOUN REFERENCE

Revise the following sentences to avoid unclear pronoun references and wordiness. (pages 140-141)

Example

1. It says in the manual that all employees must contribute to the retirement fund.
   The manual says that all employees must contribute to the retirement fund.

2. Why do they have staff meetings that waste so much time?

3. William asked to be trained in David's department so he could learn from his computer.

4. In the brochure it says that every customer will receive a 10-percent discount on every purchase over $50.

5. The employees who have worked several years at Omnicomp are generally satisfied with their supervisors, although the new ones are somewhat dissatisfied.

6. The managers told the foremen they would be making the decisions.

_____

_____

QUOTATION MARKS   Place quotation marks where they are appropriate in the following sentences.
(page 154)

1. Have you read the article The Effects of Modern Technology on Business in
Business World?

_____

_____

2. First increase sales, she said, then review the marketing strategy.

_____

3. The word *punctual* means on time.

_____

4. Repeatedly he answered no to all of her questions.

_____

5. We sell the very best computer software, bragged the salesperson.

_____

GENDER   Revise the following sentences to eliminate inappropriate use of gender, pronouns,
and terms when they are applied to people of both sexes. (page 155)

Example   1. If a customer is dissatisfied, ask him to explain his reasons.
If customers are dissatisfied, ask them to explain their reasons.

2. The chairman was fifteen minutes late for the meeting.

_____

_____

3. When the ship comes in, she will be filled with cargo.

_____

_____

4. Some people feel that modern technology is detrimental to mankind.

_____

_____

5. When a sales representative charges a customer incorrectly, he will have to make up the difference.

_____

_____

6. If a secretary has expenditures, ask her to justify them.

_____

_____

NUMBERS   Use numbers correctly by identifying the best choice for each sentence. (page 161)

Example   1. Omnicomp sold (twenty-six, 26) computers last week.
twenty-six

_____

2. It was (quarter after four, four-fifteen, 4:15 P.M.) when the meeting ended.

_____

3. (Eighteen seventy-five, 1875) is the year our company was founded.

_____

4. I am enclosing a check for (seven thousand five hundred dollars, $7500).

_____

5. My vacation starts in (five and a half days, 5½ days).

_____

6. Our administrative secretary ordered (one hundred and six, 106) technical pens, (ten, 10) pads of (nineteen-by-seventeen inch, 19x17 inch) white bond paper, and (three hundred, 300) pounds of wax.

_____

_____

7. On page (three, 3) of your letter dated January (thirteen, 13), you noted Omnicomp had a (four, 4), percent after-tax profit margin.

_____

8. The company celebrated its (fifteenth, 15th) anniversary with a party at (one hundred twenty-three, 123) (Fifth, 5th) Avenue.

_____

In the following sentences place hyphens where necessary. (page 179)

Example

1. Our boss is a well known figure in the computer science industry.
   Our boss is a well-known figure in the computer science industry.

2. The ex president of Omnicomp was responsible for reinstating bimonthly division meetings.

   _____

   _____

3. Depending on the nature of the order, we send parcels first, second, and third class.

   _____

   _____

4. Thirty five of the forty eight employees voted for the reestablishment of inservice training.

   _____

   _____

5. The public enthusiastically received the promotional package, because it was well planned.

   _____

   _____

PARENTHESES

Place parentheses where necessary in the following sentences. (pages 189-190)

Example

1. The new regional director received her M.B.A. Master of Business Administration from Stanford University.
   The new regional director received her M.B.A. (Master of Business Administration) from Stanford University.

2. Our priorities are to a increase sales, b reduce spending, and c initiate consumer interest.

   _____

   _____

3. There are many new ideas some were implemented last year that have cost the company additional money.

   _____

   _____

4. The last section of Mr. Ball's final report see page 28 was more to the point.

_____

_____

5. He had long suspected that some employees Robertson, Bellows, Shetler were embezzling company funds.

_____

_____

PREPOSITIONS Complete the sentences with appropriate prepositions. (pages 204-205)

A 1. He must account _____ the division manager _____ his photocopying expenses.

2. She continued to argue _____ improve working conditions and better benefits.

3. The credit manager and client finally agreed _____ a payment schedule.

4. Did you agree _____ work overtime?

5. Arguing _____ the supervisor won't help your relationship with her.

B Correct the prepositions where necessary, in the following sentences. (pages 204-205)

Example 1. The client argued for the manager over the present status of the overdue account.
The client argued with the manager over the present status of the overdue account.

2. She succeeded in the presidency.

_____

_____

3. She applied to credit and was rejected.

_____

_____

4. I felt that some of the committee members were reluctant to agree to me.

_____

_____

4. I felt that some of the committee members were reluctant to agree to me.

_____

_____

5. I overheard the credit manager arguing about a customer for over an hour.

_____

_____

APPOSITIVES   Underline the appositive phrases in the following sentences and circle the word or words they modify. (pages 216-217)

Example   1. Mr. Smith, the oldest employee, is retiring this summer.

A   2. The credit manager's assistant, Ms. Bellows, was first to respond. (The credit manager has more than one assistant.)

3. We will use elite type, or twelve characters to an inch, for the departmental reports.

4. All divisional members – managers, assistants, and clerk – attended the meeting.

5. A graph, or chart, will follow each page of statistics.

B   Combine the following sentences one sentence with an appositive phrase. (pages 216-217)

Example   1. The sales meeting next month will be in Texas. This is the state that has the most franchises.

The sales meeting next month will be in Texas, the state with the most

franchises.

2. My secretary's son is studying business administration. Michael will graduate next year. (The secretary has more than one son, but she's talking about the one named Michael.)

_____

_____

_____

3. The computer comes with software. Software is written or printed data.

_____

_____

4. She has intelligence and poise. These qualities will lead to her promotion.

_____

_____

COMMAS   Place commas where necessary in the following sentences. (pages 236-237)

Example   1. In 19.. 417 micro chips were defective and were therefore recalled by the company.
In 19.., 417 micro chips were defective and were therefore recalled by the

company.

2. Mr. White our department manager published a report in the January 14 19.. issue of *Business World*.

_____

_____

3. Ms. Benway added "For long reports state conclusions and recommendations at the beginning."

_____

_____

4. According to L. Wyatt computer scientist the LIX Corporation is selling outdated equipment.

_____

_____

5. They wanted to fly to the regional conference in Honolulu Hawaii but the company wouldn't pay for their tickets.

_____

_____

SEMICOLONS Place semicolons where necessary in the following sentences. (page 242)

Example   1. The retail price of the videodisc player from the New York distributor was competitive however, they refused to grant us credit.

The retail price of the videodisc player from the New York distributor

was competitive; however, they refused to grant us credit.

2. Among those attending were Scott Shetler, President of the Acme Hose Supply Company Charles Braun, President of Braun Hardware and Claudia Cassidy, President of Alpha Metals.

_____

_____

_____

3. To be cost-effective, the product must be produced in quantity therefore, we must update our production facilities.

_____

_____

_____

4. Mr. Fowler's report, based on a comparative statistical study of the five leading companies, was welcomed by the rest of the committee it confirmed the need for a revised marketing strategy.

_____

_____

_____

5. Ms. Benway's recommendations provide a conclusive analysis of the problems of employee boredom the importance of her study shouldn't be overlooked.

_____

_____

_____

The Simplified Letter

OMNICOMP INTERNATIONAL
17 BUNKER HILL ROAD, SHREWSBURY MA O1545

January 4, 19--

Ms. Barbara C. Mackie
HCI Corporation MS 34A 78N
One State Street
City, US 98765

ADMINISTRATIVE MANAGEMENT SOCIETY'S SIMPLIFIED LETTER

Ms. Mackie, this is a facsimile of the Simplified Letter recommended for many
years by the Administrative Management Society. It is a lean, clean format that
saves you time through fewer keystrokes and less typewriter movement, saves money,
boosts productivity, and enhances the look of the outgoing product.

The date is flush with the left margin from three to six lines beneath the letterhead. The inside address, also flush left, is typed three lines below the date
to facilitate the use of window envelopes. There is no salutation; this solves
the gender question in letters to correspondents who have signed previous letters
with their initials and a surname only. (In the inside address of a letter to
such a correspondent, you too can omit the courtesy title and type the person's
initials plus the surname.)

Type a capitalized subject line three vertical line spaces below the last line of
the inside address. Position the subject line flush with the left margin and omit
the words Subject or Re. The subject line encapsulates the main topic of the
message and should be brief and to the point. It is also a convenient filing
tool.

The message begins three lines below the subject line. All paragraphs are set
flush left. Paragraphs are single-spaced internally. Double spacing separates
one paragraph from another. The first paragraph opens with use of the recipient's
name in direct address as shown here--a polite way of engaging the recipient's
interest at the outset.

Enumerated lists and tabular data, if included, are set flush left with double
spacing separating one item from another. Items are single-spaced internally.
Long quotations are block indented by six character spaces. Such quoted matter
is single-spaced internally, with double spacing separating it top and bottom
from the rest of the message.

If the letter exceeds one page, use a continuation sheet matching the letterhead
in size, color, texture, and weight. Begin the heading at least six vertical
lines below the top left edge of the page. The flush-left heading includes
the recipient's name on line one, the page number on line two, and the full
date on line three. Maintain continuation sheet margins and paragraph style
as described for the first sheet. At least three message lines must be
carried over to the continuation sheet: at no time should the signature block
stand alone there.

The Simplified Letter has no complimentary close. This feature saves keystrokes. Type the writer's name and corporate title in capital letters at
least five or six lines below the last line of the message, and flush with the
left margin. A spaced hyphen separates the writer's name and title. The
writer then signs the letter in the space allowed.

Skip two spaces and typewrite your own initials flush with the left margin.
There is no need to include the writer's initials in this notation. If a
courtesy copy or enclosure notation is required, enter the material two lines
beneath your initials.

The Administrative Management Society tells us that "the Simplified Letter
stresses real economy of motion for secretaries. Its use results in better
looking letters with less effort. It will give them the pride of producing
more effective letters, and will result in increased productivity of a company's secretarial force--which ultimately saves money."

We recommend the Simplified Letter to all of our readers, and especially to
those who produce high volumes of correspondence.

JANE M. DOE - SENIOR EDITOR

ahs

cc Marietta K. Lowe
    Roberta Y. Peterson
    Candice S. Taylor

enclosures (7)

OMNICOMP INTERNATIONAL
17 BUNKER HILL ROAD, SHREWSBURY MA 01545

January 4, 19--

Mr. Peter C. Cunningham
Vice-president, Operations
CCC Chemicals, Ltd.
321 Park Avenue
City, US 98765

Dear Mr. Cunningham:

Subject: Block Letter Style

This is the Block Letter--a format featuring elements aligned with the left margin.
The date is typed from two to six (or more) lines below the letterhead, depending
on the length of the message. The inside address may be typed from two to four
lines below the date line, also depending on message length. Double spacing is
used between the inside address and the salutation. A subject line, if used, appears
two lines below the salutation and two lines above the first message line. Had an
attention line been used here, it would have been positioned two lines below the
last line of the inside address and two lines above the salutation.

The paragraphs are single-spaced internally with double spacing separating them
from each other. Displayed matter such as enumerations and long quotations are
indented by six character spaces. Units within enumerations and any quoted matter
are single-spaced internally with double spacing setting them off from the rest of
the text.

The heading for a continuation sheet begins six lines from the top edge of the page.
The heading is blocked flush with the left margin:

Page 2
Mr. Peter C. Cunningham
January 4, 19--

Skip two lines from the last line of the message to the complimentary close. Allow
at least four blank lines for the written signature. Block the typed signature
and corporate title under the complimentary close. Insert ancillary notations such
as the typist's initials two spaces below the last line of the signature block.

Sincerely yours,

John M. Swanson
Executive Vice-president

JMS:ahs

Enclosures: 4

**The Modified
Block Letter**

● ■

OMNICOMP INTERNATIONAL
17 BUNKER HILL ROAD, SHREWSBURY MA 01545

                                        January 14, 19--

CERTIFIED MAIL
CONFIDENTIAL

Sarah H. O'Day, Esq.
O'Day, Ryan & Sweeney
One Court Street
City, US 98765

Dear Ms. O'Day:

SUBJECT: MODIFIED BLOCK LETTER

This is the Modified Block Letter, the features of which are similar to those of the
Block Letter with the exception of the positioning of the date line, the complimentary
close, and the typewritten signature block. The positioning of the date line determines the placement of the complimentary close and the signature block, both of which
must be vertically aligned with the date. The date itself may be centered on the
page, placed about five spaces to the right of center as shown here, or set flush
with the right margin. Any one of these positions is acceptable.

The subject line, typed here in capital letters, is set flush left. Had an attention line been used it too would have been positioned flush with the left margin.
Note that the special mailing and handling notations appear flush left, two lines
above the first line of the inside address.

The continuation sheet heading, unlike that of the Simplified and Block Letters, is
spread across the top of the page, at least six vertical lines beneath the top edge:

Ms. O'Day   - 2 -   January 14, 19--

Notice the centered page number enclosed by spaced hyphens. Another way of styling
the page number is to enclose it with hyphens set tight to the number. Either
style is entirely acceptable.

The complimentary close--aligned with the date--appears two lines below the last
message line. At least four blank lines have been allowed for the written signature. The typed signature block is then aligned with the complimentary close.

Ancillary notations such as typist's initials, enclosure notations, and lists of
copy recipients are placed two lines below the signature block, flush with the
left margin.

                                        Very truly yours,

                                        Kathleen N. Lear

                                        Kathleen N. Lear
                                        Permissions Editor

KNL:ahs

OMNICOMP INTERNATIONAL
17 BUNKER HILL ROAD, SHREWSBURY MA O1545

February 14, 19--
Policy Number 34E 123W 9U

PERSONAL

Dr. David J. Peters
State Insurance Corporation
4556 Hightower Boulevard
City, US 98765

Dear Dr. Peters:

SUBJECT: MODIFIED SEMI-BLOCK LETTER

This is the Modified Semi-block Letter, many elements of which are positioned near or to the right or are indented. The date line determines the placement of
the complimentary close and signature block which must be vertically aligned under
it. Here, the date appears about five spaces to the right of center; it could have
been centered or aligned so as to end flush with the right margin.

A policy number (i.e., a reference line) has been used herein: notice that
it is aligned one space below the date line. The subject line is centered on the
page--a required placement in this letter style. It could have been typed in capital and lowercase letters, though.

Notice that the first line of each new paragraph is indented by six spaces.
Subsequent lines are set flush left. Displayed data and long quotations are block
indented by six more spaces:

1. A continuation sheet heading is spaced across the top of
   the page six lines below the edge, as shown in the Modified
   Block Letter.

2. The complimentary close appears two lines below the last
   message line, aligned with the date. At least four blank
   lines are allowed for the signature. The typed signature
   block, aligned with the complimentary close, includes the
   writer's name and title on separate lines.

3. Ancillary notations appear two lines below the last line
   of the signature block, positioned flush left.

If a postscript is included it is indented just like the message paragraphs
are. There is no need to introduce it with the heading "P.S."

Sincerely yours,

Donna W. Reardon
Personnel Manager

ahs

OMNICOMP INTERNATIONAL
17 BUNKER HILL ROAD, SHREWSBURY MA 01545

October 14, 19--

Dear Mr. Fitzpatrick:

This is the Executive Letter. In this styling, the inside address
appears from two to five lines below the last line of the signature space,
depending on the length of the message. It is aligned tight with the left
margin.

The Executive Letter is commonly used by secretaries to chief executive officers, especially in correspondence with their personal friends
and corporate associates. The letterhead usually contains the writer's
name and corporate title; hence this information need not be included in
the typewritten signature block.

The date appears flush with the right margin. The paragraphs are indented from five to ten spaces. Carried-over lines are typed flush left.
Paragraphs are single-spaced internally. Double spacing separates the
paragraphs one from another.

The complimentary close is vertically aligned under the date line,
i.e., flush with the right margin. Here, the typewritten signature block
is included four lines below the complimentary close because the writer's
name and title do not appear on the printed letterhead.

If the typist's initials or another notation is included, it appears
two lines beneath the last line of the inside address, also blocked flush
with the left margin.

Sincerely yours,

Michael A. Robinson
Vice President

John R. Fitzpatrick, Esq.
Fitzpatrick, Sweeney & Connon
Two Court Street
City, US 98765

MAR:ahs

Enclosure

OMNICOMP INTERNATIONAL
17 BUNKER HILL ROAD, SHREWSBURY MA 01545

June 24, 19--

Senior Buyers, Office Products
WiltonBooks Limited
1234 Clearwater Expressway
City, US 98765

Dear Senior Buyers

The Hanging-indented Letter Style

This is a facsimile of the Hanging-indented Letter, a letter style having a very
        elegant look. The Hanging-indented Letter is most often used in direct-
        mail advertising, sales, and product promotion. Since it requires much
        tabbing it is not a time-saving style appropriate to general correspondence.

Notice that we have used the minimal (i.e., open) punctuation pattern in this
        letter: the salutation, complimentary close, and ancillary notations are
        unpunctuated. We also have inserted a capitalized and lowercased subject
        line to draw attention to the topic at hand. We centered it on the page for
        a more balanced look.

The chief feature of the Hanging-indented Letter is its unusual paragraph align-
        ment. The first line of each paragraph is set flush left with subsequent
        lines block indented by at least five or six spaces. We have used the six-
        space setting in this facsimile.

The date line appears flush with the right margin in the Hanging-indented Letter,
        and the complimentary close and typed signature block are aligned under the
        date. Ancillary notations are set flush with the left margin, two lines
        below the last line of the signature block.

Continuation sheet headings, like those in the Modified Block and Modified Semi-
        block Letters, must be spaced across the top of the page about six vertical
        line spaces from the edge. At least three lines must be carried over to
        the continuation sheet: at no time should the complimentary close and the
        signature block stand alone there.

                                                        Cordially

                                                        Jan

                                                        Jan Smith
                                                        Publicity

ahs

6 enclosures

The Half-sheet

OMNICOMP INTERNATIONAL
17 BUNKER HILL ROAD, SHREWSBURY MA O1545

January 15, 19--

Mr. Lee Martin
123 Salem Turnpike
City, US 98765

Dear Lee:

    This is an example of a very short note typed on
half-sheet stationery. The half-sheet is often used
for one- or two-paragraph communications such as informal corporate invitations, letters of appreciation,
or letters of congratulation.

    Notice the narrow margins set to align with the
right and left edges of the printed letterhead. We
have chosen the Modified Semi-block Letter style here,
but you may use the Block, Modified Block, or Executive Letters also.

    Since the writer's name and title have been in-
cluded in the printed letterhead there is no need to
include it in the signature block.

               Sincerely yours,

               Executive Signature

ahs

enclosure: check

ABBREVIATIONS

A.A.	Associate in Arts
a.a.r.	against all risks (marine)
A.B.	Bachelor of Arts
A.D.	anno Domini
a.m., A.M.	*ante meridiem* (in the morning)
A.O.	account of
A/R	all risks
A/V	ad valorem
acct.	account
ad. loc.	to (or at) the place (Latin *ad locum*)
ad. val.	Ad valorem
add.	address
admin.	administration
adv., advt.	advertisement
AFL-CIO	American Federation of Labor and Congress of Industrial Organizations
agr.	agriculture
agt.	agent
AK	Alaska
AL	Alabama
Alta.	Alberta
amt.	amount
Apr.	April
AR	1. account receivable 2. Arkansas
assoc., assn.	association
asst.	assistant
atty.	attorney
attn.	attention
Aug.	August
av.	average
AZ	Arizona
B.A.	Bachelor of Arts
B.B.A.	Bachelor of Business Administration
B.C.	1. before Christ 2. British Columbia
B.D.	bank draft
B.E.	bill of exchange
B.M.	board measure
b.o.	buyer's option
B.S.	1. Bachelor of Science 2. balance sheet 3. bill of sale
B/E	bill of exchange
B/F	brought forward
B/L	bill of lading
B/P	bills payable
bal.	balance
bd.	board
bdl.	bundle
bg.	bag
bkpg.	bookkeeping
bkpt.	bankrupt
bl.	barrel
bldg.	building
blvd.	boulevard
br.	branch
bu.	bushel
bus.	business
bx.	box
C. & F.	cost and freight
c.	cent
C.B.D.	cash before delivery
c.c.	carbon copy
c.d.	cash discount
C.I.F. & C.	cost, insurance, freight, and commission
C.I.F. & E.	cost, insurance, freight, and exchange
C.I.F. C. & I.	cost, insurance, freight, commission, and interest
C.I.F.	cost, insurance, freight
C.I.F.I. & E.	cost, insurance, freight, interest, and exchange
C.P.A.	certified public accountant
C.S.T.	Central Standard Time
C.T.L.	constructive total loss
c.w.o.	cash with order
C/N	credit note
c/o	care of
C	1. Celsius 2. centigrade
c	cubic
CA	California
canc.	cancel
cc	cubic centimeter
cert.	certificate
cf.	compare
char.	charter
chg.	charge
ck.	check
cm.	centimeter
cml.	commercial
co.	company
CO	Colorado
COD, C.O.D.	1. cash on delivery 2. collect on delivery
cons.	1. consignment 2. construction
cont.	1. contents 2. continued
contr.	contract
coop.	cooperative

corp.	corporation		ex. ship	delivered out of ship
cos, c.o.s.	cash on shipment		exd.	examined
cpd.	compound		exec.	executive
cr.	Also c cubic		exp.	export
cr.	credit		F.A.A.	free of all average
CST, C.S.T.	Central Standard Time		F.A.S.	Free alongside
CT	Connecticut		F.B.	freight bill
ctn.	carton		F.C.S.	free of capture and seizure
ctr.	center		F.G.A.	free general average
cur.	currency		F.O.B.	free on board
cwt.	hundred weight		F.O.C.	free of charge(s)
d.b.a.	doing business as		F.O.D.	free of damage
D/d	delivered		F.P.A.	Free of particular average
D/D	delivered docks		F/d	free docks
D/O	delivery order		F	Fahrenheit
dB	decibel		Feb.	February
dbl.	double		fl oz	fluid ounce
DC	District of Columbia		FL	Florida
DE	Delaware		fm	frequency modulation
deb.	debenture		fpm, f.p.m.	feet per minute
Dec.	December		fr.	franc.
dept.	department		Fri.	Friday
dia.	diameter		frt.	freight
dim.	dimension		ft	foot
dir.	director		fut.	future
disc.	discount		fwd.	forward
div.	dividend		G/A	general average
dlvy.	delivery		GA	Georgia
dol.	dollar		gal.	gallon
doz.	dozen		gds.	goods
DST, D.S.T.	daylight saving time		gen., genl.	general
dup.	duplicate		gm	gram
E. & O.E.	errors and omissions excepted		GNP	gross national product
E.D.T., E.S.T.	Eastern Daylight Time, Eastern Standard Time		govt.	government
			GU	Guam
e.g.	for example (Latin *exempli gratia*)		guar., gtd.	guaranteed
E.T.	Eastern Time		ha	hectare
elec.	1. electric		hdqrs.	headquarters
	2. electrical		HI	Hawaii
	3. electricity		Hon.	honorable (title)
enc., encl.	1. enclosed		hp	horsepower
	2. enclosure		hr	hour
eng., engr.	Also e., E., engineer		ht	height
esp.	especially		I.D.	identification
Esq.	esquire (title)		i.e.	that is (Latin *id est*)
EST, E.S.T.	Eastern Standard Time		i.p.a.	including particular average
est.	established		IA	Iowa
et al.	and other (Latin *et alii*)		ib., ibid.	in the same place (Latin *ibidem*)
etc.	and so forth (Latin *et cetera*)		ID	Idaho
Eur.	1. Europe		IL	Illinois
	2. European		in trans.	in transit
ex.	1. example		in.	inch
	2. out of		IN	Indiana

ins.	insurance
int.	interest
inv.	invoice
J/A	joint account
Jan.	January
jct., junc.	junction
K	kelvin (temperature unit)
k	kilo
kc	kilocycle
kg	kilogram
km	kilometer
KS	Kansas
kW	kilowatt
KY	Kentucky
L/C	letter of credit
l	liter
LA	Louisiana
lat.	latitude
lb	pound
loc. cit.	in the place cited (Latin *loco citato*)
ltd.	limited
m.	mile
m	meter
M.A.	Master of Arts
M.B.A.	Master of Business Administration
M.E.	mechanical engineer
M.I.P.	marine insurance policy
M.O.	money order
m.t., M.T.	1. metric ton 2. Mountain Time
MA	Massachusetts
Man.	Manitoba
Mar.	March
max.	maximum
Mc	megacycle
MD	Maryland
mdse.	merchandise
ME	Maine
mech.	mechanical
Messrs.	Messieurs (plural of Mr.)
mfg.	manufacturing
mfr.	1. manufacture 2. manufacturer
mgt.	meeting
mgte.	mortgage
MI	Michigan
mi	mile
min.	minimum
min	minute (unit of time)
misc.	miscellaneous
mkt.	market

ml	milliliter
mm	millimeter
MN	Minnesota
mo.	month
MO	Missouri
Mon.	Monday
mph., m.p.h.	miles per hour
Mr.	mister
Mrs.	mistress
Ms.	feminine title of courtesy
MS	Mississippi
msg.	message
MST, M.S.T.	Mountain Standard Time
MT	Montana
mtn.	mountain
n.	net
N.A.	North America
N.B.	New Brunswick
n.b.	note carefully (Latin: *nota bene*)
N.E.	New England
n.o.s.	not otherwise specified
N.P.	notary public
N.S.	Nova Scotia
N.W.T.	Northwest Territories
N/A	1. no account 2. not applicable
N/F	no funds
N	north
nav.	1. naval 2. navigation
NC	North Carolina
ND	North Dakota
NE	1. Nebraska 2. northeast
Nfld.	Newfoundland
NH	New Hampshire
NJ	New Jersey
NM	New Mexico
no.	number
nos.	numbers
Nov.	November
NV	Nevada
NW	northwest
o.r.b.	owner's risk of breakage
o.s., O/S	out of stock
O/R	owner's risk
Oct.	October
OH	Ohio
OK	Oklahoma
Ont.	Ontario
OR	Oregon
org.	organization
oz	ounce

P.	pint		**rm.**	1. ream
p.c., pct.	per cent			2. room
P.E.I.	Prince Edward Island		**s.**	shilling
P.L.	partial loss		**S.**	south
P.M.	post meridiem (after noon)		**S.D.**	special delivery
p.n., P/N	promissory note		**S.D.B.L.**	sight draft, bill of lading
P.O.E.	port of entry			attached
p.p., P.P.	parcel post		**S.O.**	seller's option
P.S.	postscript		**S.P.A.**	subject to particular average
P.T.	Pacific Time		**S.R.O.**	standing room only
P/a	particular average		**S/D**	sight draft
p/c, P/C	1. Also p.c. petty cash		**Sask.**	Saskatechewan
	2. prices current		**Sat.**	Saturday
PA	Pennsylvania		**SC**	South Carolina
Pac.	Pacific		**SD**	South Dakota
pat.	patent		**SE**	southeast
payt., p.t.	payment		**sec.**	1. secretary
pd.	paid			2. second
per ann.	per annum		**Sept.**	September
pkg., pkge.	package		**serv.**	service
pm	premium		**sgd.**	signed
poss.	possession		**sh.**	share (capital stock)
pot.	potential		**shpt.**	shipment
pp	pages		**shtg.**	shortage
ppd.	1. postpaid		**sic**	thus; so
	2. prepaid		**sm.**	small
pr.	pair		**soc.**	society
PR	1. Also P.R. public relations		**SOP**	standard operating procedure
	2. Puerto Rico		**SOS**	1. international distress signal
pro tem	for the time being; temporarily			2. any call or signal for help
	(Latin *pro tempore*)		**sp.**	special
prop.	1. property		**sr.**	senior (after surname)
	2. proprietor		**St.**	1. saint
PST, P.S.T.	Pacific Standard Time			2. street
pt.	1. pint		**sta.**	station
	2. point		**std.**	standard
	3. port		**stk.**	stock
q.	quart		**sub.**	also subst. substitute
qt.	1. quantity		**suff.**	sufficient
	2. quart		**Sun.**	Sunday
Que.	Quebec		**supt.**	superintendent
R.D.	rural delivery		**SW**	southwest
R.O.G.	receipt of goods		**T.**	1. ton
r.p.m.	revolutions per minute			2. troy
R.R., RR	railroad		**T**	temperature
r.s.v.p., R.S.V.P.	please reply		**t.**	teaspoon
rd.	road		**T.B.**	trial balance
re.	concerning; in reference to		**tbs., tbsp**	tablespoon
rec	receipt		**T.L.O.**	total loss only
recd.	received		**T.O.**	turnover
rev.	revenue		**T.T.**	telegraphic transfer
RFD, R.F.D.	rural free delivery		**tech.**	technical, technology
RI	Rhode Island		**tel.**	1. telegram

	2. telegraph		**w.**	**1.** width
	3. telephone			**2.** also **W.** west; western
Thurs.	Thursday		**W.A.**	with average
tkt.	ticket		**W.B.**	waybill
TN	Tennessee		**w.i.**	when issued (financial stock)
tnpk.	turnpike		**w.o.c.**	without compensation
trans.	transaction		**W.P.A.**	with particular average
treas.	**1.** treasurer		**W/W**	warehouse warrant
	2. treasury		**WA**	Washington
Tues.	Tuesday		**Wed.**	Wednesday
TV	television		**whse.**	warehouse
TX	Texas		**whsle.**	wholesale
U/w	underwriters		**WI**	Wisconsin
uhf, UHF	ultra high frequency		**wk.**	week
USA, U.S.A.	United States of America		**wkly.**	weekly
UT	Utah		**wt.**	weight
V.P.	vice president		**WV**	West Virginia
VA	Virginia		**WY**	Wyoming
var.	**1.** variable		**XL**	extra large
	2. variety		**y.**	year
	3. various		**Y.T.**	Yukon Territory
vhf, VHF	very high frequency		**yr.**	**1.** year
VI	Virgin Islands			**2.** your
VIP	very important person (informal)		**z.**	**1.** zero
vol.	volume			**2.** zone
VT	Vermont			

MONETARY UNITS

Country	Basic Unit	Standard Subdivision	Symbol
Afghanistan	afghani	100 puls	Af.
Albania	lek	100 quintars	L
Algeria	dinar	100 centimes	DA
Andorra	franc	100 centimes	Fr.F.
Angola	kwanza	100 lwei	Kz
Argentina	peso	100 centavos	$a
Australia	dollar	100 cents	$A
Austria	schilling	100 groschen	S
Bahamas	dollar	100 cents	B$
Bahrain	dinar	100 fits	BD
Bangladesh	taka	100 paise	T
Barbados	dollar	100 cents	B$
Belgium	franc	100 centimes	BF
Belize	dollar	100 cents	$B
Benin	ngultrum	100 chetrums	CFAF
Bolivia	peso	100 centavos	Bs
Bourkina	franc	100 centimes	CFAF
Bulgaria	lev	100 stotinki	LV
Burma	kyat	100 pyas	K
Burundi	franc	100 centimes	FBu
Cameroun	franc	100 centimes	CFAF
Canada	dollar	100 cents	Can$
Central African Republic	franc	100 centimes	CFAF
Ceylon	rupee	100 cents	Cey R
Chad	franc	100 centimes	CFAF
Chile	escudo	100 centesimos	E°
China, People's Republic of	renminbi	10 chiao	$
China, Republic of (Taiwan)	yuan	100 cents	N.T.$
Colombia	peso	100 centavos	Col$
Congo, Republic of	franc	100 centimes	CFAF
Costa Rica	colon	100 centimos	¢
Cuba	peso	100 centavos	$
Cyprus	pound	1000 mils	LC
Czechoslovakia	koruna	100 halers	Kc
Denmark	krone	100 ore	DKr
Dominican Republic	pesos	100 centavos	RD$
East Germany	ostmark	100 pfennigs	OM
Ecuador	sucre	100 centavos	S/
Egypt	pound	100 piasters	LE
El Salvador	colon	100 centavos	¢
Ethiopia	dollar	100 cents	Eth$
Finland	markka	100 pennis	Fmk
France	franc	100 centimes	Fr
Gabon	franc	100 centimes	CFAF
Gambia	dalasi	100 butut	LG
Ghana	cedi	100 pesewa	N¢
Greece	drachma	100 lepta	Dr
Guatemala	quetzal	100 centavos	Q
Guinea	syli	100 cory	S
Guyana	dollar	100 cents	G$

Country	Basic Unit	Standard Subdivision	Symbol
Haiti	gourde	100 centimes	G$
Honduras	lempira	100 centavos	L
Hong Kong	dollar	100 cents	HK$
Hungary	forint	100 filler	Ft
Iceland	korna	100 aurar	IKr
India	rupee	100 paise	R
Indonesia	rupiah	100 sen	Rp
Iran	rial	100 dinars	RI
Iraq	dinar	1000 fils	ID
Ireland, Republic of	pound	100 pence	Llr.
Israel	pound	100 agorot	1L
Italy	lira	100 centesimi	Lit
Ivory Coast	franc	100 centimes	CFAF
Jamaica	dollar	100 cents	J$
Japan	yen	100 sen	¥
Jordan	dinar	1000 fils	JD
Kenya	shilling	100 cents	K Sh.
Khmer Republic (Cambodia)	riel	100 sen	CR
Kuwait	dinar	10 dirhams	KD
Laos	kip	100 at	K
Lebanon	pound	100 piasters	LL
Lesotho	rand	100 cents	R
Liberia	dollar	100 cents	S
Libya	dinar	1000 dirhams	Din
Luxembourg	franc	100 centimes	Lux. F
Malagasy Republic	franc	100 centimes	FMG
Malawi, Republic of	Kwacha	100 tambala	KW
Malaysia	dollar	100 cents	M$
Maldive Islands	rupee	100 larees	MRp
Mali	franc	100 centimes	MF
Malta	pound	100 cents	LM
Mauritania	ouguya	100 khoums	Oug
Mauritius	rupee	100 cents	MRp
Mexico	peso	100 centavos	Mex$
Monaco	franc	100 centimes	FR
Mongolian People's Republic	tughrik	100 mongo	Tu
Morocco	dirham	100 centimes	DH
Nauru	dollar	100 cents	
Nepal	rupee	100 pice	NR
Netherlands	guilder	100 cents	Fls.
Netherlands Antilles	guilder	100 cents	C Fls.
New Zealand	dollar	100 cents	$NZ
Nicaragua	cordoba	100 centavos	C$
Niger	franc	100 centimes	CFAF
Nigeria	niara	100 kobes	N
North Korea	won	100 jun	W
Norway	krone	100 ore	NKr
Oman	riyal-omani	1000 baiza	RS
Pakistan	rupee	100 paisas	PR
Panama	balboa	100 centesimos	B

Country	Basic Unit	Standard Subdivision	Symbol
Philippines, Republic of the	peso	100 centavos	Esc
Poland	zloty	100 groszy	Zl
Portugal	escudo	100 centavos	Esc
Qatar	riyal	100 dirhams	R
Rumania	leu	100 bani	L
Rwanda	franc	100 centimes	CFAF
Saudi Arabia	riyal	100 halalas	SRI
Senegal	franc	100 centimes	CFAF
Sierra Leone	leone	100 cents	Le
Singapore	dollar	100 cents	S$
Somali Republic	shilling	100 cents	So. Sh
South Africa, Republic of	rand	100 cents	R
Southern Yemen	rial	40 bugihas	R
South Korea	won	100 chon	W
Spain	peseta	100 centimos	Pta or Pts (plural)
Sudan	pound	100 piasters 1000 milliemes	SdL
Surinam	guilder	100 cents	Sur. Fls.
Swaziland	emalangeni	100 cents	
Switzerland	franc	100 centimes	SwF
Syria	pound	100 piasters	SL
Tanzania	shilling	100 cents	T. Sh.
Thailand	bahat	100 satangs	B
Togo	franc	100 centimes	CFAF
Tonga	pa' anga	100 seniti	
Trinidad and Tobago	dollar	100 cents	TT$
Tunisia	dinar	1000 milliemes	D
Turkey	lira	100 kurus	TL
Uganda	shilling	100 cents	U. Sh.
Union of Soviet Socialist Republics	rouble	100 kopecks	R
United Kingdom of Great Britain and Northern Ireland	pound	100 pence	L
United States of America	dollar	100 cents	$
Uruguay	peso	100 centimos	UR$
Venezuela	bolivar	100 centimos	B
Vietnam	dong	100 chong	D
Western Samoa	tala	100 cents	Tala
West Germany	Deutsche mark	100 pfennigs	DM
Yemen	rial	40 bugshas	R
Yemen Democratic People's Republic	dinar	1000 fils	SYD
Yugoslavia	dinar	100 paras	Din
Zaire	zaire	100 makuta	Z
Zambia	kwacha	100 ngwee	KW
Zimbabwe	dollar	100 cents	Z$

METRIC CONVERSION TABLE

Unit Measure	Equals	Measure
Barrel (Oil)	42	Gallons (Oil)
Centimeter	0.3937	Inch
Centimeter	0.01	Meter
Centimeter	10	Millimeters
Cubic foot	28320	Cubic cms.
Cubic foot	1728	Cubic inches
Cubic foot	0.02832	Cubic meter
Cubic foot	0.03704	Cubic yard
Cubic foot	7.48052	Gallons
Cubic foot	28.32	Liters
Cubic foot	59.84	Pints (liq.)
Cubic foot	29.92	Quarts (liq.)
Cubic inch	16.39	Cubic centimeters
Cubic inch	0.000578	Cubic foot
Cubic inch	0.00001639	Cubic meter
Cubic inch	0.004329	Gallon
Cubic meter	1	Cubic centimeters
Cubic meter	35.31	Cubic feet
Cubic meter	61.023	Cubic inches
Cubic meter	1.308	Cubic yards
Cubic meter	1000	Liters
Cubic meter	2113	Pints (liq)
Cubic meter	1057	Quarts (liq.)
Decigram	0.1	Gram
Decimeter	0.1	Meter
Degree (Angle)	60	Minutes
Degree (Angle)	0.01745	Radian
Degree (Angle)	3600	Seconds
Dekagram	10	Grams
Dekaliter	10	Liters
Dekameter	10	Meters
Fathom	6	Feet
Foot	30.48	Centimeters
Foot	12	Inches
Foot	0.3048	Meter
Foot	1/3	Yard
Gallon	3785	Cubic centimeters
Gallon	0.1337	Cubic foot
Gallon	231	Cubic inches
Gallon	0.00378	Cubic meter
Gallon	4	Quarts (liq.)
Gallon, Imperial	1.20095	U.S. Gallons
Gallon, U.S.	0.83267	Imperial Gallons
Gallon, water	8.3453	Pounds of Water
Gram	980.7	Dynes
Gram	15.43	Grains
Gram	0.001	Kilogram
Gram	1000	Milligrams
Gram	0.03527	Ounce
Gram	0.03215	Ounce (troy)
Gram	0.0002205	Pound

Unit Measure	Equals	Measure
Hectoliter	100	Liters
Hectometer	100	Meters
Inch	2.540	Centimeters
Kilogram	980.665	Dynes
Kilogram	2.205	Lbs.
Kilogram	0.0011	Ton (short)
Kilogram	1000	Grams
Kiloliter	1000	Liters
Kilometer	100000	Centimeters
Kilometer	3281	Feet
Kilometer	1000	Meters
Kilometer	0.6214	Miles
Kilometer	1094	Yards
Liter	1000	Cubic centimeters
Liter	0.03531	Cubic foot
Liter	61.02	Cubic inches
Liter	0.2632	Gallon
Liter	2.113	Pints (liq.)
Liter	1.057	Quarts (liq.)
Meter	100	Centimeters
Meter	3.281	Feet
Meter	39.37	Inches
Meter	0.001	Kilometer
Meter	1000	Millimeters
Meter	1.094	Yards
Milligram	0.001	Gram

GLOSSARY

Accounts payable: A current debt representing the amount owed by an individual or business to a creditor for service or merchandise on credit

Accounts receivable: Money owed to a business for merchandise purchased on open account

Addendum: An addition, such as an appendix

Adjustment letter: A customer's request to remedy a problem in a product or service

Ad Valorem: According to value

Against: In foreign commerce, used as synonym for "upon"

Air express: A method used for mailing packages when next-day delivery is necessary

Antecedent: The word, phrase, or clause that a pronoun refers to

Apparent good order: Statement that a shipment is free from damage and in good condition, as far as appearance is concerned

Appended parts: A supplement to a report or other communication, such as a bibliography or postscript

Appendix: Supplementary material included after the text or report body, such as a sample questionnaire or working papers usually providing additional information not crucial to the conclusion or recommendations

Application letter: A letter, usually sent with a résumé, for the purpose of obtaining a job interview

Application series: The résumé, application letter, interview, and any follow-up letters that provide a detailed description of the applicant

Applications software: Software programs written to perform particular business functions such as accounts payable, inventory control, and analysis of sales

Backup storage: Copies of data files (usually magnetic tape) used as a precautionary measure against damage or loss of the original

Batch system: A computer system that stores input and output data on a deferred- or delayed-processing basis: for example, invoice data for an entire day is entered all at once before any of the invoices are printed. In contrast, an interactive system handles small amounts of input and output data at any time, and usually gives the user immediate results

Baud rate: A rate measuring units of information (usually bits) transmitted per second

Bibliography: A list of publications used as sources of information for a communication or report

Bill of Exchange: A written order addressed by one person (the drawer) to another person (the drawee), directing the drawee to pay a specified sum of money to the order of a third person (the payee)

Bill of lading: A contract between a shipper and a rail or ocean carrier for the delivery of a product

Bit: A unit of information represented by binary digit 0 or 1

Breach of contract: A violation of the conditions of a legal agreement

Broker: A middleman between the buyer and the seller

Brokerage: A commission paid to a broker for services performed

Bubble memory: A computer memory that uses magnetized "bubbles" to store information represented by binary digits

Budget: An estimated summary of revenue, including itemized costs and expenses incurred during a given time

Byte: A unit consisting of eight bits representing the storage space of a character

CRT (Cathode-Ray Tube): A video screen that displays computer data, instructions and responses

Cashier's check: A check that is drawn by and on the same bank

Certificate of origin: A certificate covering the shipment of goods stating the origin of material or labor used in the production of such merchandise

CPU (Central Processing Unit): The element of a computer system that processes data in accordance with specific instructions by the software

Coherence: The selection of words, sentences, paragraphs, and thoughts connecting a message in a logical and understandable manner

Collate: Combine media in a specific order

Commendation letter: A letter of recommendation expressing desirable qualifications

Commission: The amount paid, usually a predetermined percentage, for consummating a transaction involving sale or purchase of assets or services

Communication: An exchange of information or ideas that results in understanding between the sender and the receiver of a message

Computer: a machine which accepts information or data (input), processes it (central processing unit) and either stores the information processed (memory), or supplies it on a screen or as hard copy (output)

Computer language: The code in which a program is written

Computer search: The use of computers to find sources of information, bibliographies, and related materials from files or data banks

Computer system: A system is comprised of the computer, the software and any peripheral equipment

Consignee: The receiver of goods

Consignor: The shipper of goods

Console: The keyboard of a computer system which is used to recall and enter data

Connotations: Implications and associations beyond the literal meaning of a word or phrase

Consular invoice: An itemization of goods shipped in another country, certified by the Consul of that country, who in turn verifies value, size, quantity, and description of merchandise

Culture: The way of life established by a society

Data: Digital or alphanumeric information expressed in characters, quantities, or amounts used as input for data processing; often used as a synonym for "information"

Data base management: A storage and retrieval system that allows easy access to stored information and efficient compilation of special reports. In data base management, a complete item of data (e.g., a product number and a description of the product) is stored in the data base only once and can be referred to by one or more short names or code numbers, rather than having to be described in full each time it is needed (e.g., in each invoice file where the part appears)

Data Center: A computer processing central location

Data Processing: Refers to the conversion of data to a desired form for further use

Debugging: The elimination of an error in a computer program

Distributed processing: Access to a computer system by individual processors linked to a common data base. (This is in contrast to a time-sharing system, in which several users share a single Central Processing Unit.)

Dividend: A percentage of the value of a stock paid to the stockholder as determined by the Board of Directors of a company or corporation

Dun: An unreasonable demand for payment

EDP (Electronic Data Processing): Converting data by electronic means to a desired form

Empathy: The ability to project yourself into another's situation to understand feelings and motives

Emphasis: Special importance, weight, or stress applied for a given purpose

Enclosure: A supplement attached to or included with a letter

Encoding: The process of writing a message into code form suitable for automatic reading

Endorse: To sign one's name on the back of a document

Entrepreneur: A person who initiates and assumes the risk of a business venture

Ethics: A system of moral values or principles

Exaquatur: A government's authorization of another country's consul

Expenditure: A payment plan for a service or product

Expense account: An account set aside to repay charges incurred by an employee while performing work

Floppy disk: A flexible magnetic disk (resembling a 45-rpm record) used to store computer data

Face value: The apparent value on coin, paper currency, or other negotiable documents

Facsimile: A duplicate copy or reproduction

Feedback: A response to an issue or a communication

First draft: The rough, unrevised composition of a written communication

Gerund phrase: The -ing verbal form and an object, which functions as a noun (*a working paper*)

Graphics: A photograph, drawing, table, chart, or graph used to illustrate

Hardware: Refers to the computer itself or to computer equipment

Idiom: An expression or style of speaking peculiar to a group or to a given language

Impromptu speaking: A presentation without advance notice or specific preparation

Inference: The act of reasoning or drawing conclusions

Infinitive phrase: The word *to* and a verb, which is used as a noun

Interactive system: A computer system that provides immediate results and allows an exchange of information

Inventory: A detailed list of items, goods, and materials in stock; assets

Invoice: An itemized bill prepared by the seller or shipper for the convenience of the buyer or receiver

Jargon: A specialized, technical language used in a particular profession

Job Market: The prospective employers' locations, job opportunities, and needs as studied by the job applicant

Letter of credit: A document issued by a bank on another bank or banks, foreign or domestic, or upon itself. The letter of credit gives the buyer the financial backing of the bank that issues the letter of credit in his behalf. The acceptance by the bank of drafts drawn under the letter of credit satisfies the seller in the handling of the transaction

License: A document officially permitting a certain activity

Magnetic tape: a coated, usually plastic tape that is sensitive to magnetic fields

Mailgram: A telegram delivered by postal services

Mailable copy: Copy ready for distribution, free from errors

Mainframe/maxi: Terms referring to "large" computer systems

Main selling point: The aspect of a product or service most attractive to a buyer; usually differentiates a product or service from its competitors

Management Information System (MIS): A data processing system which furnishes management personnel with current information in real time speed

Marketability: The ease with which an item can be sold

Memorandum: A short, informal written communication within a company

Memory: The part of the Central Processing Unit that holds data for processing

Merge: The combination of two or more things into one

MOS (Metal Oxide Semiconductor): The technology applied to create the microprocessor and memory portions of many computers

Methodology: The procedure used to research and collect data

Microcomputer/minicomputer: A microcomputer is a small, comparatively inexpensive computer system; a minicomputer refers to a larger and more complete system

Microprocessor: A semiconductor unit, or "chip," which functions as the core of the Central Processing Unit

Microwave transmission: A quick, efficient communications system using voice or data transmission through radio beams of ultra-short wave lengths

Mixed punctuation: The use of a colon following the salutation and a comma following a complimentary close in a business letter. See open punctuation

Mode: In data processing, the term *mode* denotes a method of operation

Modem: A device that links a computer or terminal to a telephone line for the purpose of long-distance data transmission and reception

Nonverbal communication: A message conveyed through gestures, motions, or facial expressions

Offline: Computer equipment that is not dependent on a central processing unit

Online: Computer equipment that is dependent on a central processing unit

Onionskin: A thin, lightweight paper used for copies and for airmail

Open punctuation: The use of no punctuation after the saluation and the complimentary close in the business letter. See mixed punctuation

Paraphrase: A restatement of a message in one's own words

Participative management: A philosophy of management that emphasizes the participation of subordinates in decision-making policies that directly affect them

Participial phrase: The -ing form of a verb and an object, when used as an adjective

Peripheral equipment: Devices which store data and input-output material such as printers, keyboards, CRT's remote terminals, and tape and disk drives which are not physically a part of the computer

Positive tone: The use of timeliness, empathy, and the "you-attitude" in communications

Postage-paid envelope: An envelope on which postage has been prepaid, used as a courteous gesture when a reply is desired

Postscript: An added thought indicated by the initials "P.S.," usually appearing below the signature

Prefatory parts: Parts preceding the body of a text, such as the table of contents, preface, abstract, or summary

Problem statement: A statement of the purpose of a report

Promotional letter: A descriptive letter written about a product or service to potential customers

Public Relations: Activities of a business designed to promote a favorable relationship with the public

Punched tape: An input/output device which stores data using a binary code system in the form of punched holes on tape

Questionnaire: A list of questions sent out for the purpose of obtaining information for a report or other research

RAM (Random-Access Memory): This memory in a

computer is random, volatile, easily accessed, and quickly lost when the electrical power to the computer is turned off

ROM (Read-Only Memory): The permanent, non-expandable memory of a computer, which is built into the computer, and which operates what are called "housekeeping" programs

Ream: A 500-sheet package of paper

Redundancy: Saying the same thing twice in one communication

Research: The collecting and reporting of data in an objective and systematic manner

Respondent: One who answers an inquiry or a questionnaire

Service bureau: A company hired by a client to run computer programs

Software: Programs that instruct a computer how to respond to specific user commands

Solid state: Pertaining to materials that convey or control electrons within solid materials

Solicited application: A job application in response to announcements of openings, or classified advertisements. See *Unsolicited application*

Sort: A function of computer processing which groups information alphabetically or alphanumerically in accordance with given instructions

Stock: The capital raised by a corporation by selling shares of ownership that entitle "stockholders" to dividends as profits are gained

Storage: The external devices (cards, tapes, disks, cassettes) that store data and software

Synopsis: A brief summary

System software: Software programs that deal with the internal functions of a computer system

Table: A written "visual" usually arranged in labeled rows or columns for reference or categorization purposes

Telecommunications: Communications by telephone, telegraph, television, teletypewriter, and computers over telephone lines or related equipment

Terminal: An instrument of input or output often equipped with a keyboard and a printer and connected to a computer

Time-sharing: Simultaneous access to one CPU in which each user has a terminal but the computer is based in one location allowing shared use

Warranty: A guarantee by the seller of a product that it will perform as announced or be repaired for a specific period of time free of charge

INDEX

COMMUNICATING IN BUSINESS _____

To the student:

One of the best ways to improve the next edition of our textbook is to get reactions and suggestions from you, the student. You have worked with *Communicating in Business*, and we want to know what you like about the book and how it could be better. Please answer the questions below. Tear out this page and mail it to:

> Joseph Buschini/Richard Reynolds
> Houghton Mifflin Company
> One Beacon Street
> Boston, Massachusetts 02108

Be honest and specific in your comments. Tell us both what is good and what is bad about *Communicating in Business*. Thank you.

1. Overall, how would you rate *Communicating in Business*? (Check one)
   ( ) excellent   ( ) average
   ( ) good   ( ) poor

2. Which chapters did you find especially helpful? Why?

   _____

   _____

   _____

   _____

   _____

   _____

   _____

   _____

3. Which chapters did you find least helpful? Why?

   _____

   _____

   _____

   _____

   _____

   _____

   _____

   _____

4. Were any chapters too difficult or confusing? Which ones?

_____

_____

_____

_____

_____

_____

5. Do any chapters need more explanation or practices? Which ones and why?

_____

_____

_____

_____

_____

_____

6. What material would you like to see added to future editions of
Communicating in Business?

_____

_____

_____

_____

_____

_____

7. Do you have any additional suggestions, criticisms, or reaction to
Communicating in Business?

_____

_____

_____

_____